Ⓖ Masaccio: *The Baptism of the Neophytes*

Ⓙ Masaccio: *The Alms Giving*

Ⓗ Masolino and Masaccio: *The Healing of the Cripple and The Resurrection of Tabita*

Ⓚ Filippino Lippi: *The Dispute with Simon Magus and The Martyrdom of St. Peter*

Ⓘ Masolino: *Original Sin*

Ⓛ Filippino Lippi: *The Liberation of St. Peter*

ANATOMY *of a* RESTORATION
The Brancacci Chapel

ANATOMY *of a* RESTORATION

The Brancacci Chapel

Ken Shulman

WALKER AND COMPANY NEW YORK

First published in the United States of America in 1991 by Walker Publishing Company, Inc.

Published simultaneously in Canada by Thomas Allen & Son Canada, Limited, Markham, Ontario

Color insert photographs courtesy of Antonio Quattrone

Library of Congress Cataloging-in-Publication Data
Shulman, Ken.
Anatomy of a restoration : the Brancacci Chapel / Ken Shulman.
Includes bibliographical references.
ISBN 0-8027-1121-9
1. Mural painting and decoration, Italian—Conservation and restoration—Italy—Florence.   2. Mural painting and decoration, Renaissance—Conservation and restoration—Italy—Florence.
3. Brancacci Chapel (Florence, Italy) I. Title.
ND2757.F5S5   1990
751.6'2'094551—dc20   90-12256
CIP

Printed in the United States of America

2 4 6 8 10 9 7 5 3 1

To the Restorers, and the Memory of Dino Dini

Table of Contents

Contents

Acknowledgments

I WOULD LIKE TO THANK the following persons for their willing and vital assistance during my research: Dr. Ornella Casazza, for her good cheer and patience; Professor Paolo Parrini, for his clarity; Professor Enzo Ferroni, for his passion and his narrative gift; Engineer Maurizio Seracini, for his genuine interest; Dino Dini, for a life lived entirely for art; Sabino Giovannoni, for his enthusiasm and honesty; Gioia Germani, for her solidarity and unselfish support; Lydia Cinelli Bianchi, for her unpretentious cooperation.

I am also particularly indebted to Paolo and Laura Mora for their kind hospitality, to Dr. Clemente Marsicola of the ICR for his fresh ideas, to Carlo Bigliotti for sharing his expertise in marble, to Leonetto Tintori for his memory, to Guido Botticelli for his intelligence, and to Gianluigi Colalucci for allowing me to touch the Sistine vault.

In addition, I would like to thank Dr. Giuseppe Pizzigoni, Dr. Andrea Polli, Professor Nazzareno Gabrielli, Marcello Chemeri, Professor Mauro Matteini, Professor Arcangelo Moles, and Professor Umberto Baldini. I would also like to thank the Kunsthistorisches Institut in Florenz for the use of its exceedingly well organized library and reading facilities.

A special thank-you to Francesca, who played the part of Ariadne in leading me through the treacherous labyrinth of physical chemistry; to Daniela Dini, for her friendship, and to Dr. and Mrs. Ugo Procacci, who more than anyone convinced me that this fascinating project was truly within my reach.

Introduction

THE RESTORATION OF the Brancacci Chapel officially began in 1981 under the direction of Professor Umberto Baldini, at that time head of the Opificio Delle Pietre Dure restoration laboratory in Florence. Drawing on more than thirty years of experience in restoration, Baldini directed an eclectic team of scientists, restorers, and art historians in a splendidly executed operation, which will be remembered as the pinnacle of his career and will serve as a model for all similar interventions in the future.

But the story of the Brancacci Chapel restoration, exceptional in all aspects, begins much earlier. Since the turn of the century, critics, historians, and artists had expressed their dismay at the sorry state of this remarkable temple of art. The series of frescoes by Masaccio that had literally given birth to an artistic explosion known as the Italian Renaissance and had served as a school for generations of Italian painters including Beato Angelico, Domenico Ghirlandaio, Sandro Botticelli, Leonardo Da Vinci, and the "divine" Michelangelo, was obscured by a thick layer of filth.

The lifelike figures that the young Masaccio fashioned with unprecedented skill and manner, including "the one who trembles" in *The Baptism of the Neophytes,* which Giorgio Vasari so admired, were thoroughly blackened. Far from being exquisite and moving, the cycle of frescoes was a murky blur.

In 1932, Dr. Ugo Procacci, founder and director of the department of restoration at Florence's Uffizi Museum and *maestro* to Umberto Baldini, removed two small pieces of a marble altar, which had been mounted in the Brancacci chapel at the beginning of the 1700s. This was nearly three hundred years after Masaccio

The Baptism of the Neophytes detail of "the one who trembles" which so impressed Manetti and Vasari.

climbed down from the scaffolding in the chapel to depart for Rome.

What Procacci discovered beneath the marble exceeded even his greatest expectations: bright colors—lucid, full of light and contrast. Masaccio had been ordained as the father of Renaissance painting because of his revolutionary use of perspective and his expressive modelling technique. His classical and realistic cadences were based on the innovations that his friends Donato Donatello and Filippo Brunelleschi had applied to sculpture and architecture. Masaccio turned his back totally on the prevailing International Gothic style, a style which found one of its most accomplished exponents in Masolino, Masaccio's Brancacci Chapel colleague.

Yet no one had thought of Masaccio as a brilliant colorist. The unearthing of Masaccio's true tones was a stunning and disorienting surprise.

"All of art history will have to be rewritten after the Brancacci Chapel is restored," Procacci wrote shortly thereafter. "We will see that the revolution of color, traditionally attributed to Beato Angelico and Domenico Veneziano, was already present in the work of Masaccio."

Nearly fifty years would pass before Procacci's prophecy could be fulfilled. These were years of bureaucratic delays, frustration, excuses, petty rivalries, and stubborn opposition by those who see all restoration as an unbridled and unwarranted violence perpetrated on works of art. All of these obstacles would combine to dampen the substantial efforts of Procacci and his colleagues.

As the decades passed, many of the scholars, historians and art lovers who had studied the Brancacci and hoped to witness its restoration saw their dreams descend into desperation. Others, perhaps out of a sense of helplessness, began to nurture unrealistic and inflated expectations for an eventual restoration that would not only return the chapel to its original splendor but would also definitively resolve what most historians agree to be "the most intricate and delicate case of attribution in all of art history."

For five centuries, scholars have grappled with the shroud of mystery that surrounds the chapel. Most indications point to Felice di Michele Brancacci as the patron of the Brancacci Chapel, and support the theory that the original commission for the cycle of frescoes based on episodes from the life of St. Peter was awarded to Masolino of Panicale. However, we possess no documents to confirm this hypothesis. No contract exists linking Felice Brancacci, a wealthy Florentine silk merchant, to Masolino or to Masaccio. There are no recorded payments to the artists, nor specifications as to the subjects, style, or materials to be used in the decoration of the chapel.

Many of those who had impatiently awaited the restoration of the Brancacci Chapel hoped that the Baldini–Casazza team would clarify once and for all the enigmatic relationship that bonded a stunningly innovative painter like Masaccio to a traditional, courtly, decorative artist like Masolino.

Scholars in earlier ages naturally assumed that Masaccio, seventeen years younger than Masolino, was an apprentice to the *maestro*. According to Giorgio Vasari's *Lives of the Artists,* Masolino began work in the Brancacci Chapel alone. Masaccio took his place two or three years later when the older artist died.

Later generations of historians revised the perception, casting Masaccio as a sort of foreman in the Masolino workshop, present in the chapel either from the outset of the project or shortly thereafter. A few scholars have even preferred to view him as an independent collaborator who was instrumental, if not dominant, in the conception, design, and execution of the sublime series of frescoes.

Many art lovers hoped that the restoration would also demonstrate whether Masaccio deliberately left the chapel unfinished when he left for Rome in 1428, or whether the completed frescoes were destroyed by vandals after the Brancacci family was exiled from Florence in 1434. Others waited for a discovery that would illuminate the role of Filippino Lippi, the artist who completed the chapel's fresco cycle in the early 1480s, more than fifty years after Masaccio's death.

The Brancacci Chapel restoration finally began in late 1981 with Baldini, Procacci's pupil and restoration heir, at the helm. Following a plan, which Procacci submitted to the Superior Council of Fine Arts in 1970, Baldini's Opificio Delle Pietre Dure restorers first dismantled the baroque marble altar that had been mounted on the rear wall of the chapel during an eighteenth century renovation.

The removal of the altar brought several fragments of fresco to light, including two decorative heads painted as cameos along the chapel's gothic window jamb and the remnants of a destroyed central fresco panel. Aside from their intrinsic historical value, these fragments would also prove indispensable as a chromatic meter for the restorers who were later to clean the chapel's priceless frescoes.

The Opificio restorers proceeded with the historical research that Procacci had prescribed, searching beneath the actual Eighteenth century lunettes and vault created by painter Florentine Vincenzo Meucci in hopes of finding traces of Masaccio and Masolino's original upper register and ceiling frescoes. The hunt yielded just two preparatory drawings. The rest of the original work had been destroyed.

Toward the end of 1982, because of a dispute, which broke out between the Florence and Rome authorities over jurisdiction of the restoration, the state funds that had financed the operation were suspended, and the restoration stalled. Another two years would pass before Baldini, who in 1983 moved to head the Central Institute of Restoration at Rome, obtained funding from the Olivetti Corporation and resumed the operation. This time, with his wife and longtime collaborator Ornella Casazza as technical director, Baldini would finish the job.

Like an expert medical doctor at the head of a well-trained staff, Baldini ordered a battery of tests, which would furnish him with a detailed bill of health for the frescoes. All foreign substances on the surface of the wall paintings were identified by sophisticated photographic techniques and chemical analyses in order to facilitate their removal. The consistency of the frescoes and the walls beneath them was measured with an ultrasound probe. A complete micro- and macro-environmental survey provided Baldini with many of the probable causes that had led to the chapel's decay, and with a chance to eliminate this decay at its source.

The history of restoration demonstrates that the favorable effects of an operation, even the most successful, are hardly eternal. If the cause of the ailment is not eliminated, art restoration is nothing more than a topical and temporary cure.

The Brancacci Chapel was much more than a pictorial facelift. While Ornella Casazza's team of restorers removed the murky layer of grime that masked the frescoes, biologists, engineers, chemists, physicists, and meteorologists worked to eliminate dust, humidity, and other noxious elements from the atmosphere, which circulated about the exquisite wall paintings. In the Brancacci Chapel, and throughout his illustrious career, Baldini has demonstrated that conservation is the most vital component of art restoration.

The Baldini-Casazza restoration will not go down in history as the one that solved the sphinx-like riddle posed by the Brancacci Chapel. The team made several important discoveries, which support the contemporary conception of Masaccio and Masolino as something akin to equal partners. However, the nature of their participation appears destined to remain unknown, at least until the invention of a technology that can provide us with a foolproof method of identifying the author of any painting, relief or sculpture. (Professor Vito Cappellini, who supervised the spectroscopy analyses of the pigments used in the Brancacci Chapel, is currently working on a software program to that effect; at present, the project is barely in its embryonic stage.)

A detailed examination of Filippino Lippi's work has illuminated his part in the story to some extent, and appears to bolster the theory that certain segments of Masaccio's work were indeed destroyed. Still, even at restoration's end, the evidence is at best circumstantial.

The aesthetic results of the restoration are extraordinary. Baldini's finely-attuned team of first-rate technicians, expert historians, and, most of all, patient and passionate restorers has lifted the suffocating layer of grime from the precious frescoes. The long-buried colors have been revived without upsetting the delicate harmony of the chapel. Pictorial gaps that were produced when previous repaintings were removed have been aptly filled in with Casazza's unobtrusive technique of chromatic abstraction.

In keeping with the Baldini philosophy, the restoration did not end when the restorers had finished retouching the paintings. To insure that the paintings of Masaccio, Masolino, and Filippino Lippi remain in their current condition, an environmental control system filters the Brancacci Chapel air. Humidity, temperature, and air pressure are maintained at safe levels. Technicians perform regularly scheduled analyses of the air inside the Carmine Church (the home of the Brancacci Chapel) to isolate and eliminate any potentially noxious particles.

For the restoration profession, the Brancacci operation will serve as a laboratory model of a productive and harmonious interaction between technician, historian, and restorer. This collaboration is the cornerstone of the Baldini restoration method, and a monumental contribution to the field.

Because of its extreme artistic importance, the restoration of the Brancacci Chapel was very much a showcase for the profession. Generous funding from the Olivetti Corporation allowed for a quantity of technical participation not often within the meager economic possibility of most restorers.

"The Olivetti Corporation did not select a random sum of money and dump it in our laps," says Baldini. "They undertook the project with the same commitment as we did, followed it from beginning to end, and were always ready to provide the necessary assistance. Because of this, we experienced no delays during the project."

Aside from the now traditional examinations used in fresco restoration—ultraviolet and infrared flourescence, x-ray photography, chemical analysis of pigments and intonaco—a number of other analyses were applied to art restoration for the first time in the Brancacci Chapel: ultrasound exploration, thermovision, infrared reflectography, holography, and color spectroscopy.

The Brancacci Chapel is likely to remain a historic, thematic, and artistic mystery until the time when its colors are no longer visible, or when the walls of the Carmine Church collapse into a heap of stones and rubble. What Umberto Baldini and Ornella Casazza have done is to allow us to view the work of Masaccio, Masolino, and Filippino Lippi unfettered, and to create the best possible conditions for us to come to our own conclusions about the small Florentine chapel where a twenty-five-year-old indigent painter named Masaccio ushered in the Renaissance.

The HISTORY

CHAPTER ONE

La Cappella Brancacci
(The Brancacci Chapel)

The work of art to be restored is the work of art which exists in the world

CESARE BRANDI
Central Institute of Restoration Bulletin
Rome 1951

I F ALL ARTWORKS had simply been left untouched at the moment of their completion, and if the only causes that contributed to their decay were those due to exposure to the elements, the work of the twentieth-century restorer would be decidedly easier. Instead of having to sift through centuries of patchwork repairs and ill-advised additions in an impossible search for the original "soul" of the work of art, the restorer could concentrate on assessing the state of health of the original materials. He could then proceed toward eliminating the factors responsible for the artwork's decomposition while reversing or arresting the damage wherever possible.

If a restorer could apply his craft with the absolute certainty that the object before him had not been modified since the artist declared that piece complete, the cloud of controversy that has plagued the restoration profession and promoted long and vitriolic debates might never have arisen.

Unfortunately, almost all works of art come down to us with some modification. A healthy slice of Leonardo Da Vinci's *Mona Lisa* was trimmed off in the seventeenth century in order to fit the

4   painting for a new frame. Two columns in the background were eliminated in the process, radically disrupting Leonardo's delicately complex perspective.

Michelangelo's marble *David* suffered a broken arm during a riot in Florence's Piazza Signoria when the statue was inadvertently struck by a bench, which someone had dropped out of a window in the nearby Palazzo Vecchio. The arm snapped off at the elbow and split into three pieces, which were alertly collected by Michelangelo's friend and biographer Giorgio Vasari. Vasari later repaired the *David,* attaching the fragments of the forearm to the exposed elbow with three copper screws.

Countless paintings, frescoes, and statues have been manhandled throughout history. Most Byzantine icons have undergone so many repaintings and revisions that the original work is buried beneath a sort of temporal collage. Other icons were smashed by fanatic reformers whose major contribution to world culture would be the word "iconoclast." It is mind-boggling to think about the numbers of wooden statues and paintings that were burnt during religious conflicts or revivals.

Art history is all too full of similar episodes. Man tends to transform the artworks with which he lives in the same manner as he tries to modify the landscape around him, in an effort to suit his tastes or needs. Yet even the wanton destruction that man has perpetrated through caprice or violence does not compare to the incalculable damage he has wrought through care. More artworks have been ruined by well-meaning but inept restorers than by all the King's horses, mobs, and men. Ironically, man has demonstrated that he is never quite so effective at ruining his artworks as when he tries to save them.

"In art, as in medicine, there are cases of neglect, of abuse, and also cases of too much or improper care," says Ornella Casazza. "I'd say that the Brancacci falls into the latter category."

Restorers and especially historians who work in restoration are fond of using the medical profession as a metaphor for their work. In the Umberto Baldini restoration method, the historian is a sort of general practitioner who helps to coordinate a team of specialized surgeons (restorers) and laboratory analysts (technicians).

Yet while there are many similarities between the fields of medicine and art restoration, there are also many differences. A physician usually can find out nearly everything he needs to know about a patient's history by simply consulting a chart or file. Data concerning previous surgeries, illnesses, and medication are readily available.

Art historians are not nearly as fortunate. Until very recently, it was extremely rare for a restorer to leave any sort of record about his work. There are a few notable exceptions. The Catholic Church, renowned throughout history for its meticulous record-keeping, filed a detailed report each time Michelangelo's Sistine Chapel vault was touched by restorers. These documents, containing vital information regarding the date, range, and most importantly the techniques and materials used by previous restorers, were invaluable to the team that worked on the vault between 1981 and 1990.

Unfortunately, the Carmine order was decidedly less diligent than the Papal State in monitoring its artistic treasures. The only text to which the Baldini/Casazza team could refer was the Brancacci Chapel itself. And the chapel was barely legible.

Despite its very modest size—in theory, one could probably pack one hundred Brancacci Chapels into Michelangelo's Sistine Chapel at the Vatican in Rome—the Brancacci Chapel has suffered more assaults, modifications, decorations, and disasters than most major cities. The walls, vault, entry arch, marble basements, floor, and most of all the frescoes bear ample evidence of more than five centuries of precarious existence.

Aside from a domelike ceiling, which varies in height from thirty to forty feet, the Chapel is no larger than a good-sized den or dining room. Its entrance measures twenty-two and one-half feet from the rear wall on which Masolino's *St. Peter Preaching to the Crowd* and Masaccio's *The Baptism of the Neophytes, St. Peter Healing with his Shadow,* and *The Alms Giving* appear. The two lateral walls that support the remaining scenes stand seventeen feet apart.

The celebrated frescoes are also smaller than one might expect them to be. Masaccio's *Adam and Eve Driven from Paradise* expresses the sum of all human pathos within the very human dimensions of six and one-half feet by two feet nine inches. Even the larger

6 scenes, like Masaccio's *The Tribute Money* and Masolino's *Tabita* are less than twenty feet across.

The cornerstone for the Church of Santa Maria Del Carmine in Florence was laid on June 11, 1268. The first notice of the Brancacci Chapel appears in 1389 in the Carmelite book of entries and exits; this was the register where all monies received or paid out by the church were recorded. That year's ledger mentions a payment to a group of monks for the construction of three walls and a vault in the chapel belonging to the Brancacci family of the Oltrarno zone of Florence.

The Carmine church was eminently public in character and intrinsically linked with the life and fortunes of the city. When landlocked Florence defeated Pisa in 1406, thereby acquiring the Mediterranean port so vital to its textile trade, the victory celebration was held in the Carmine church. As part of the festivities, a joust was held across the river in the piazza of Santa Croce; the joust was won by a young man named Felice Brancacci.

Brancacci was a wealthy silk merchant who performed several important diplomatic and military missions for the Florentine Republic, including a dangerous sea voyage in 1422 to the court of the Sultan of Egypt. Because of the decline in the wool trade (the staple of the Florentine economy) and the corresponding rise in silk, the wealth, prestige, and influence of the Brancacci family increased dramatically under Felice.

Like any influential Florentine, Brancacci was wary of arousing the envy of any of his fellow citizens, prudently avoiding any ostentations of opulence or political ambition. One of the few gestures of affluence permitted by the unwritten Florentine code of conduct was the commissioning of a work of art, preferably that of an altarpiece or the decoration of a chapel.

Sometime after 1423 and before 1425, commissioned by Brancacci, Tommaso di Cristofano di Fino, known as Masolino or "little Tommy," began work in the Carmine chapel on a series of frescoes based on episodes from the life of St. Peter. St. Peter was the patron saint of the Brancacci family and also the symbol of the authority of the Vatican. Like most Florentine merchants, Brancacci was a staunch supporter of Pope Martin V during the great schism and later during his wars in Emilia-Romagna. The choice of St. Peter as a subject was anything but casual for Brancacci, and

the frescoes, which he commissioned would serve as an unequivo-
cable endorsement of Papal authority in all ecclesiastical matters.

The forty-year-old artist began work with the four-leafed
gothic style vault that he decorated with frescoes representing the
four Evangelists. The standard architecture of the chapel's ceiling,
and the artistic conventions of Florence in the 1400s made this an
almost mandatory subject.

Having finished the vault, Masolino began work on the upper
register. We cannot be certain of the subjects that Masolino chose
to depict in his frescoes, since the original paintings of the upper
register no longer exist. Historical accounts of the chapel provide
some assistance, although none are precise enough to allow for a
definitive reconstruction.

In the 1550 version of *The Lives of the Artists,* Giorgio Vasari
writes that in addition to the vault Masolino painted a scene in
which

> Christ frees Andrew and Peter from the fishnet; and made
> there his [St. Peter's] weeping for the sin when he denied
> Christ and then his homily to convert the people. He made
> the tempest and shipwreck of the Apostles, and when St. Pe-
> ter frees from the sickness his daughter Petronella, and in the
> same story when he and [St.] John go to the temple, where
> before the gate lies the poor cripple who asks him for alms,
> whom unable to give neither gold nor silver, with the sign of
> the cross, he frees.

At some point during the decoration, for reasons that are still
unclear, Masolino was joined by a second artist named Tommaso
Cassai, better known to his contemporaries as Masaccio. The
name can be translated to mean either "large," "slovenly," or even
"bilious" Tom, depending upon the translator's wholly arbitrary
impression of Masaccio.

The two painters divided work on the six scenes of the middle
register. Masolino abandoned the job in the Brancacci Chapel, either to leave for Hungary in September of 1425 or for Rome in
1427. Masaccio, still in his early twenties, completed the scenes of
the middle register and then moved to the bottom register. Like
his senior colleague, he too would leave the chapel incomplete,

St. Peter Enthroned featuring supposed self-portrait of Masaccio—third figure from right staring out at viewer.

departing for Rome to join Masolino in the fall of 1427 or the spring of 1428, having painted only three of the six projected frescoes in the bottom register.

In 1433 a cabal of Florence's most powerful families—the Uzzano, the Strozzi, and most of all the Albizzi—staged a successful coup d'etat and drove the family of Cosimo de Medici into exile. Although he was related to the extremely wealthy Palla Strozzi by marriage—Brancacci had married Strozzi's daughter Lena in 1431—Felice tried vainly to avoid siding with either faction. But when Cosimo de Medici returned to rule Florence after just one year of comfortable exile in Venice, the Brancacci were one of the seventy Florentine families whom Cosimo had declared enemies of the Republic and subsequently exiled.

Bearing the name of a banished family, the Brancacci Chapel suffered substantial damage at the hands of Medici supporters and common vandals in the years following Cosimo's return. Many of the portraits that Masaccio had painted in his *The Resurrection of Teofilo's Son* were scratched out or erased altogether. It is possible that large chunks of the fresco, presumably those containing the effigies of citizens who had fallen into disgrace, were removed.

Toward 1460, with the ever-increasing popularity of the Madonna, the Brancacci Chapel was rededicated in her honor. A fresco on the rear wall was destroyed to accommodate the installation of a large twelfth-century icon that according to legend had arrived at the Carmine from Byzantium. Undoubtedly the principal painting of the chapel, this fresco in all probability featured the scene of St. Peter's crucifixion, and was almost certainly the work of Masaccio.

The central fresco on the rear wall was not the only painting to suffer because of the icon. When the Byzantine piece was mounted, the chapel's original gothic mullioned window was substantially shortened, causing a considerable reduction in the amount of light that entered into the chapel. Although the loss of light did not physically damage the remaining frescoes, it did disrupt the intricate color scheme, which Masaccio and Masolino had conceived to best exploit the natural light. The original beauty of the chapel, so dependent on the artists' innovative use of shading, was seriously compromised.

Reconsecrated as the Chapel of the Madonna of the People, the

The Martyrdom of St. Peter detail of self-portrait of Filippino Lippi.

Brancacci Chapel became the meeting place of a fervent cult whose members expressed their devotion by lighting countless candles before the sacred image, candles made from tallow or animal fat, which gave off a thick, sooty smoke while burning.

In or around 1480, a twenty-four-year-old painter named Filippino Lippi began the task of finishing the series of frescoes that Masolino and Masaccio had left incomplete more than fifty years earlier. Son of a painter, the defrocked Fra Filippo Lippi, Filippino had learned his art in the *bottega* of Sandro Botticelli where he worked as an assistant since 1472. Botticelli in turn was the disciple of Filippino's father Filippo. And Filippo Lippi, who grew up as an orphan in the Carmelite monastery and took his vows in 1421, was perhaps the only painter to know the privilege of watching the Brancacci Chapel frescoes take form before his eyes.

Adapting his own style to blend with that of Masaccio, Lippi completed the story of *The Resurrection of Teofilo's Son.* He preserved Masaccio's choreography while dressing the scene with portraits of Tommaso Soderini, Pietro Giucciardini, and Pietro Pugliese—all heroes of the Florentine Republic who have returned from the dead to witness the miracle that St. Peter performs before the moved eyes of Teofilo, prefect of Antioch. In addition to *Teofilo*, Lippi painted three other frescoes in the bottom register to finally complete the decoration of the chapel.

Presently, only three of Masolino's frescoes are visible in the Brancacci Chapel. Five of Masaccio's panels are still in place, along with a sixth Masaccio panel that Filippino Lippi completed in the early 1480s. The remaining three paintings in the Brancacci are Lippi's.

Beginning at the left in the upper register, we see Masaccio's *Adam and Eve Driven from Paradise*. Based on the story from the book of Genesis, the compelling 2.08 × .88 meter (7 × 3 foot) panel provides the thematic base for a fresco cycle, which begins with man's original sin and culminates in his redemption. Masac-

The Tribute Money by Masaccio, central group.

12 cio's strikingly modern scene also functions as an effective visual anchor for the chapel's intricate geometry.

Next to the Genesis scene stands what many critics maintain to be the most important painting in all of the Italian Renaissance. A masterpiece of rhythm, gravity, and composition, *The Tribute Money* spans the remaining 5.98 meters (20 feet) of wall and stands 2.55 meters (8'6") tall. The scene, skillfully fusing three separate episodes in the same panel, depicts Christ as he commands St. Peter to pay a tribute to the tax collector. Long assumed to be an illustration of Christ's well-known "render unto Caesar that which is Caesar's" dictum, the episode is actually based on a passage from the gospel according to St. Mark.

On the rear wall, perpendicular to *The Tribute Money*, Masolino has painted *St. Peter Preaching to the Crowd.* Taken from the Acts of the Apostles, it represents, along with the crucifixion, one of the most fundamental moments in the life of the father of the church.

Across the altar, still on the first register, the decoration resumes with Masaccio's evocative *The Baptism of the Neophytes.* At 2.55 × 1.62 meters (8'6" × 5'4",) its dimensions are identical to the Masolino panel. Thematically, Masaccio's composition is in perfect concert with Masolino's as it illustrates St. Peter performing another of his divine offices. Chromatically, the two frescoes are in harmony. But Masaccio's lifelike rendering of St. Peter and the nude figures waiting to be baptized are ages away from Masolino's idealized dramatization in *St. Peter Preaching to the Crowd.*

Passing on to the right wall, we find *The Resurrection of Tabita,* a wide, brimming, symphony of color and fable. Directly across from Masaccio's *The Tribute Money,* on a panel of identical size, Masolino's fresco is based on two separate miracles that appear in the Acts of the Apostles. To the left of the panel, St. Peter heals a cripple while heading to the temple with St. John. On the right, St. Peter resurrects a young woman named Tabita to the astonishment of the crowd.

Masolino's *Original Sin,* a representation of Adam and Eve from the book of Genesis at the precise moment of the Fall, completes the first register. Facing Masaccio's *Adam and Eve Driven from Paradise,* and identical in measure, the delicate, stylized couple serves as a visual counterpoint to punctuate the design of the chapel's upper register.

Original Sin by Masolino.

The Resurrection of Teofilo's Son and *St. Peter Enthroned* by Masaccio and Filippino Lippi.

14   Filippino Lippi's *St. Paul Visiting St. Peter in Prison* begins the
lower register. On the left wall beneath Masaccio's *Adam and Eve
Driven from Paradise,* the panel measures 2.30 × .88 meters (7'6" ×
3.) Like many of the lower register panels, the subject is taken
from The Golden Legend, a thirteenth century ecclesiastical text
by Jacob of Voragine. The legend recounts the story of St. Peter's
journey to Antioch in Syria, his imprisonment, his release, his
conversion of the town to Christianity, and his martyrdom.

Next to the slender Lippi panel stands *The Resurrection of Teofilo's
Son,* a Lippi-Masaccio collaboration and the last work Masaccio
executed in the Brancacci Chapel. Directly beneath *The Tribute
Money,* the painting shows St. Peter as he resurrects the son of
Antioch prefect Teofilo before the eyes of the stunned tyrant. The
scene ends with St. Peter enthroned, symbolizing the conversion
of Antioch to Christianity, and St. Peter's primacy as head of the
Church.

Like *The Tribute Money* above it, *Teofilo* is a monumental group
scene and of equal visual gravity. The 5.98 meter (20 foot) *Teofilo*
fresco also completes a thematic cycle that Masaccio began in *The
Tribute Money.* In the upper panel, St. Peter as an emissary of the
Church bows to the power of the State, as represented by the tax
collector. In *Teofilo,* St. Peter inverts the relationship and subjects
the secular authority of the State to the clerical dominion of the
Pope.

Teofilo also contains a wealth of portraits and iconography. Masaccio's figure of Teofilo is generally assumed to be modelled after
Gian Galeazzo Visconti, Duke of Milan and Florence's most hated
enemy at the beginning of the fifteenth century. His conversion
would have had a special significance for the people of Florence.

To the far right, beside St. Peter's throne, Masaccio has painted
portraits of Filippo Brunelleschi, Leon Batista Alberti, and his
own enigmatically defiant self-portrait, presumably done while
staring into a mirror.

On the rear wall, we find Masaccio's *St. Peter Healing with his
Shadow.* Like Masolino's *St. Peter Preaching to the Crowd* above it,
the 2.30 × 1.62 meter (8'8" × 5'5") panel takes its subject from
the Acts of the Apostles and shows St. Peter healing the sick and
lame with his shadow as he strides through a city lane.

On the other side of the altar stands Masaccio's *The Alms Giv-*

The Dispute with Simon Magus and The Martyrdom of St. Peter by Filippino Lippi.

ing, a scene of poor Christians donating their worldly goods to St. Peter. The body of Ananias, a man who fell dead after he attempted to keep the proceeds of the sale of his house instead of giving them to St. Peter, lies at the pilgrims' feet.

Viewed together, the four frescoes on the rear wall of the chapel are a graphic illustration of St. Peter's four principal duties on earth: to preach the word, to baptize, to heal the sick, and to give alms.

To the right of *The Alms Giving,* beneath *Tabita,* we find Filippino Lippi's largest and most ambitious Brancacci scene. *The Dispute with Simon Magus and the Martyrdom of St. Peter* has the same dimensions as *The Resurrection of Teofilo's Son.* Depicting St. Peter's debate with the charlatan Simon Magus before Emperor Nero and St. Peter's horrendous crucifixion (the father of the Church was crucified upside down), Lippi takes his subject matter from The Golden Legend.

On the lower right, at the entrance to the chapel, Lippi has painted *The Liberation of St. Peter.* Set beneath Masolino's *Original Sin,* Lippi's St. Peter is set free from his prison cell in Antioch by a radiant angel while a guard slumbers on his sword at the gate. With the same dimensions as *St. Paul Visiting St. Peter in Prison* and set directly across from it, Lippi's *The Liberation of St. Peter* passes from bondage to freedom, and from despair to hope, lighting the way to redemption to complete the chapel's thematic cycle.

The first known cleaning of the Brancacci frescoes dates back to

1565. Alessandro Allori, a popular painter, recalled the event in his *Rules of Design and Drawing.*

"And now we'll have a look at the lovely chapel of Masaccio," he writes, "and so much more so now that the monks have had it washed, like new, that one can see much better than one did before."

There is no mention of the technique used by the Carmelite friars. Most likely, the monks dusted the frescoes with a linen cloth, or with chunks of soft bread that could be dampened in the case of a particularly tough stain.

From the seventeenth century onward, the Chapel was repeatedly modified to suit the ever-changing tastes and styles of Florence. In 1660, a noblewoman named Costanza Sforza donated a giant lamp which was placed in the center of the chapel. The twelfth-century image of the Madonna that had supplanted the fresco on the rear wall was covered with pearls and precious stones. In 1670 a stonecutter named Agnolo Tortori was hired to construct a marble base along the bottom of the walls. Eight years later Niccolo Guicciardini, a prominent Florentine citizen, paid for a marble floor.

The frescoes of the Brancacci Chapel were very nearly destroyed in 1690. An extremely rich Marchese named Ferroni announced his intention to demolish and rebuild the chapel in the manner of the more modern chapel that the Corsini family had built in 1675 across the apse from the Brancacci Chapel in the Carmine Church. Ferroni encountered little resistance from the Carmelite monks who apparently were more than happy at the prospect of no longer having to view what one monk described as "those bearded farmers dressed in their mantles and robes in the antique fashion."

The work of Masaccio and Masolino found a very unlikely savior in Vittoria Della Rovere, a noblewoman from Urbino who had married into the Medici family and whose son became Grand Duke of Tuscany. She intervened to oppose Ferroni's plan to demolish the chapel, apparently after solicitation from members of Florence's Academy of Design and Fine Arts.

Ferroni was not easily dissuaded. After the first rejection of his project, the wealthy marchese offered to saw off the lower register "where the important scenes were" in order to preserve them.

This too was denied him, and Ferroni eventually built his chapel across the river in the church of the Santissima Annunziata.

The gradual evolution of the Brancacci Chapel continued into the 1700s. In 1707, four iron lamps made by a certain Arcangelo Finari were suspended from the entry arch. In 1714, a Carmelite monk named Angelo Benedetti donated a silver *paliotto*—a richly embroidered cloth that was used to cover the front of the altarpiece—weighing thirty-two pounds.

In 1734, the monks commissioned a painter named Antonio Pillori to clean and restore the frescoes. As with the 1565 restoration, we have no documents that describe Pillori's method. It is probable that, aside from ample repainting, Pillori also coated the frescoes with the *beverone,* an egg or animal glue-based mixture that was commonly used by restorers to revitalize a painting's dull or fading colors.

In 1746 the chapel was drastically and irretrievably modified. According to Carmelite records, Angela Tempesti, the mother of Carmine Prior Lorenzo Gaspari Masini

> . . . had the vault of the chapel painted by the esteemed painter Signore Vincenzo Meucci who, observing that the chapel suffered for darkness, undertook to illuminate it as much as possible using vivid colors which would allow for maxium reflection of the rays of light, and since the figures of the third [upper] order had nothing of value he covered them with his work, and he also retouched the scratches and abrasions of the good pictures, but with such delicacy that in fact the pictures appear untouched, and to render the chapel more luminous the religious benefactress had a large window opened and worked and embellished to perfection. And all this industry including the cost of the first facade cost . . . 1500 ducats. [the work] Was terminated in the month of July of 1748.

> This chapel lacked an altar and steps of marble to accompany all the rest, and Fra Andrea Spezzini soon supplied a remedy. And now that this chapel is adorned with its lamps, candlesticks, *paliotto* in pure silver, wax, flowers, mantel, etc., the impression is not unpleasant, and we poor brothers can be content.

18   While it is tempting to refer to the Meucci intervention as the rape of the Brancacci Chapel, it must be said that Masolino's vault probably did suffer from darkness, and that Meucci most likely found the frescoes of the four Evangelists in an advanced state of decay due to the consistently high level of moisture in the chapel's ceiling.

In 1771, during the night of January 29, a terrible fire broke out in the Carmine Church. The blaze originated in a pile of wood and straw left by workmen who were repairing the church's roof. By morning, the church lay in ruins. Miraculously, the Brancacci Chapel was left intact. Along with the Corsini Chapel, it is the only original structure standing in the Carmine today.

Still, the Brancacci Chapel suffered more than superficial damage during the fire. The searing heat caused the calcium-based decorations that had been mounted between the upper registers in 1748 to broil, leaving a dark stain along the walls. The extreme temperatures also caused the iron-based pigments in the frescoes to shift, visibly altering the color scheme of the chapel. Two large chunks of *intonaco*—one from Masaccio's *The Tribute Money,* the other from *The Resurrection of Teofilo's Son*—crumbled to the ground. And all the paintings were veiled by a thick layer of soot and dust left by the smoke.

The Chapel was extensively restored during the years following the 1771 Carmine fire. In 1780, the remaining branch of the Brancacci family, at the time residing in France, renounced all claims of ownership of the chapel so as not to have to pay for its maintenance.

The Brancacci Chapel then passed into the hands of the Riccardi family. Its new patron, Marchese Gabriele Riccardi, celebrated the acquisition by purchasing a bronze candelabra for the chapel. Riccadi also commissioned a painter named Carlo Sacconi to execute a thorough cleaning and repainting of the frescoes. Although Sacconi left no record of his work in the Brancacci Chapel, it is almost certain than he, too, basted the surface of the frescoes with an egg-based protective layer which also gave the paintings a temporary transparent clarity.

By 1830, scholars were already calling for a general restoration of the chapel. In 1864, another proposal was advanced to remove the "sordid deposits which cover many parts of divine frescoes."

In 1904 the paintings were once again restored. "It was deplorable that they [the frescoes] were veiled and half-concealed by a thick layer of dust which the humidity had nearly affixed onto the precious paintings," one journalist commented in the Florence daily *La Nazione,* after the operation. "Now that the inconveniency has been removed, and the frescoes cleaned with the greatest cure and diligency, we see them in all their admirable beauty."

Whatever the nature of this "greatest cure and diligency,"—the use of the *beverone* is almost certain here, judging from the rapidity with which the layer of grime reformed across the paintings—its salutatory effects were fleeting. Voices began calling for yet another intervention by the mid-1920s.

In 1929, the Fascist Union of Architects and Engineers proposed the removal of the twelfth century Madonna del Popolo to honor Masaccio on the five-hundredth anniversary of his death. This proposal, along with that of a cleaning of the frescoes, was held in abeyance by an administration that soon had other, far more pressing concerns.

During the Second World War, Ugo Procacci, then Superintendent of Monuments and Director of Restoration for the province of Florence, supervised the construction of an internal brick support to buttress the walls of the Brancacci Chapel during allied bombings. In 1946 the protective supports were dismantled, and the frescoes were dusted to remove a layer of fine red dust that the bricks had left across the surface of the paintings.

Florence. October 25, 1988. The International
University of Art.

Umberto Baldini is visibly a busy man. Paradoxically, he is much busier since his official retirement in 1987 than he ever was as Superintendent of the Opificio Delle Pietre Dure restoration laboratory in Florence or as Director of the Central Restoration Institute in Rome. In October alone he has travelled five times to Napoli and twice to Venice for consultations. It is only due to my good fortune that I find him in his office at the International University of Art where he holds the title of Dean.

"It's been my entire life for the past forty years," he comments, conspicuously consulting his wristwatch. "Art and art restoration. Always in the laboratory, or on the scaffolding at a fresco site. Or in the

Umberto Baldini in the Brancacci Chapel.

gallery. This is the only way to truly enjoy a work of art. To have it become an inseparable part of your existence."

Few men seem more suited for a life of incessant activity than Baldini. His raw and boundless energy is overwhelming. I have barely taken my seat across his desk and he has already shifted into overdrive. "I have no hobbies," the professor proclaims. "I have no other interests. All my free time is spent with art, or with my restorers, or with my chemists and technicians. My work is my recreation."

Baldini is the most respected and accomplished restoration director in Italy. Even his professional rivals admit a grudging admiration not only for his managerial ability but for his knowledge and acute intelligence.

"By now the restoration team is indispensable in our field," he says, as an introduction to his method. "And in our case the team is composed of three elements: the restorer, the scientist, and the historian. The role of the scientist is to analyze the material at hand. The role of the restorer is to heal that material. And the role of the historian is to form a link between these two mechanical specialists and guide them during their work. The historian adds his aesthetic and historical knowledge of the work at hand to the specific material knowledge of the restorer and the scientist.

"Each one of these disciplines, if taken to excess, can be deleterious for the work of art," Baldini says, shifting in his seat. "The scientist, for example, sees only the physical nature of the materials used in the work of art. While it is true that Michelangelo's *David* is made out of marble, it is also a piece of marble which has been treated like no other piece of marble on earth. The scientist, by definition, looks at the material but not at the work of art, whose existence extends well beyond the sum of materials used in its composition."

Everything about this man is animated; he cannot sit still. His empty hands seem to struggle against some invisible restraint, as if unable to bear even a moment's inactivity. Unconsciously, Baldini takes the sheet of paper containing the list of questions I have prepared for him and begins to fold it aggressively into halves.

"The restorer, too, must operate within certain limits. The restorers of the 1800s were full of presumption. They imitated Giotto, Raphael, Titian, Leonardo. They painted over these great artists and thought that no one would be able to tell. Some of them even believed that they were improving the pictures. To do such things they must have believed that they were as good as any painter who ever lifted a brush.

"There was a well-known painter and restorer in the 1800s," Baldini says, springing forward in his chair, "a man named Gaetano Bianchi, who once stated that Giotto was a superb painter whose only failing was that he hadn't properly understood the technique of perspective. This man, this Bianchi, set out to *correct* Giotto when he was hired to restore the frescoes in the Bardi Chapel at Santa Croce. And not only did he attempt to *correct* Giotto, he also artificially aged the fresco segments that he had painted in so they would blend in with Giotto's five-hundred-year-old colors. The only problem was that he didn't calculate that his work would also age, and in a different manner than the rest of the chapel. When we restored the chapel in the late 1960s, with the cleaning of the frescoes, the difference between Bianchi's work and Giotto's work was painfully visible. We had to remove all of the segments which Bianchi had painted.

"The restorer must force himself to be as objective as possible. But then again," Baldini races on; the sheet of paper is now folded into eighths. He slips it into his shirt pocket, his eyes either uninterested or entirely unaware of what his hands are doing. "Then again, the restorer must not be purely scientific. He must know how to read the piece. Restoration is not arbitrary. It is ultimately interpretation.

"I could give Sabino Giovannoni and Marcello Chemeri the same fresco painted by the same artist and each would do it differently. But each of them would remain within the limits dictated by the work of art.

22 Certainly there are limits in the text of the work of art. But there is room for interpretation within those limits. There is room for interpretation. We are lost if it were any other way. We are lost!" he exclaims, his dark eyes flaring.

"And then the third element, the historian." Here Baldini pauses and momentarily folds his once again unemployed hands. "The historian is the case doctor, the man who orders the tests and reads the charts and consults with the surgeons before and after the operation."

It is hardly a coincidence that Baldini has afforded himself the most important role in the three-member team. Gifted with an assertive, forceful character, and an agile, eclectic mind that is capable of absorbing and processing an astoundingly wide breadth of data, Baldini naturally strives to lead. His insistence on the predominance of the historian within the restoration team has caused some resentment among restorers, particularly among the older ones who had grown accustomed to their autonomy and to a greater share of participation in the many decisions that must be made during any operation. Yet restoration, as a profession, has drawn enormous benefits from Baldini's contribution. His method has provided a homogenity of approach which has allowed restorers to obtain consistently satisfactory results. His emphasis on specialization has attracted many of Italy's leading technicians and scientists to restoration. These scientists and technicians have applied their various techniques to art and dramatically increased the number of diagnostic and therapeutic options available to restorers.

Most important, under Baldini's direction, and due to the irrepressible energy that has permitted him to circumvent an often static bureaucracy, teams of restorers and scientists have collaborated to save some of the most valuable artworks in Italy.

"The historian is similar to the director of an orchestra who must decide on the interpretation of a particular piece and communicate that interpretation to his musicians," Baldini says, using an analogy to illustrate his vision. "He is the man who knows the sheet of music not for the notes which are written on it but for the music it represents.

"When Zubin Mehta first arrived to direct the Florence Philharmonic," Baldini leans back in his chair; his eyes dart toward the office door, which has cracked open. In a flash his gaze returns. "At his first press conference as musical director of the Florence Communale, he said that he hoped to do with the Orchestra what Baldini and Casazza had done with Botticelli's *Primavera*."

The *Primavera* was one of Baldini's most publicized and most successful restorations during his thirteen years as director of Florence's Opificio

Delle Pietre Dure. Botticelli's restored panel painting, a sensuous, colorful allegory of Spring, is on display in the Uffizi Gallery.

"Needless to say, aside from being very flattered, we were also pleased that an internationally acclaimed *maestro* had recognized that our work, at least in our approach, did in fact resemble his.

"The restoration team works only with what it finds before it," Baldini says, picking up speed once more after a momentary diversion. "With what is written in the painting. We don't add anything. We don't modify. We don't try to recover the original colors. Original. What does that mean? What happens if I wake up one morning and look in the mirror to find that I've got white hair and wrinkles?" he asks, pointing to his own face. "Does that mean I'm not original? Does that mean I'm not Baldini? Of course I'm still Baldini. I'm simply aged. These are my original colors in their natural state after sixty-some odd years. Now I could re-dye my hair jet-black if I wanted to, but I think it would look rather foolish.

"The work of art is no different. We lose the peaks over time. Colors fade, and some colors fade more than others. Imagine you had an old wax phonograph record of Caruso," he proposes as analogy. "A record of Caruso which is generally in terrible shape—scratches, gouges, etc.—but in which you can still hear a few perfect notes. But those perfect notes, mixed in with the rest of the record, only increase the cacophany. Taken out of context, that is, without the rest of the music to support it, those perfect notes are jarring, even unpleasant. It is virtually impossible to appreciate the music, except in fragments. At this point you have to make a decision. Which do you prefer? A couple of perfect high Cs, or a harmonic whole, a record which, although muted, allows you to appreciate the genius of Caruso?

"The same is true for art. Aging is inevitable, just as it is in man. And like people, various materials age at various rates. The chromatic balance which may have existed when a painting was finished in the 1500s may not exist today. And that balance, that harmony, is the basis of that painting's ability to transmit its message. We cannot confer eternal life on paintings or statues or frescoes. At best we can prolong the period of their expressive potential, that is, preserve, restore, and protect both the details and the whole of the artwork so that its significance—its music, if you will—can still be heard."

CHAPTER TWO

From Out of Nowhere

> After Giotto, art declined, because all artists imitated other
> paintings, and continued to decline, until Tomaso Fiorentino, known
> as Masaccio, showed with perfect work how all others who chose a
> maestro other than nature, maestro of maestros, labored in vain.
>
> LEONARDO DA VINCI
> Treatise On Painting *1500 cir*

ASIDE FROM A FEW scattered decades during which the artist's reputation waned, Masaccio's stature has been universally affirmed and magnified since Leonardo first credited him with having resurrected the art of painting. With his innovative modelling technique, his unprecedented use of perspective, and most of all his stark expressive power, Masaccio has been the object of an unabated veneration, which at times approaches a cult-like devotion.

Hundreds of thousands of pages have been written about the revolutionary nature of Masaccio's art, about his sheer, innate creativity, about the five brief years during which the young genius would lay the foundation for all painters who would follow him.

In themselves sufficient means to achieve immortality, Masaccio's astonishing achievements are even more alluring due to the veil of mystery that surrounds them, a veil that centuries of historians have attempted in vain to unravel. Very few documents regarding the artist's early life exist. We do not know, for example, in which artist's *bottega,* if any, the young Masaccio learned his trade. In this void, scholars have had no choice but to launch themselves into a freefall of speculation in identifying Masaccio's dramatic and irreversible departure from the popular International Gothic style.

As it was the site of the revolution that was to be known as the Renaissance, the Brancacci Chapel became the source of inferences as historians tried to piece together a plausible scenario. The oft-modified text was full of omissions and contradictions. But one element confused historians above all else.

How was it possible, they asked, for Masaccio to have given vent to his miraculous vein while working under the tutelage of a steadfastly traditional painter like Masolino di Panicale? The nature of the relationship that bound the two artists came to be considered as the lost chord that would complete the unfinished Masaccio-Masolino symphony.

At the heart of the matter was one question. Did the two artists share responsibility for the entire Brancacci project, or was Masaccio, as Vasari had written, called to the Carmine to finish the fresco cycle after Masolino abandoned the job? The issue would have been long resolved had the chapel's vault and upper register survived. As chapels were always decorated from top to bottom, a Masaccio fresco in the first register would be compelling proof that the young artist had worked alongside Masolino from the outset of the project. Unfortunately, the chapel's vault and upper register had been repainted during the chapel's dramatic 1748 renovation.

Few men have worked harder at ferreting the truth out of the Masaccio legend than Professor Ugo Procacci. A towering figure in art history since the 1930s, and the father of the Florentine school of restoration, Procacci put the history back into art history. As a young man he had studied with renowned Italian historian Gaetano Salvemini until Salvemini, an ardent anti-facist, lost his Florentine University chair. Therefore, Procacci came to the study of art with a historian's innate suspicion of the subjectivity that had characterized art history for decades.

In a radical departure from tradition, Procacci insisted that art historians support their often arbitrary conclusions with physical or documentary evidence. He demanded that historians familiarize themselves not only with the images and colors they saw before them on the canvas, but also with the materials and techniques, which the artist had used to create those images. By imposing his empirical historian's rigor, Procacci profoundly altered the nature of the study.

Procacci has done much to untangle the web of hearsay that
previous ages have wound around the figure of Masaccio, his relationship with Masolino, and his role in the Brancacci Chapel.
But in the absence of a written contract between Felice Brancacci
and the artists who would fresco his family's chapel, not even Procacci was able to arrive at the core. And he was convinced that his
last possible chance of resolving the riddle lay beneath the eighteenth century frescoes in the upper register of the Brancacci
Chapel.

December 21, 1988.

It is Masaccio's birthday, a happy coincidence for my first meeting
with Ugo Procacci. The restoration of the Brancacci frescoes is nearly
done. Most of the restorers have moved on to other jobs. Still, due to the
inertia of the Superior National Council of Fine Arts, which has yet to
decide what to do with the dismantled baroque altar, the chapel remains
closed to the public.

Professor Procacci is 84 years old. Because Florence is in the midst
of a two-week cold spell, and because Procacci has just recovered from

Ugo Procacci in his study.

the flu, he has invited me to his home in Piazza della Madonna D'Aldombrini, a few meters away from the Medici Chapel and the Church of San Lorenzo. His housekeeper escorts me from the elevator through a series of rooms until we reach the professor's study.

The room is an elegant, careless clutter of treasures: bookshelves overripe with first printings and rare volumes; a layer of prints and color photographs strewn across the furniture like a carpet of autumn leaves. The furniture, in good repair but showing signs of age, is eighteenth century Florentine. After a minute or so, Procacci appears.

One always expects old men to be small and curved, bent inevitably over their canes. But Procacci, despite his age, is still a giant. Well over six feet, he lumbers slowly but steadily into the study, barely lifting his large feet from the floor. His hands proceed him, hanging limply, almost immobile, from his wrists. His hair, still thick, is completely white. His mouth, seemingly atrophied into a marbled, whimsical grin, makes him appear infinitely benign.

"Buongiorno," he greets me, warm and genteel. The hand that had seemed so still awakens now to grasp mine like stone coming to life.

In 1932, one year after he entered service at the Uffizi Gallery, Procacci supervised the removal of two "ears" that protruded from the marble altar on the rear wall of the Brancacci Chapel. "It was not a difficult operaton," Procacci recalls today. We sit across an elegant cherry or chestnut desk which is sprinkled with books, photographs, and various correspondence.

"The two slabs merely leaned against the wall," he says. "They weren't supporting it. There was no danger in removing them. We did it with a handsaw."

The operation uncovered two small half-ovals, one in Masaccio's *The Baptism of the Neophytes,* the other in Masolino's *St. Peter Preaching to the Crowd.* These tracts of *fresco* had been sealed beneath the marble since the altar's construction in 1748.

"I saw the original colors," Procacci glows, his youthful eyes sparkling almost in defiance of the aged mask imposed by time. "It was a revelation.

"I knew that there was a thick layer of grime covering the frescoes, and that they had been darkened during the 1771 fire. But I hadn't expected to find such a dramatic contrast. The difference between the colors that had always been visible and the colors we discovered that day was enormous.

"These were the colors of the 1600s," Procacci gleams, "when the frescoes were still in excellent condition. The colors before the fire. And especially before the work of the many restorers who tried their hand in

the Brancacci. In that moment I saw that, as a colorist, we knew next to
nothing about Masaccio."

A few days after the removal of the slabs, Procacci had one of his
restorers paint a *fresco* copy of the newly uncovered sections to record the
colors as they first appeared. Today these copies can be found at the restoration laboratory in Florence's Fortezza Del Basso.

"I had the copies made in *fresco* because in those days color photography was not very common," Procacci explains. "It was a fortuitous
decision, because we discovered later that color prints did not have a very
long life span. The colors tend to fade or shift. In *fresco,* if properly preserved, the colors remain unchanged for centuries."

The discovery so inspired Procacci that a short time afterward he
declared that all of art history would have to be rewritten when the Brancacci Chapel had been restored.

"Historians had traditionally attributed the revolution in color to
Piero Della Francesca, Beato Angelico, or Domenico Veneziano," the
professor explains. "After having seen what lay beneath those two small
sections of altar, I realized that all these supposed innovations were already to be found in Masaccio."

Despite Procacci's enthusiasm, there were few echoes of his discovery in the academic world. The professor tried for decades to mount an
effort at restoration. "We even did a piece of trial cleaning," he says,
proudly, "in the panel where St. Peter heals with his shadow. Down near
the legs. Not the way they've cleaned it now, but with the techniques
that we used then, working slowly with a scalpel under a microscope.
The results were excellent."

Evidently, Procacci's "excellent" results were still not enough to obtain the approval of the national Fine Arts authorities. Year after year,
Procacci's proposal was blocked by a lack of funding and by a general
diffidence toward restorers.

"Historians have always been reluctant to make this sort of decision," the professor admits magnanimously. "In all fairness, I must say
that a part of their reticence is well-founded, given the widespread damage that restorers have inflicted. And when it comes to authorizing the
restoration of an important milestone like the Brancacci Chapel, everything moves twice as slowly."

In 1970, Procacci drafted his definitive plan for an eventual Brancacci
Chapel restoration. The professor's strategy, aside from a thorough
cleaning of the frescoes, prescribed that the restoration team was to
search beneath the Meucci vault and beneath Sacconi's architectonic decorations in the upper register for any remaining traces of the original
Masolino or Masaccio paintings.

His blueprint also included a clear idea of how the chapel would appear at restoration's end. "There is no need to disrupt the 1700s architecture," the professor wrote. "The entry arch and vault may be left as they now stand. But the altar must be removed along with the baroque window in order to recover the original decorations on the gothic window jambs, and more importantly, to recover the original light which Masolino and Masaccio surely took into consideration when designing the chapel."

The project was submitted to the Superior National Council of Fine Arts—of which Procacci was a member—and was, after a short debate, approved. Yet Procacci would retire before the Brancacci restoration finally got under way.

"Baldini got the go-ahead the year after I left the Uffizi," Procacci observes. There is not the slightest hint of bitterness in him.

"I'd fought all my life to be able to restore the Brancacci. While I never stopped crying out for it, even after I retired, I had begun to think that I wouldn't see the work done in my lifetime. And now, with the work completed, it is extremely gratifying for me to see my intuitions confirmed.

"My line has not been changed," he says, implying that Baldini, his former pupil, has presided over the Brancacci restoration the same way that Procacci would have. "All of the research has been conducted as I'd suggested. And at last, we see for certain that in Masaccio, there was everything one could possibly desire in a work of art. His work is one of the highest expressions in the history of mankind."

CHAPTER THREE

Masaccio

T OMMASO CASSAI, better known as Masaccio, was born on December 21, 1401, in Castel San Giovanni, known today as San Giovanni Valdarno, a small walled town about halfway between Florence and Arezzo. His father was a rural notary and came from a family of trunkmakers or *Cassai;* this was also the origin of the family's name. Masaccio's mother, Monna Jacopa di Martinozzo, was the daughter of an innkeeper in the nearby village of Barberino di Mugello.

The artist's birthdate is stated in Antonio Manetti's *Lives of Fourteen Outstanding Men of Florence,* published at the end of the fifteenth century. Manetti obtained his information about Masaccio from Giovanni "La Scheggia" Cassai, Masaccio's younger brother. Manetti's portrait of the artist begins:

> Masaccio painter, wonderful man, who painted in Florence and elsewhere . . . He worked also in other places, in Florence, in churches, for private persons; and at Pisa and Rome and elsewhere; from his time, among those who know, reputed to be the finest maestro. . . . He painted in the Brancacci Chapel more stories, and the best there is . . . it is painted by the hand of three maestros, all fine, but him, marvelous."

Twenty years passed between the artist's birthdate and his next documentary footprint, a receipt documenting Masaccio's first payment to the Florence Guild of Doctors and Spice Merchants on January 7, 1422. Guild membership was a prerequisite for any artist who aspired to receive important commissions. The Florentine

32   painters had allied themselves with the Doctors' Guild, as it was
the guild that controlled the commerce of pigments and other
products vital to painting.

At age twenty, Masaccio became an independent painter in Florence. Before that, nothing is recorded. It is known that Masaccio's
father died when the artist was five, and that shortly thereafter his
mother married an elderly spice merchant named Tedesco del
Maestro Feo. It is also known that Masaccio had a younger
brother. But there is nothing which might lend depth to our impression of the young artist.

We cannot even make a reasonable guess as to the date of Masaccio's arrival in Florence from Castel San Giovanni. Ugo Procacci
has discovered a document which mentions a payment made by
the Cassai family of Castel San Giovanni to one Piera di Bardi for
lodging in Florence between 1417 and 1421. It is more than probable that this was a rental agreement for the young Tommaso,
especially in light of the death of Masaccio's stepfather in 1417.
But the fact the artist's name does not appear anywhere in the
document leaves just enough space to allow for a reasonable doubt
about the identity of the tenant.

The next document that specifically mentions Masaccio is dated
1424. It is the certificate of the artist's entry into a second, more
selective painters' union, the Company of St. Luke.

It is 1426 before more hard evidence comes to light of the artist
and his whereabouts. A series of contracts and payment receipts
place Masaccio in the Carmine church in Pisa in 1426, from February 19 until December 26. Masaccio worked during that period
on a polytich for the altar of the chapel of Pippo di Giovanni di
Ganti for which he received 80 florins. (It is nearly impossible to
translate that sum into its twentieth century equivalent. In comparison with what most artists received for similar work, Masaccio
earned what might be considered the union wage for his work on
the Pisa Polytich.)

In 1427, with the city's coffers gaping after having born the cost
of a second war against Milan, the Florentine ruling oligarchy was
forced to levy a new tax. Under this tax, known as the *catasto,* a
citizen's contribution was calculated according to a flat percentage
of his net worth. Aside from being the forerunner of all graduated

taxation systems, the *catasto* is an incredibly rich vein of information, which has been amply mined by Renaissance historians.

From the vgarious *catasto* declarations we learn that Palla
Strozzi, the father-in-law of Felice Brancacci, was Florence's
wealthiest citizen with an estimated net worth of over nine million
florins. Brancacci himself figures as number 526 in the city's 1427
scale of wealth.

As a struggling independent artist, Masaccio's financial situation was quite different from those of Strozzi or Brancacci.

"We are in family we two together with our mother who is
forty-five years of age," he writes in his July 29, 1427, *catasto* declaration.

"I Tommaso mentioned above am of years twenty-five and Giovanni my brother mentioned above is of years twenty. We live in
the house of Andrea Macigni for which we pay a yearly rent of ten
florins. . . .

"I Tomasso keep part of a *bottega* (workshop) near the Badia of
Florence for which I pay a yearly rent of two florins."

A list follows naming all of the family's creditors and the various amounts owed them. The list includes monies owed to two
bakers that were secured by household objects placed in hock to
purchase bread. A debt of six florins owed to Andrea del Giusto,
an apprentice who assisted Masaccio on the Pisa Polytich, is also
mentioned.

The total debt declared in Masaccio's *catasto* comes to just over
44 florins. Under credits, Masaccio writes that his widowed
mother was supposed to receive the dowry of 40 florins that had
gone to the family of her first husband, and one of 60 florins that
had gone to the family of her second husband Tedesco del Maestro
Feo, and that neither of the two families seemed disposed to return
the money. Nor did the family of Tedesco del Maestro Feo appear
to have any intention of ceding a small house with an adjacent
vineyard in Castel San Giovanni, which had been promised to
Masaccio's mother in her second husband's will.

"I do not write the yield of the vineyard nor the dimensions, as
we do not know them," Masaccio concludes. "Nor does our
mother perceive any income from the vineyard, nor does she live
in said house."

And here Masaccio disappears. Two years later, in the spring 1429, the only notice of his death appears.

"Said to have died in Rome," the author of the declaration scribbled in the margin of that year's *catasto* next to the name of Tomasso Cassai, knowing full well that the family's tax liability would be lessened as a consequence of having lost a member.

No one knows exactly when or under what conditions Masaccio began work in the Brancacci Chapel. Nor is there a reliable account, which catalogues the panels of the lost upper register and vault.

Contemporary descriptions of the chapel are of scarce utility. "He [Masaccio] painted in the Brancacci Chapel," reads the text of *Magliabecchiano Code,* an early sixteenth-century compendium, "where the greater part is by his hand."

The Book Of Antonio Billi, also published in the first decades of the 1500s, contains a similar entry, differing only in that "the greater part" becomes "a part of which." Giorgio Vasari, the man most responsible for fixing Masaccio's star into the firmament of art's greatest geniuses, was no more precise.

". . . he finished a part of it," the historian writes about Masaccio in his 1550 volume *The Lives of the Most Excellent Architects, Painters, and Sculptors from Cimabue until Our Times,* "that is, the story of the chair, the liberate the infirm, raise the dead and heal the sick with the shadow while going to the temple with Saint Giovanni."

These three seemingly innocent lines have spawned enough hair-splitting among art historians to have satisfied a troop of Talmudists. Century after century of scholars have wrestled with Vasari's description in a vain effort to compel it to coincide with what they saw before them on the walls of the chapel. Vasari, in what would prove history's last opportunity to solve the riddle of the Brancacci Chapel, comes decidedly short of his mark.

The author of the *Lives* proved to be far more gifted as a myth-maker than as a chronicler.

He was an extremely abstract person and very casual. As one who had applied all his soul and will exclusively to art, he took little care for his own person and less for others. And because he didn't wish to think in any manner of the worries or things of this world, and not in the least about his clothes, and because he rarely went to collect monies from his debtors except when he found himself in extreme need, Thomas, which was his name, was called by everyone 'Masaccio.' Not because he was malignant, being as he was naturally good-natured, but for the total neglect for his own person while nonetheless performing services and favors for others with great affection. . . .

As fiction, Vasari's quaint and wholly subjective character sketch of Masaccio is innocuous enough. As artistic criticism, it is the historic equivalent of a rave review. Vasari begins his paean by observing that nature rarely creates an exceptional person without providing him with equally exceptional companions.

"And this is true," he illustrates, "in Florence, having produced in the same age Filippo (Brunelleschi,) Donato (Donatello,) Lorenzo (Ghiberti,) Paolo Uccello, and Masaccio."

These five men, Vasari explains, were not only responsible for erasing "the rough and clumsy style" that had governed artistic canons until their time, but also for laying the foundation for all artists who would succeed them. "And to whom," the biographer continues, "all of us, in truth, are singularly obliged, they who through their efforts showed us the right path. . . ."

After acknowledging the debt that his generation of artists owes its illustrious predecessors, Vasari turns to render that which is Masaccio's to Masaccio:

> And insofar as painting, to Masaccio in maximum, for having before any other made feet rest firmly on the ground, thereby putting an end to the clumsy manner of painting figures always on their toes which all painters had used until that time. And then for having given such vivacity and such relief to his paintings, a feat which merits no less recognition than if he had invented the art itself.

If Vasari is to take credit for having recognized in Masaccio the birth of a new era in painting, he must also shoulder the blame for

Adam And Eve Driven from Paradise by Masaccio.

having propagated one of art history's most monumental misunderstandings.

"He [Masaccio] began the art around the time Masolino di Panicale was painting in the Carmine," Vasari writes, explaining how after a period spent working in Rome, during which time "occured the death of Masolino, for which, remaining unfinished the

Chapel of the Brancacci, Masaccio was recalled by his great friend
Ser Filippo di Brunelleschi to Florence, and through him commissioned to finish the chapel.''

From the 1429 *catasto* of Masaccio's family, it is now evident that
Vasari, perhaps in haste, somehow exchanged Masaccio's death for
Masolino's. Masaccio died in 1428 or at the latest in 1429, while
Masolino is documented through 1432, and is estimated to have
lived well into the 1440s.

Despite its many errors, Vasari's *Lives* and the information it
contained was accepted with blind biblical devotion well into the
1900s. And his account of Masaccio's early formation, and the
circumstances that brought him to the Brancacci Chapel would be
held as a tenet until 1940, when another Florentine historian
named Roberto Longhi would use a newly-restored panel painting
in the Uffizi Gallery to turn Masaccio-Masolino scholarship on its
head.

Saint Anne and the Madonna

The Brancacci Chapel is neither the sole nor the earliest surviving product of the Masaccio-Masolino partnership. In one of the
first rooms of the Uffizi Gallery in Florence, there is a painting
that nearly all critics agree to be a work on which the two artists
collaborated before the first stage of scaffolding was erected in the
Brancacci Chapel.

The *Sant'Anna Metterza* (Saint Anne, the Madonna, and Five
Angels) is a panel painting meauring 1.75 meters at its apex and
just over a meter in width. The subject was a common one for
painters in the fourteenth and fifteenth centuries. Like almost all
Saint Anne paintings of the period, the Uffizi panel contains the
same, standard components: Saint Anne seated in a throne that is
surrounded by angels; the Virgin Mary seated before her mother
(Saint Anne); and the Holy Child in the Virgin's lap.

The *Sant'Anna Metterza* was apparently done for the Florentine
church of Sant'Ambrogio. Neither signed nor dated, it is cited by
Vasari, but only in the second edition of his *Lives*. As Vasari had
attributed the work entirely to Masaccio, his opinion, like his
opinion on the division of labor in the Brancacci Chapel, was ac-

The *Sant' Anna Metterza* by Masaccio and Masolino. Panel painting. 1423?
Uffizi Gallery, Florence.

cepted by nearly all leading scholars well into the twentieth century.

While a few important critics in the late 1800s did observe certain Masolino-like characteristics in the work, the observation was used to support the then-accepted premise that Masaccio conceived and completed the work while under Masolino's tutelage and therefore under his influence.

In 1935, the *Sant'Anna Metterza* was removed from display and transported to the Uffizi's restoration workshop where it was subject to a restoration that was to last nineteen years. Severely dam- aged by a disastrous 1700s restoration, the *Sant'Anna Metterza* had been liberally repainted during successive interventions.

From 1935 to 1953, the Uffizi restorers cleaned the panel's surface and removed the colors that previous restorers had added in an attempt to conceal its numerous gaps and abrasions. In 1954, a 33-year-old gallery inspector named Umberto Baldini supervised a final pictorial "accompaniment" before the *Sant'Anna Metterza* was returned to its place in the public gallery.

Longhi, who at the time was ruminating the revolutionary fodder that would become the daring central thesis of *Fatti Di Masolino E Di Masaccio* (*Facts of Masolino and Masaccio,*) was the first historian to decry the evidence of a second hand in the painting of the *Sant'Anna* panel. After a close examination of the *Sant'Anna* in 1940, he declared that the painting was the result of a collaboration between two artists.

The Madonna and Child, set firmly in real space toward the center of the picture, were, as Vasari had assumed, the work of Masaccio. But the weightless, somewhat wooden Saint Anne in the background was painted by Masolino di Panicale.

Not satisfied with having contradicted over three hundred years of history, Longhi proceeded to infer the nature of Masaccio's early rapport with Masolino from the visual evidence that he gleaned while following the restoration of the *Sant'Anna* panel. According to Longhi's reading of the painting, Masolino, after having designed the work, decided or was forced by other commitments to allot a certain amount of space to his assistant or collaborator. As *maestro,* Masolino naturally reserved the most important sections of the painting for himself, in this case the section encompassing the figure of Saint Anne.

The figure of the Madonna had always been subjugated by the more majestic Saint Anne in fourteenth and early fifteenth century renditions of the subject. There is no reason to believe that Masolino would have had any reason to invert the conventional hierarchy. But Masaccio's Madonna is so dynamic and vibrant that it steals the show from Masolino's Saint Anne, despite its inferior position on the panel. Masaccio's Madonna, modelled with a ribbed internal structure that Longhi likens to that of Brunelleschi's famous Duomo *cupola,* completely dominates the scene.

In his liberal but engaging analysis, Longhi also claims to perceive a visible attempt by Masolino to modify his own style in the figure of Saint Anne. The older artist, either aggravated or astonished by his assistant's unexpected prowess, tries to imbue his Saint Anne with some of the plasticity and power of Masaccio's Madonna in order that she regain visual supremacy. His effort is only partially successful.

All Masaccio-Masolino scholars now agree that the *Sant'Anna Metterza* is a work on which the two artists collaborated. Apart from a minor dispute regarding the angels in the background, historians also concur with Longhi's view of the division of the work. And while the debate regarding an approximate completion date for the panel is still open—the various estimates range from 1420 to 1425—no one has dreamed of disputing Longhi's assertion that the *Sant'Anna Metterza* was painted by Masaccio and Masolino before the two artists began work in the Brancacci Chapel.

Roberto Longhi's earthshaking inferences are subjective and by definition open to interpretation. It is impossible to know whether Masolino was in fact intimidated by his younger collaborator during work on the *Sant'Anna,* and whether he indeed was bullied into changing what had been for him a very successful painting style. Theoretically, it is even conceivable that Masolino had already begun experimenting with perspective on his own, and that Masaccio, painting according to his *maestro*'s instructions, simply demonstrated himself to be a far more gifted vehicle for this daring sort of innovation.

But the virtually undeniable testimony that Masaccio and Masolino had worked together prior to the Brancacci Chapel project, and that Masaccio, albeit in a work of less importance, had been allowed this sort of freedom, had profound historical ramifications. From 1940, until Baldini started research in the Chapel in 1979, the *Sant'Anna Metterza* was the strongest argument that Masaccio and Masolino could have worked together in the Brancacci Chapel from day one.

CHAPTER FOUR

Masolino from Panicale

NLIKE MASACCIO, with whom he is inextricably linked in history, Masolino di Panicale has been generally regarded as a gifted, lyrical painter who had the misfortune of collaborating with one of art's rarest geniuses. This is not to say that Masolino was not productive, or that his work was second-rate. During his lifetime, Masolino was an extremely popular artist who successfully adapted the International Gothic style to satisfy the lyrical, courtly tastes of the early fifteenth century Florentine bourgeoisie. Yet despite his delicate calligraphy, his exquisite use of color, and his inviting, enchanting, fabled landscapes, Masolino's reputation is inevitably trampled beneath the titanic, triumphant march of his younger and more celebrated partner.

The coauthor of the frescoes in the Brancacci Chapel has certainly received his share of recognition. Masolino's three surviving Carmine panels are universally admired. And more than one critic has hailed his *Pieta* fresco in the Saint Stefano Church in Empoli as one of the greatest masterpieces in all of art. Still, as history has dubbed Masaccio the noble conqueror of space and gravity, the fortunes of his fellow peers have visibly wilted in comparison.

History has been harsher with Masolino than with any other artist of the period. Critics have faulted and derided him for having been unable or unwilling to assimilate the artistic novelties that were taking form and shape on the wall opposite the one on which he worked. This may in part be true. However, with the recent cleaning, Masolino's Brancacci frescoes appear to demonstrate that the artist was much more aware of the science of perspective and the use of *chiaroscuro* than had been previously imagined. And,

La Pieta by Masolino. 1424? La Collegiata, Empoli.

Masolino is certainly not the only artist who failed to intuit that Masaccio's unusual, jarring, explosive style was not a momentary deviation but a decisive turn in the evolution of painting.

Tommaso di Cristofano di Fino, nicknamed Masolino, was most likely born in 1383 in the town of Panicale in the Valdelsa (a valley region about twenty miles outside of Florence). Cristofano di Fino, Masolino's father, was a whitewasher.

The first surviving document specifically referring to Masolino di Panicale is dated January 18, 1423. This is the receipt of Masolino's entry into the Florence Guild of Doctors and Spice Merchants. If the artist's estimated birthdate is accurate, Masolino would have been forty at the time. It is also interesting to note that Masolino became an independent painter one year after Masaccio. This alone casts serious doubts on Vasari's claim that Masaccio "began the art around the time when Masolino di Panicale painted in the Carmine."

As in Masaccio's case, nothing is known of Masolino's activity before his matriculation into the Doctors' Guild. But from the moment he appears in guild records, Masolino seems to have been inundated with important commissions. Aside from various Madonnas and panel paintings attributed to Masolino in museums in Europe and America, the painter from Panicale was also hired to decorate two chapels between 1423 and 1425: the Brancacci Chapel in Florence, and the Chapel of the Cross in the Saint Stefano Church of Empoli. The Empoli job is documented by a receipt, which mentions a payment of 74 florins made to Maso di Cristoforo on November 2, 1424.

Masolino next appears in the records on July 8, 1425, when he received a payment from the Company of Saint Agnes for his work on the decorations for that year's festival of the Ascension in the Florence Carmine. It is assumed that by this time the Brancacci Chapel vault and lunettes were already underway, and that Masolino began the job either shortly after becoming a member of the Doctor's Guild in January of 1423, or upon his return from Empoli. Several scholars are convinced that Masolino's inscription into the Doctors' Guild was simply a necessary formality in order for him to be eligible to accept the Brancacci commission.

What is certain, and we owe this certainty to Procacci, is that on September 1, scarcely two months after receiving the payment from the Company of Saint Agnes, Masolino di Panicale left the Brancacci job to set out for Hungary, where he had been summoned by a certain Pippo Spano.

Pippo Spano, whose name was actually Filippo Scolari, was a Florentine mercenary in the service of King Sigismondo of Hungary. The nickname "Spano" is an adaptation of the Hungarian title "bano," which roughly corresponds to the English "duke" or "earl."

Spano, who evidentally earned his title on the battlefield, founded a flourishing Tuscan colony in Hungary during the early part of the fifteenth century. Florentine and Roman ambassadors who visited him there speak glowingly in their reports of the one hundred and eighty chapels that Spano had erected. Although a Florentine by birth, Spano had been absent from his native city since the turn of the century. He had returned for a short visit in

44   1410, during which time he gave lavish parties and banquets and invited all those who wished to follow him back to Hungary.

It is curious that Pippo Spano would summon an artist whose work he had presumably never seen. Equally curious is Masolino's frenetic Florentine activity from the moment of his entry into the Doctors' Guild. Both anomalies strongly suggest that Masolino was already an affirmed artist. And if Masolino did not operate in his own name in Florence until 1423, it follows that he was active elsewhere, either in other parts of Italy or abroad. It is quite probable that Masolino had already acquired a substantial reputation for his work in Hungary. This would explain why he was summoned there, apparently out of the blue, in 1425, as well as the flurry of commissions that Masolino received in Florence after 1423.

Procacci's finding completely discredits Vasari's claim that Masaccio was summoned to the Brancacci Chapel to finish the frescoes that Masolino, upon dying, had left unfinished. It is possible, however, that Masaccio did arrive at the Carmine after Masolino's departure for Hungary in September 1425.

Before the current restoration, it seemed logical to suppose that Masolino had subcontracted the job to Masaccio shortly before leaving for Hungary, perhaps to avoid having to pay a penalty to Felice Brancacci for failing to fulfill his contract. But nearly all the evidence unearthed by the Baldini team buttresses the theory that both Masolino and Masaccio were present in the Brancacci Chapel from the beginning of the drama. This makes the idea of Masaccio bounding to center stage as a last minute understudy for Masolino highly untenable.

It is also quite improbable that Masolino could have abandoned the Brancacci job without his patron's consent. Felice Brancacci, who was a silk merchant, may well have released Masolino from the Carmine contract as a personal favor to Spano in exchange for an advantageous commercial accord. Pippo Spano controlled the major trade routes in Hungary, and Hungary was an important market for Italian silk.

All speculation aside, Masolino arrived in Hungary where he worked for Pippo Spano until the mercenary's death in December of 1426. The artist left Hungary for Italy in August or September of 1427. There is no indication that Masolino ever returned to

Florence. Chronologically, it is possible that the artist returned to the Brancacci chapel to finish the second register with Masaccio before leaving for Rome in May of 1428 at the bequest of Cardinal Branda Castiglione.

In Rome, Masolino frescoed the Cardinal's personal chapel in the Basilica of San Clemente with scenes from the lives of Saint Catherine and Saint Ambrogio. Aside from a handful of scholars who claim that the San Clemente Chapel was painted by Masolino and Masaccio during a hypothetical 1423 voyage to Rome, which is mentioned in many historical texts, including Vasari, historians generally vacillate between 1428 and 1429 as the starting date for work on the San Clemente frescoes. The earlier date is chosen by those who, having detected the hand of Masaccio in the central Crucifixion scene, need a chornology that allows for the possibility of his participation.

Masolino also painted a polytich for the church of Santa Maria Maggiore while in Rome. Like Masaccio's Pisa polytich, this altarpiece was also dismembered. The central scenes now reside in the Capodimonte Museum in Napoli, while other surviving panels are on display at the Vatican Museum, at the London National Gallery, and in the Johnson Collection in the Philadelphia Museum of Art. As in the case of the San Clemente Chapel, many prominent historians attribute a part of the work to Masaccio.

In 1432, Masolino received a payment for a fresco he painted in the Church of San Fortunato in Todi, Umbria. This is the last time the painter will appear in any record.

As in the case of Masaccio, the standard historical texts are of little assistance in outlining the life and work of Masolino. The *Magliabecchiano Code* and *The Book of Antonio Billi* both make only summary mention of the artist. Vasari's "life" of Masolino is even more muddle than is his "life" of Masaccio.

According to the author of the *Lives,* Masolino was

> a disciple of Lorenzo di Bartoluccio Ghiberti, and during his adolescence an excellent goldsmith, and on the work on the door [the door in question is the north gate of the Baptistry in Florence] was the best assistant that Lorenzo had, in the robes of the figures he was quite able and valid, and in finishing had much good manner and intelligence.

46   Because it was written in Vasari's "bible," the presence of Masolino in the Ghiberti *bottega* was accepted as gospel for centuries. In the 1403 and 1407 contracts for the north doors of the Baptistry, a certain Maso di Cristofano does appear as one of Ghiberti's helpers. This name has traditionally been identified with Masolino. Delving into the Florentine Archives, Ugo Procacci has discovered that there were actually three men named Maso di Cristofano in Florence between 1400 and 1409. One of these men, a Maso di Cristofano di Braccio, was a goldsmith who was regularly inscribed in the Silk Guild. Masolino, whose grandfather's name was Fino and not Braccio, does not appear in that guild's register.

"He took up painting at the age of nineteen," Vasari continues, "and this became the art which he would forever practice, having learned the technique of color from Gherardo dello Starnina."

Gherardo Starnina is a mythical Florentine figure who straddles the transition between late gothic and early renaissance art. Aside from a panel painting in the Uffizzi Museum that has been attributed, and not unanimously, to Starnina, his work has survived only in fragments. While Starnina spent a good deal of time away from Florence—his presence is documented in Spain from 1389 to 1401—Masolino could have conceivably worked as an apprentice or aide in his *bottega* before Starnina died around the year 1410.

Historically, Starnina crosses paths with Masolino in several locations. Starnina frescoed the Serragli Chapel in the Florence Carmine Church ten or fifteen years before Masolino began the Brancacci cycle across the nave. And both Starnina and Masolino decorated chapels in the Saint Stefano Church in Empoli—Starnina in 1409 and Masolino in 1424.

Still, as with the Ghiberti legend, we have no documents that could conclusively confirm this second stage of Masolino's education. Nor do we possess any evidence that could support yet another theory that suggests that Masolino may have worked as an apprentice in the *bottega* of Bicci di Lorenzo, an extremely popular and productive fifteenth century painter. Along with works in all of Florence's major cathedrals, Vasari credits Bicci di Lorenzo with having decorated chapels in the Florence Carmine church and also in Saint Stefano Church in Empoli. There are strong similarities

between his work and Masolino's, especially when working in
fresco.

And there is more. Andrea di Giusto, who assisted Masaccio in 1426 on the Pisa Polytich, was listed as a *garzone* or "gopher" in the Bicci di Lorenzo *bottega* a few years earlier. There is also another *garzone* working there, a certain Giovanni di San Giovanni. Several historians have not hesitated to identify this other lad as Giovanni "La Scheggia" Cassai, a second-rate painter from Castel San Giovanni who is better known to scholars as Masaccio's younger brother.

Vasari's version maintains that Masolino, after having learned to color with Starnina, travelled to Rome where he worked

> in the house of Orsina Vecchia in monte Giordano, and, for an illness which the air caused to his head, returned to Florence, where he made in the Carmine beside the Chapel of the crucifixion [Starnina's Serragli Chapel] the figure of Saint Peter which we still see today. And given that this piece of artifice was highly praised, it was decided to entrust him in that church with the chapel of the Brancacci with the stories of Saint Peter, and this work with every study he completed a part . . .

The account in the *Lives* follows with a description of the vault and the lunettes of the upper register, all of which were destroyed when the Chapel was renovated in 1748 by Vincenzo Meucci and Carlo Sacconi. Vasari's inventory also includes a description of *The Resurrection of Tabita* which he erroneously entitles *Saint Peter Who Liberates from Evil his Daughter Petronella*. In blatant negligence, Vasari mentions neither *Original Sin* nor *Saint Peter Preaching to the Crowd,* Masolino's two other surviving Brancacci frescoes.

After his incomplete list of Masolino's Brancacci Chapel scenes, and after an obligatory and transparently fulsome piece of praise, Vasari commits his most colossal and most inexplicable error.

"These stories," he sustains, "due to his death, he left unfinished. . . . Masolino died young at the age of twenty-seven, truncating the hopes which the people had harbored for him."

St. Peter Preaching to the Crowd by Masolino.

Consistent even in his mistakes, the author of the *Lives* has once more confused the biographies of the two artists who collaborated in the Brancacci Chapel. It was Masaccio, seventeen years Masolino's junior, who died young, after a brief but brilliant career.

Castiglione D'Olona

While Vasari credits Masaccio with a healthy volume of paint-ings, very few of these works have survived. Because of this scar-city, those historians wishing to delve deeper into the relationship between Masaccio and Masolino have been forced to search for evidence in the more numerous surviving works of Masolino.

Castiglione D'Olona is a stately, serene *borgo* perched on a hill-top in the Varese region of northern Lombardy. Seen from afar, even today, the village appears to be the incarnation of the distant, genteel, courtly settlement so often depicted by early fifteenth century painters like Gentile da Fabriano, Lorenzo Monaco, Ar-cangelo di Cola, and especially by Masolino di Panicale.

Castiglione D'Olona was the family seat of Cardinal Branda Castiglione. The enlightened prelate who commissioned Maso-lino (and perhaps Masaccio) to decorate his chapel in Rome's San Clemente Basilica is entombed in the *collegiata* there.

In 1843, while cleaning the white calcium walls of the vault above the choir in the *collegiata* church at Castiglione D'Olona, a workman, perhaps scrubbing just a bit too arduously, accidentally discovered what appeared to be a series of Latin characters chis-elled into the stone wall. Further scraping revealed a large inscrip-tion which read Masolinus Di Florentia Pinsit (Painted by Maso-lino of Florence).

Aroused by this unexpected find, regional officials eagerly sanc-tioned the careful removal of the white plaster that covered the *collegiata* vault in hopes of finding traces of a heretofore undocu-mented Masolino work.

The results of the excavation exceeded even the most optimistic expectations; an entire fresco cycle, designed and painted for the most part by Masolino, was recovered. Similar excavations in the Castiglione D'Olona *battistero* revealed yet another cycle of wall paintings done by Masolino and his *bottega*.

It was not at all uncommon for a chapel's frescoes to be plastered or whitewashed by a later age for whom the paintings have lost appeal or meaning. Giotto's sublime frescoes depicting the life of Saint Francis in the Bardi Chapel in Florence's Santa Croce Cathe-dral were also ignominiously buried beneath a layer of stucco. Ma-

50   solino's *Chapel of the True Cross* in Empoli suffered a similar fate in 1792.

Aside from exasperating, these unfortunate burials are also extremely unhealthy for wall paintings. Sealed from the air by a thick layer of plaster or stucco, the natural process of decay to which all artworks are subject is accelerated tenfold. We cannot know how long the Castiglione D'Olona frescoes were suffocated beneath their white shroud. They were already badly disintegrated when exhumed in 1843.

Despite their condition, fragmentary state, the discovery of Masolino's Castiglione D'Olona fresco cycles reignited the still smoldering debate regarding the relationship between Masaccio and Masolino. With no documents on which to base their estimates, historians are still deeply divided over the possible dating of the Castiglione D'Olona frescoes. Ironically, both camps use identical evidence to support two contradictory interpretations.

The fabled, courtly, fantasy world depicted in the Castiglione D'Olona paintings is ages away from the more modern work that Masolino did in the Brancacci Chapel and in the *Pieta* at Empoli. Still, even without the autograph of the artist, the Castiglione D'Olona frescoes would have been almost unanimously attributed to the painter of Panicale. Aside from his documented historical relationship with Cardinal Branda Castiglione, the late-medieval technique and subject matter of the *collegiata* and *battistero* paintings point overwhelmingly to Masolino. No serious historian has even thought to question their authenticity.

Much thought, however, has been given to assigning a year to them. A minority of scholars has embraced the obvious conclusion: the Castiglione D'Olona frescoes, being technically inferior to Masolino's work in Empoli in 1424 and to his work in the Brancacci Chapel (at a date most likely after Empoli), could not conceivably have been painted after these more accomplished works. Most of these historians agree on 1421 as a probable starting point. This was the year the Pope Martin V gave Cardinal Branda Castiglione permission to remodel his church in Castiglione D'Olona.

A second theory, and that espoused by the majority of Masolino scholars, asserts that the artist arrived in Castiglione D'Olona in the year 1435. Chronologically, the coauthor of the Brancacci Chapel frescoes would have left Florence for Rome in 1428, Rome for Todi in 1432, and shortly thereafter made his way to Castiglione D'Olona to decorate yet another chapel for Cardinal Branda, a patron who was already a great admirer of his work.

The collocation of these works toward the latter end of the artist's life requires a leap of the imagination that borders on faith. Masolino's Castiglione D'Olona frescoes appear rude and primitive in comparison not only to his Brancacci paintings, but also to the work he did in the Branda Castiglione Chapel at San Clemente in Rome. While the painter's documented works denote a growing mastery of the techniques of perspective and modelling—techniques which Masolino either assimilated from working alongside Masaccio or acquired through his own diligence—none of this skill is employed at Castiglione D'Olona. On the contrary, in his *battistero* and *collegiata* frescoes, Masolino seems to have painted in total ignorance of the many novelties that he assimilated during his long career.

If the 1435 date is to be accepted for Castiglione D'Olona, Masolino's apparent about-face requires some plausible justification. A sudden dramatic improvement, although inexplicable, is a very common occurrence in art. An equally sudden decline is much rarer. This is not to say that Masolino's Castiglione D'Olona frescoes are less appealing or successful than his other works, merely that they do not contain the slightest hint of an array of techniques that had become standard numbers in his artistic repertoire long before 1435.

Roberto Longhi expresses the majority opinion on Castiglione D'Olona in his revolutionary and ingenious interpretation of the Masaccio-Masolino myth. Centuries of historians sought to identify the benign influence that Masolino might have worked on his junior colleague. Longhi argues that is was the older painter from Panicale who was dragged out of his stately orbit when chance or fate steered a blazing meteor named Masaccio across his path.

According to Longhi, Masolino's art deviated drastically during the years of his collaboration with Masaccio. Overwhelmed and easily influenced, Masolino capitulated before Masaccio as if surrendering himself to the pull of a greater gravitational field. Longhi even goes so far as to imagine a heated discussion between the two artists in the Brancacci Chapel. An impatient Masaccio tries in vain to impart the basics of the science of perspective to a hopelessly befuddled Masolino, then reproaches the confused colorist for his feeble efforts at applying the technique in *Tabita.*

Longhi believes that Masaccio was a powerful, frightening, but above all temporary influence on Masolino. On Masaccio's death, with Masolino freed from the tyranny of the father of modern painting, the artist from Panicale once more becomes himself. Longhi is among those historians convinced that Masaccio did indeed participate in the decoration of the San Clemente Chapel in Rome. He even claims to be able to distinguish between the work Masolino did in San Clemente while Masaccio was still alive, and those parts that he painted after Masaccio had died.

Viewed through Longhi's eyes, Masolino's Castiglione D'Olona frescoes are merely the unadulterated expression of an artist who has at long last recovered his wits after his violent collision with Masaccio. Awakened from his nightmare, with all memory of Masaccio erased, Masolino once more sought refuge in the world of gothic illusion that was so dear to him.

Baldini remains wisely above the fray here, limiting himself to the diplomatic observation that the dating of Castiglione D'Olona is still widely disputed. He does observe that after the recent cleaning, Masolino's Brancacci Chapel frescoes, and particularly the *Tabita* panel, show that the artist was far more advanced than any historian had believed possible:

> Longhi wrote that the *loggia* where Tabita lay looked like a "rickety shack held together with nails." But now, with the full range of Masolino's chromatics recovered, we see how he used various tonalities of color to create a realistic illusion of space. The *loggia* has weight now, is solid. It exists in space. Before the removal of the *beverone,* the artist's subtle use of shading was concealed. Now, with the cleaning, we see an entirely new Masolino, an artist who was not only aware but also adept in using *chiaroscuro* to shape his figures.

Strangely enough, both the 1421 and the 1435 camps concur that there is no trace of Masaccio or of his influence in the Castiglione D'Olona frescoes. The 1421 faction explains this absence by pointing out that Masaccio and Masolino did not meet until at least 1423, and probably not until 1424 or 25. The 1435 wing interprets it instead as evidence that Masolino had shaken off any lingering suggestion left over from his short but harrowing collaboration with Masaccio.

It would even be possible to argue that Masaccio, either directly or indirectly, participated in the decoration of the Castiglione D'Olona *battistero*. In the panel that depicts *The Baptism of Christ,* several of the neophytes awaiting the plunge into the icy river waters bear a discernible resemblance to Masaccio's shivering figures in *The Baptism* in the Branacci Chapel. Although the *battistero* landscape and figures are almost certainly the work of Masolino, the painter has swaddled his males in the same undergarments that Masaccio uses to clothe his nudes in the Brancacci Chapel. There is even "a one who trembles" in the Castiglione D'Olona scene.

The Brancacci Chapel frescoes, despite the heavy *beverone,* were in relatively good condition before the Baldini-Casazza restoration. Unfortunately, the frescoes of Castiglione D'Olona have been ruined by time, the elements, and by repeated attempts at restoration. Little remains of the original work. We cannot know whether Masaccio may have based his Brancacci *Baptism* on the Masolino panel in Castiglione D'Olona, whether Masolino included these subtle but undeniable similarities as an homage to his dead collaborator, or whether some restorer, having visited the Brancacci Chapel, chose to repaint Masolino's *battistero* baptism scene in Castiglione D'Olona with Masaccio's superb Brancacci panel in mind.

Castiglione D'Olona, although a fascinating find, offers us little help in coming closer to understanding Masolino or Masaccio. Instead of supplying a potential solution to the riddle of these two men, the *collegiata* and *battistero* frescoes add yet another measure of mystery to an already-garbled tale.

The Chapel of the True Cross

The town of Empoli, about twenty miles from Florence, was an extremely affluent urban center in the fourteenth and fifteenth centuries. Many of the period's leading artistic *botteghe,* including those of Gherardo Starnina and Bicci di Lorenzo, were hired to fresco chapels in Santo Stefano degli Agostiniani, the town's central cathedral.

Since the turn of the current century, many historians believed that it was probable that Masolino, too, had worked in Empoli. And in 1938, Giovanni Poggi, then Fine Arts Superintendent for the provinces of Florence and Arezzo, found a document that confirmed their suspicions. The document, dated January of 1469, comes from the records of the Compagnia della croce cappella st'elena empoli (the Company of the Cross of the Chapel of Saint Helena Empoli).

> . . . and still we find that said chapel already mentioned above which the company had painted and completed on 2 November MCDLXIX we paid Maso di Cristofano painter of Florence florins 74 in gold as is written in our ancient books.

The Company's ancient books also confirmed that in 1792, a panel of Agostinian friars voted 6-1 to strip and then replaster the walls of the chapel that the Company of the Cross had commissioned Masolino to decorate.

". . . and when we do not believe that it causes any displeasure or offense to the public to demolish these rude paintings which have no existing virtues, and once replastered, to give these walls a background of gallant color . . ." an anonymous friar wrote in the church diary.

The passage from the confirmation that the Chapel had existed to the discovery of its current location was by no means certain. The church of Santo Stefano had undergone several architectural revisions since the early fifteenth century. There was no way of guessing whether the Chapel walls still stood, and if they did, whether any of Masolino's frescoes had survived.

Delving deeper into the Company of the Cross records, Poggi concluded that the Masolino frescoes had been painted in the fourth chapel in the right hand nave. The Superintendant's restorers removed the layer of plaster to discover a few scattered fragments of *fresco,* along with the artist's *sinopie,* the preparatory drawings done in a red-clay pigment directly on the chapel wall.

Neither the *sinopie* nor the fragments seemed typical of Masolino. The isolated *fresco* patches were especially puzzling as the

Band of Saints painted on entry arch. By Masolino (or bottega.) Fresco. 1424. The Chapel of the True Cross, Empoli. This band was discovered by Ugo Procacci and Dino Dini in 1956. It is probable that the Brancacci Chapel had a similar entry arch with similar decorations.

56 color scheme was far darker than any of Masolino's known works. The fact that the so-called Chapel of the True Cross had been decorated with scenes that depicted the life of Mary Magdalene gave historians further reason to pause. Still, as the decorations were undeniably the work of an artist from the early 1400s, and as the Company documents had indicated this chapel as the site of Masolino's Chapel of the True Cross, Poggi's attribution was accepted for many years.

Ugo Procacci began his career in 1931 as an assistant to Poggi. The pair worked together for more than thirty years in a partnership based on a complete professional and personal respect. But in 1954, after a careful reexamination of the Empoli documents, Ugo Procacci realized that his former *maestro* had misread the data. Masolino's chapel, if still in existence, and if Procacci's geometry was correct, was located in the first chapel along the right hand nave, and not the fourth as Poggi had believed.

In 1956, Procacci sent Dino Dini, his best restorer, to Santo Stefano. Working with the utmost patience, Dini removed the plaster from the walls of the chapel that the Superintendent believed to be The Chapel of the True Cross. When the entire surface was uncovered, it was clear that Procacci had hit the spot. Like the Mary Magdalene Chapel three niches down, only a few fragments of *fresco* were discovered beneath the demolished plaster. But those fragments were unmistakably the work of Masolino.

The *sinopie* were found to be in excellent shape. The episodes depicted—Christ Carrying the Cross, Christ on the Cross, Christ Arisen from the Sepulchre, Christ with the Eucharist—were perfectly consonant with the theme of Christ and the True Cross. And from an aesthetic and technical standpoint, Masolino's preparatory drawings were astonishing.

"These are among the most beautiful *sinopie* in all of the 1400s," Procacci proclaimed. "They show us a new concept of space, avoiding the crowding which was so typical of the period. In Empoli, Masolino had already evolved beyond the late gothic. We may not yet be at the Renaissance, but we are certainly on the threshold."

Interesting in itself as an example of Masolino's surprisingly advanced knowledge of design and spacing, the Chapel of the True Cross is even more valuable for the clues it provides regarding a possible reconstruction of the lost sections of the Brancacci Chapel. As with many chapels of the period, the four-leafed vault of the Empoli chapel is decorated—in *sinopia*—with the four Evangelists. According to Vasari, Masolino painted the same figures on the vault of the Brancacci Chapel.

Along with the Santo Stefano *sinopie* and *fresco* fragments, Dini also uncovered a decorative band that Masolino had painted along the bottom of the chapel's entry arch. Unlike the frescoes in the Chapel of the True Cross, this decorative band was uncovered in fairly good condition; a healthy portion of the artist's original colors had survived.

The band, jeweled with medallions that featured the heads of ten saints, was also a common motif in the early fifteenth century; almost all frescoed chapels from Giotto onward contained an analogous decoration. The entry arch in the Branda Castiglione Chapel in Rome's San Clemente Basilica is dressed with a strip that is nearly identical to the one unearthed in Empoli.

As the original Brancacci Chapel architecture almost certainly resembled that of the Santo Stefano Chapel of the True Cross, it is more than logical to conclude that the Brancacci Chapel had an entry arch that resembled that of the Empoli chapel. It is also safe to assume that the original gothic arch in the Carmine was decorated with the same conventional bands and saint's heads.

The discovery of the Santo Stefano *sinopie* caused a modest reassessment of Masolino's ability among art historians, and offered a stringent opposition to Longhi's view of the Masolino-Masaccio relationship. Having attested to the painter's unexpected facility in the designing of a *fresco* cycle, it became much more feasible for historians to accept the possibility that Masolino could have been capable of plotting and projecting the complex geometry of the Brancacci Chapel frescoes without any assistance from Masaccio.

The Sagra

Ugo Procacci did not always return from his artistic argosies with trophy in hand. He was responsible for several major discoveries during his long years of service, discoveries that included Masolino's Chapel of the True Cross and the missing bottom sec-

58 tion of Masaccio's *Trinity* fresco in Florence's Santa Maria Novella Cathedral. Unhappily, the find that more than any other lost work represented Procacci's golden fleece would ultimately elude him.

On April 4, 1422, the Carmine Church was consecrated by a trio of bishops. "And Masaccio, in remembrance of this," writes Vasari in the second version of his *Lives*, "painted in *verde terra*, with *chiaroscuro*, above the door that leads to the convent, within the cloister, the entire procession as it was."

The scene was set in the Piazza Del Carmine where Masaccio

> depicted an infinite number of citizens, in cape and gown, taking part in the procession, as if they were alive, among whom were Filippo di Brunelleschi, in wooden clogs, Donatello, Masolino di Panicale who was his *maestro*, Antonio Brancacci who hired him to do the chapel, Niccolo da Uzzano, Giovanni di Bicci de' Medici. . . .

With unusual attention to detail, Vasari observes approvingly that Masaccio had arranged the figures

> in rows of five or six, diminishing, according to the point of view, and not all in the same measure, but with a certain observance, that distinguishes those which are small and large from those who are tall and thin.

The fresco is mentioned and lauded in all pre-Vasarian sources. Antonio Manetti, in his *Lives of Fourteen Outstanding Men of Florence,* comments that not only did Masaccio "make natural likenesses of these gentlemen, but also of the door of the convent, and even of the gatekeeper with the keys in hand."

The painting was lost between 1598 and 1600 when the Carmelite friars restructured the church's cloister. Its destruction is virtually certain, although one seventeenth century source asserts that the monks deliberately preserved the *Sagra* by erecting a wall over it during the renovations. In the 1860s, a half-hearted attempt to locate traces of Masaccio's *Sagra* proved fruitless.

Aside from the regret that accompanies the loss of any great work, the disappearance of the *Sagra* is particularly acute for art historians who are already starved for evidence pertaining to Ma-

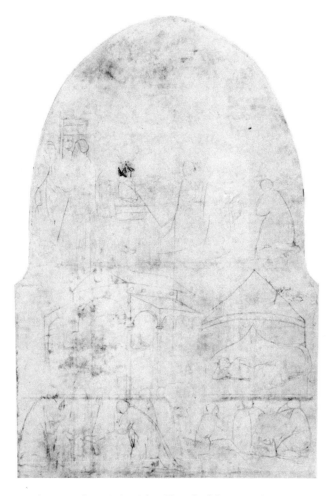

Synopia by Masolino. 1424. The Chapel of the True Cross, Santo Stefano degli Agostiniani, Empoli.

saccio. Had it survived, the *Sagra* would have constituted a welcome foothold for scholars. Many wring their hands in private at the idea of being able to compare Masaccio's fresco in *terra verde* to his work in the Brancacci Chapel. While the *Sagra* might not have burnt off all the mist that surrounds the Brancacci Chapel, it would have provided an invaluable point of reference in the study of Masaccio's development, and more importantly, of his development as a *fresco* painter.

Partial drawing of Masaccio's *La Sagra* by Andrea Boscoli, sixteenth century. Uffizi Gallery.

Fortunately, historians have not had to rely on the surviving literary descriptions and on their imaginations in order to reconstruct the lost *Sagra*. Six known drawings of the painting exist, including an early drawing by Michelangelo now at the Albertina Museum in Vienna, and a late 1500s drawing by an anonymous Florentine in Procacci's private collection.

The correspondence between the drawings and the historical descriptions is exact enough to cancel any reasonable doubt. Even in reproduction, the sharp, dynamic modelling of the figures, and most of all the powerful, kinetic spatial cadences, so utterly diverse from the static gothic crowding that characterized the period, point conclusively to Masaccio as the only possible author of the scene.

In two of the partial drawings, the gatekeeper with a ring of keys at his belt appears. The standard profile of Brunelleschi is easily recognized in four of the drawings, and always as the first figure in the third row. These four drawings also allow ample reason to infer that the third and fourth figures of the third row, a tall man and a shorter one both facing the spectator, are none other than Masaccio and Masolino (little Tommy.)

As might be expected, there is little concord about a possible date for the composition. Procacci believes that Masaccio began work on the *Sagra* months or even weeks after the consecration of the Carmine in April of 1422. Other historians argue for a later date, some as late as 1425. Most agree that the work could not have been painted before 1424.

Several scholars suggest that Masaccio may have begun the *Sagra* after he and Masolino had painted the first few scenes in the Brancacci Chapel. Vasari writes that "while he was working on this work [the Brancacci Chapel], that the said Church of the Carmine was consecrated . . . and Masaccio, in memory of this, in *verde terra* . . ."

Yet in his usual haste, Vasari has overlooked a fundamental contradiction. We know for certain that the Carmine was consecrated in April of 1422. While the estimates for the first Brancacci scenes vary, it is virtually impossible that Masolino and Masaccio were already at work in the chapel by that date.

Between 1932 and 1933, Procacci directed a series of historical investigations in the Carmine in an effort to ascertain whether any of the church's many frescoes lost or destroyed during the centuries of revision still existed. Climbing onto the convent roof, the young professor found traces of the walls of a chapel, which the painter Lippo Fiorentino had decorated in the late 1300s.

After a careful analysis, Procacci also located the site of the Chapel of Saint Girolamo, which Gherardo Starnina had frescoed for the Pugliese family in 1409. Although Carmine documents

62   maintained that the frescoes had been preserved, Procacci discovered only fragments of Starnina's work beneath the plaster. One fragment, a section of San Girolamo's library, was, however, sufficient proof that once more Procacci had hit the bull's-eye.

While of considerable historical importance, the Lippo and Starnina discoveries were of little consequence when compared to the eventual unearthing of Masaccio's *Sagra*. Procacci was well aware that other teams had searched, and in vain, for the vanished *terra verde* masterpiece. But the possibility that his historical predecessors had once again misread the documents and looked for the missing work in the wrong spot, and the seventeenth century legend that the *Sagra* had been preserved behind a wall during the 1598 cloister renovations were enough to fan his embering hopes.

The results of Procacci's documentary research were quite promising. According to his reconstruction, the *Sagra* had not been painted in the cloister along the church wall as everyone had supposed, but on the wall adjacent to it. This would place the original *Sagra* beside the site of the destroyed Chapel of the Passion. Working from the inside of that chapel, Procacci found traces of the original chapel door, which provided access to the chapel from the cloister.

Convinced that he had pinpointed the wall on which Masaccio had commemorated the consecration of the Carmine, Procacci gave orders to demolish the overlying plaster. Sadly, he and his team found nothing. Several centimeters had been shaved off the original wall. The *Sagra* had been destroyed. Even the two stone stairs that appear in almost all descriptions of the painting had been so thoroughly removed that no trace of them remained. The naked, chiselled wall, with wordless eloquence, testified conclusively that the *Sagra* was lost forever.

CHAPTER FIVE

The Green Light

I N 1979, after nearly a decade spent monitoring the condition of the Brancacci Chapel, Umberto Baldini concluded that the restoration of the celebrated *fresco* cycle could no longer be postponed.

"It's a misconception to think that we intervene on a work of art because some critic has decided that he'd like to see it with brighter colors, or without certain additions," Baldini asserts. "Or that frescoes can be removed from their walls at the whims of historians who simply want to see what's beneath them to satisfy some remote curiosity."

We are once more in his office at the International University of Art in Florence. Our interview, barely begun, is immediately interrupted by a phone call; it is Professor Paolo Parrini calling from the Syremont company in Milan. Baldini fields three demanding technical questions from the Brancacci team's scientific coordinator like a soccer goalie taking warmups. At the end of the conversation, he thanks his friend for calling and hangs up the receiver.

"The restorer doesn't touch the piece unless the piece has reached a critical point in its conservation," Baldini says, picking up exactly where he had left off. "Unless he is convinced that the original materials will deteriorate irreparably if he does not intervene to halt the decay."

Italy's most prominent and best known restoration figure recalls that as early as 1948, Florence Gallery Superintendent Monica Beccalucci had wanted Procacci to restore Botticelli's *Primavera*. "She always said that the artist hadn't meant to paint an allegory of Spring in brown," Baldini recalls.

"And of course she was right. The colors which we were seeing were obviously distorted by an organic lacquer which some restorer had painted over the panel. Certainly it would have been a great honor to restore such an important work. And who wouldn't prefer a fresh and lively Botticelli to one in which three sere and yellowed graces disported on a burnt brown lawn?"

"But these are not the factors upon which we base our decision to intervene." The professor's mouth pulls into a tight and anxious smile. "In the cases of the *Primavera,* it would have been irresponsible of us to clean it at that time. The original materials were not in danger. And the painting, although somewhat obscured, could still be read clearly. It was only when the colors began to flake off—this was in 1982—that we elected to intervene."

According to the data that Baldini received from his scientists at the Fortezza Del Basso and from several veteran restorers, the frescoes in the Brancacci Chapel had reached a state of decomposition that required immediate action.

"We had kept the Brancacci under observation since Procacci's time," Baldini elaborates. "For years, the results of our analyses were reassuring. Every so often an article would appear in the papers, calling for a restoration, decrying the sorry state of Masaccio's frescoes, denouncing the Uffizi or the Opificio Delle Pietre Dure or the Ministry of Fine Arts for its negligence."

"But what the people failed to understand was that the condition of the Brancacci Chapel did not change from year to year. The *fresco* cycle, although very dirty, was stable. In fact, I'd say that the Brancacci Chapel was chronically stable.

Baldini cannot emphasize this point enough. "Grime is not always a sickness," he stresses. "Grime is not always deleterious to the health of an art work. Sometimes the grime or the *beverone* even acts to preserve the original materials. But above all, grime is a momentary state. And as long as the work of art is still legible, there is no reason for the restorer to intervene.

"What worried us far more than the grime," the professor leans toward me in his chair, "were the humidity stains which appeared and disappeared on some of the frescoes during certain seasons. Humidity which inevitably brought mineral salts to the surface of the frescoes and left them there when the water evaporated. This, too, must be evaluated case by case. If these salts merely appear as

stains and do not pose a threat to the colors, they are not to be 65
considered hazardous. In the early 1970s, this was the situation in
the Brancacci Chapel. Unfortunately, towards 1977, we observed
that these stains had begun to erode the original materials and
threatened to cause a substantial color loss. This was when we
decided that the restoration was necessary."

The moisture that menaced the frescoes of the Brancacci
Chapel, and specifically Masaccio's *Baptism of the Neophytes* and
Masolino's *St. Peter Preaching to the Crowd,* both of which are on
the chapel's rear wall, was not a new phenomenon. Legendary
restorer Leonetto Tintori, who today at the age of eighty-two
teaches the art of *fresco* painting and restoration in his home outside Prato, remembers an inspection he did in the 1940s with Fine
Arts Superintendent Giovanni Poggi.

We are sitting in the living room in Tintori's rustic *colonica*
house. Above the fireplace hangs a copy of the central crucifixion
panel from Masaccio's dismantled Pisa Polytich. Tintori did the
copy himself, working from the original panel a four-day stint at
the Capodimonte Museum in Naples.

It is a faithful reproduction. Aside from a good imitation of
Masaccio's brush technique, Tintori was scrupulous in using materials that were nearly identical to those which the twenty-six-
year-old genius from Castel San Giovanni had used in Pisa in
1426. The radiant background is done in authentic gold. The restorer also found a way to age his panel to simulate the effect that
time would have had on the colors and on the wooden support.
Even the gold background is seasoned with a patina that would
convince all but the most expert eyes.

During his fifty-year career Tintori has applied his art to some
of Italy's most precious paintings. He is best known for his resto-
ration of Piero Della Francesca's *fresco* cycle in the Church of San
Francesco at Arezzo. And for his meticulous cleaning of *La Trinita,*
Masaccio's masterpiece of perspective in Florence's Santa Maria
Novella Cathedral.

"There was a substantial leak which trickled through the back
wall of the chapel every time it rained. At first we assumed that the
leak was somewhere in the roof," Tintori recalls. The restorer's
voice is mercurial and high; the difference in tone from one word

La Trinita by Masaccio.
Fresco. 1425?
Santa Maria Novella, Florence.

to the next make it sound almost as if he is singing. "But in examining the wall from the outside, we found a ledge about halfway up where the rainwater gathered after dripping down off the roof. It was there that the water entered into the wall. This was easy enough to remedy. We simply placed a sheet of glass over this ledge in such an angle that the water would run off of it and down onto the ground."

In 1957, Tintori returned to the Brancacci Chapel, this time with Procacci. "There were more moisture stains," Tintori explains. "On the same two frescoes, but higher up, near the corners. What made matters much worse this time were the mineral salts which had formed there. With Procacci we mapped the distribution of these salts. Evidently, a drainpipe which ran from a sink or bathroom above the chapel and down through the rear wall had cracked. And the entire wall was contaminated with the minerals which the water, leaking through it, had left behind. Even as far back as 1957," Tintori shakes his head, "it was a serious problem."

In 1972, Professor Mauro Matteini, chief chemist at Florence's Fortezza Del Basso restoration laboratory, accompanied Baldini for another series of tests on the rear Brancacci wall. "In restoration, even at the diagnostic level, you always begin with what you can see," the chemist says. "In the Brancacci, we were at the beginning of what could be called a chromatic crisis."

Returning to the same moisture stains that Procacci and Tintori had examined fifteen years earlier, Matteini took samples of the mineral salts for both a qualitative and quantitative analysis. "We found the minerals to be either sulfates or nitrates," he says. "Both of which can be extremely dangerous to the *fresco* materials if left alone."

Analyzing the origins of the various saline samples, Matteini also plotted a map that gave the approximate distribution and concentration of the salts. "For the most part we found the stains to be concentrated in two main zones," the professor explains. "As the moisture was not diffused, we concluded that it was the result of a relatively recent leak."

A second survey, performed in 1977, confirmed Matteini's deduction. "The stain was much less dense," he says. "And the salts had migrated considerably. From this we concluded that the cause of the infiltration, that is the leak, had been eliminated. Still, the wall was full of salts, and these salts continued to surface."

Matteini left a successful career in industrial chemistry in 1971 to accept a low-paying post at the Fortezza Del Basso. During his first two years in restoration, the professor had to teach junior high school in order to make ends meet.

"I came here most of all because it is increasingly difficult for a

68   chemist to practice chemistry in Italy," he says from behind his desk at Florence's Fortezza Del Basso. "Most of the time you get pigeonholed into one branch of analysis, or into testing one specific material. Coming to the Fortezza represented an opportunity for me to deal with an extremely wide variety of materials: bronze, gold, copper, *terra cotta,* tapestries, marble, *fresco,* panel and canvas paintings."

At the Fortezza, particularly during Baldini's aggressive reign, Matteini was blissfully busy with all sorts of artworks. In addition to his work in the Brancacci Chapel, he performed or supervised diagnostic examinations on *La Primavera,* Ghiberti's Baptistry *Doors of Paradise,* Donatello's bronze *Judith and Holifernes,* and the Piero Della Francesca frescoes in Arezzo.

"I've always been fascinated by ancient knowledge," Matteini confesses. "And particularly ancient technical knowledge. Nowadays, when we think about a civilization of the past, we tend to overemphasize that culture's humanistic achievements while virtually ignoring its surprising technical prowess. A twelfth- or thirteenth-century *maestro* of painting was first and foremost a *maestro* of technique. Giotto, aside from being a brilliant painter, was also a brilliant technician. How else could so many of his works have survived? The same holds true for Michelangelo, or Masaccio."

In early 1979, along with his colleague Dr. Arcangelo Moles, Matteini returned once more to the Carmine for a series of preliminary diagnostic tests on the Brancacci Chapel frescoes. Baldini, whose prestige in Italy was at its peak, lobbied intensely among the various ad hoc committees that had sprung up to deliberate this latest proposal to restore the Brancacci Chapel. A skilled and able politician, Baldini succeeded where Procacci had failed. The restoration of the Brancacci Chapel, nearly fifth years after Procacci pulled away two small pieces of the altar to unveil the colors that lay dormant underneath, was finally about to begin.

In any repair or renovation work, it is almost always preferable to perform all of the labor in one interval. Anyone who has built an addition onto his house or redone his den will attest to the discomfort that the work-in-progress creates around the home. Contractors are hired to schedule and coordinate—often with dubious success—the seemingly endless invasion of plumbers, plas-

terers, carpenters, tilers, masons, and painters in an effort to econ-
omize in both time and expenses.

The shattering of personal routine, especially in one's home, is never pleasant. Still, once the workers have arrived, and once the house has been gutted, most homeowners tend to take advantage of the interruption by executing all the small repairs they have procrastinated over for years.

In restoration, and especially in an on-site restoration, these logistical problems are multiplied. The restoration of a painting or small statue that can be transported to the laboratory has virtually no adverse effect on the gallery where it has been displayed. A few visitors may regret that they were unable to view Botticelli's *Primavera* during their visit to the Uffizi, but most will be so thoroughly overwhelmed by the museum's collection that any momentary disappointment will be quickly erased.

The case is different when the work of art in question cannot be moved. The prolonged indisposition of a major landmark or artwork inevitably creates ill-will, particularly among foreigners and tourists who may have travelled across an ocean to visit that particular piece. Rome's Trevi Foundation was barely visible through the jungle of scaffolding erected around it during the 1989–1990 restoration. The frescoes on the inside of Brunelleschi's dome in the Florence Duomo have been masked by bridges and green safety nets for the past ten years. Florence's Piazza Della Signoria, considered by many to be the most beautiful square in the world, was crudely transformed into an unruly construction site for nearly five years in the late 1980s while historians, archaeologists, and architects debated over the materials to be used in the new pavement.

Michelangelo's Sistine Chapel vault was a fortunate exception. The Vatican restoration team that worked on the ceiling *fresco* built an ingenious scaffolding bridge that spanned the chapel and could be slid from one end of the vault to the other along two steel girders that served as runners. This bridge, roughly thirty feet wide, concealed only the section of the ceiling actually under restoration and left the remainder of Michelangelo's *fresco* in plain sight of the visitors below. Although the view of the ceiling was partially obstructed—it can be argued that the opportunity for a tourist to compare the vivid colors of the already restored sections of the

70   vault with those sections that had yet to be cleaned was well worth the price of admission—the Sistine Chapel remained open throughout the ten-year intervention.

The structure of the Brancacci Chapel did not allow for this sort of partition. Its much more modest dimensions dictated that the chapel be closed to the public for the duration of the restoration, however long it might take. No one expected a rapid intervention. While Baldini had obtained the go-ahead for the Brancacci project because of the alarming situation on the rear wall, it was understood that his restoration would far exceed a mere removal of the discolorations caused by the mineral salts.

Once the chapel was sealed, and once his team was on the job, it made sense that they should also perform the historical research, which Procacci had outlined when he first submitted his definitive outline for the Brancacci restoration in 1970. No better opportunity to look for Masolino's lost vault, or to locate traces of the original first register beneath the Meucci decorations had or would arise.

In addition to its detective work, Baldini's team would also effect the long-overdue cleaning of the entire *fresco* cycle. Most important, Baldini had projected a thorough revision of the environment in and around the Brancacci Chapel, a project that included air filters, humidity and temperature controls, and periodic checkups to monitor the health of the frescoes and their supporting structure. In plotting to eliminate all possible causes of future decay, the Brancacci operation combined a program of immediate cure with an unprecedented long-range strategy of prevention. This accent on conservation was to be one of the project's greatest contributions to the fields of restoration.

It is unfair and inaccurate to call the moisture stains a pretext that Baldini used to launch what would be seen by much of the art world as the be-all and end-all of restorations. A much more realistic interpretation would be that the stains were the last and most intractable argument in a series of arguments whose sum effect was to shake the various Ministries and Superintendencies out of their habitual inertia.

Once convinced however, the governing bodies were all of one mind. If there had ever been a time to conduct the definitive search for artifacts that might write the final page in the mystery of Masaccio and Masolino, that time had come.

CHAPTER SIX

The Dismantling of the Altar

T HE FIRST AND SIMPLEST step prescribed in Procacci's Brancacci blueprint called for the removal of the baroque altar that Signora Angela Tempest—the mother of Carmine Prior Lorenzo Gaspari Masini—had mounted on the rear wall in 1748. The altar had been inserted as a final complement to the frescoes that Vincenzo Meucci and Carlo Sacconi painted over Masolino's vault and first register panels during the dramatic two-year Brancacci Chapel renovation.

Ostensibly, Procacci had used the recovery of the chapel's original light as his primary motive in justifying the altar's removal. The altar and the baroque window above it had been constructed at the expense of the chapel's gothic mullioned window, thus disrupting the natural illumination that Masaccio and Masolino had undoubtedly taken into account when painting their frescoes. In order for these paintings to be read properly, it was indispensable that they be lit from the identical source around which they had been designed.

Privately, Procacci nursed hopes that the removal of the altar might also lead to an even more important discovery. At Masolino's Chapel of the True Cross at Empoli, Procacci's restorers had discovered a healthy piece of the artist's original window decoration buried beneath a layer of eigtheenth century plaster. When decorating the Empoli Chapel in 1424, Masolino had painted an ornamental band along both window jambs. The band was jeweled with medallions featuring cameo-like portraits of young men and maidens; two of these medallions were found intact by restorer Dino Dini. Given the many architectural and decorative par-

Window decoration by Masolino. Fresco. 1424. The Chapel of the True Cross, Santo Stefano degli Agostiniani, Empoli. An identical decoration was found along the rear Brancacci Chapel wall when the baroque altar was dismantled.

allels between the Chapel of the True Cross and the Brancacci Chapel, Procacci thought it probable that Masolino—or Masaccio—had painted the same sort of ornamental band along the splayed jambs of the original Brancacci window. And his innate optimistic curiosity led him to hope that at least a part of this window, and a few fragments of these decorations still lay beneath the baroque alter, waiting to be discovered.

"Dr. Procacci came here in 1979 to ask me whether I thought it was possible that the artisan who had mounted the altar over the window in 1748 might have done so without destroying the decorations," recalls Carlo Bigliotti, chief of the marble workshop at Florence's Opificio Delle Pietre Dure. We are in the courtyard in the Opificio, seated among the pile of marble and *pietra serena* fragments that the students at the Opificio have used for their experiments in sculpting.

Bigliotti was born in Via Degli Alfani, just fifty meters from the Opificio. His father Alfonso had worked as a stone restorer at the Opificio since 1934 and was assistant technical director from 1947 through 1975. Carlo began spending his afternoons at the Opificio at the age of five. In 1957, when he turned sixteen, he was hired as a full-time restorer of stone monuments and sculpture.

"Dr. Procacci was seventy-five at the time and had been retired for several years. Baldini was director of restoration here. Naturally, the relationship between the two men was excellent. Procacci had been Baldini's *maestro*. The two men shared the same ideals and ambitions, particularly with the Brancacci, which had been Procacci's pet project since the 1930s. Even though he was retired, Procacci kept himself very busy in those days, almost as if he were still in service. You still see him in and about the city today," Bigliotti smiles affectionately; "at various restorations. He just moves more slowly now that he's nearly eighty-five.

"After having a look at the altar, I told him I really couldn't say whether there might be traces of *fresco* beneath it," Bigliotti remembers. "But in terms of work, it was certainly within our capabilities. We've dismantled dozens of simliar pieces. The altar in the Brancacci didn't promise to be of any great difficulty."

Unlike its extraordinary *fresco* cycle, the Brancacci Chapel baroque altar was ordinary in its every aspect. Hewn of white Carrara marble, the structure was composed of two essential parts: the

74 altar, and the *pala d'altare.* Centered against the rear wall of the chapel, the lower section—the altar itself—was rectangular in construction and was preceded by two steps. The altar's marble lintel which generally served as a table for a series of candelabrae stood 1.75 meters from the floor, a few centimeters above the base of the lower *fresco* register. There was a space of approximately sixty centimeters between the base of the altar and the rear wall of the chapel, a space wide enough to allow for easy passage.

Unlike the altar base which was freestanding, the *pala*—the ornamental upper segment of the altar—was flush against the wall. This was where Procacci had hoped to find his buried treasure. Aesthetically, the *pala* was a standard baroque reinterpretation of Greek architectural elements: two marble columns adorned with sculpted floral decorations rose from the altar lintel. The ornate baroque capitals at the top of the columns supported an architrave, which in turn supported a freize that was decorated with rectangles of red-polished marble. A triangular tympanum—elongated to conform with the tastes of the 1700s—which framed a heraldic stem was perched atop the freize.

Aside from its decorative and ceremonial functions, the *pala d'altare* also served as a dramatic frame for the Byzantine *Madonna Del Popolo* icon which had been placed in the Brancacci Chapel during the 1460s. From the altar lintel to the peak of the tympanum, the *pala* measured 4.85 meters in height. At its peak the structure touched the upper border of the second *fresco* register.

"The various pieces were anchored to the wall with a series of iron rods," Bigliotti explains. "When the altar was first mounted, the workmen drilled holes into the blocks of stone. The iron rods were then inserted and fused into place with molten lead. Once the lead had hardened, the piece was hoisted and fitted into holes which had been drilled into the wall to accommodate the rods. These altars were not sculpted out of a single piece of marble; they were constructed block by block."

Like its essentially hellenic design, the support system that the eighteenth-century artisans had used to erect the *pala d'altare* also had its origins in ancient Greece. "I've seen identical constructions in several Greek ruins in southern Italy," Bigliotti says. "The only difference was that in the fifth century B.C. the Greeks used bronze instead of iron for their metal brackets."

In the spring of 1980, with the full approval of Opificio Director Umberto Baldini, Bigliotti took a group of his students from the Opificio across the river to the Carmine Church where they would begin the disassembly of the Brancacci altar. The project did not appear to present any unexpected difficulties.

"I've worked here for over thirty years," Bigliotti says, with a smoldering pride. It is a pride, which could easily be mistaken for humility, the pride of a man who values a delicate manual skill enough to have spent his life cultivating it.

"In our work, you generally know what to expect before you set up a *cantiere.*" *Cantiere* is an Italian word which is used for all types of construction sites including shipyards and quarries. In restoration, a *cantiere* is the term used to signify any on-site intervention. "When you see a piece of stone which protudes nearly a full meter from the wall," Bigliotti explains, "you know that the piece cannot possibly be resting on the two slender columns beneath it. It has to be supported by some other method."

The *cantiere* at the Brancacci was erected quickly. The chapel was sealed with a plywood barrier, and a series of scaffolds and platforms erected. The work structure was also fitted with a system of pulleys and cranes to assist in the transportation of the various altar segments. "You have to remember that a piece of solid marble as wide as this," Bigliotti spreads his arms, "can weigh up to half a ton."

Working patiently, Bigliotti and his students took apart the upper section of the altar piece by piece. The iron rods that anchored the blocks to the chapel wall were either sawed in half or loosened with an electric drill and then removed. Each piece was numbered and catalogued to allow for a complete reconstruction in the future. The operation, which lasted nearly three months, held no unpleasant surprises in store for the marble restorers.

For Baldini, and Procacci, the results of the project were more than pleasant; they were astonishing. Day by day, with each piece that was removed, another fragment of the chapel came to light.

"It was a magical time." Bigliotti's face shines as he recalls the exuberance that accompanied his work in the Brancacci. "Every day brought forth a new surprise. In our work, when this sort of thing occurs, we consider ourselves very, very fortunate to have taken part in it."

The first article that Bigliotti's team uncovered was the bottom half of the original gothic mullioned window. "Evidently, the top half had been destroyed," Bigliotti surmises, "either when the baroque window was opened when the chapel was renovated, or during the fire. The bottom section of the gothic column is still in place along the base of the window."

Moving farther downward, as Procacci and Baldini had hoped, the team began to uncover fragments of *fresco*. The Brancacci artists had painted a band of geometric floral decorations along the inside of the window jambs. As with the two crescents that Procacci had uncovered in 1932, the newly-discovered colors were far more vivid than those of the rest of the chapel.

But there were even more discoveries, finds that would far eclipse the important reconfirmation of the chromatic reality of the Brancacci frescoes. The floral decoration continued, and in relatively sound condition, along the concave folds of the wall that ran from the window jambs down toward the floor. And just above the border that divides the two *fresco* registers, another of Procacci's hunches paid off. The team found two decorative medallions.

It was the sort of discovery that all historians dream of making and very few live to make. The work of Masolino and Masaccio, exhumed after more than two hundred years. "When we first saw them," Bigliotti recalls, "it was as if we'd discovered something as dazzling as the sun."

There was no question of the two medallions being anything other than original. The medallion on the left, featuring a delicate feminine figure, was a virtual copy of the medallion that Procacci's team had discovered along the window of the Chapel of the True Cross at Empoli in 1952. The medallion was obviously the work of Masolino.

The second medallion was a bit more enigmatic. Unlike the left-side medallion, this right-side cameo featured the head of a young man. While the colors were the same as those in the left-side medallion, the male figure appeared to differ from its feminine counterpart in style. The graphic elements were far less acute than in the left-side medallion; the young lad's cameo seemed to have been achieved through a skillful use of color and shading.

After an assiduous comparison, Baldini was certain enough to venture an attribution. The right-side medallion had been painted by Masaccio. "Even without the Empoli medallion as contrast, I wouldn't have hesitated to attribute the first Brancacci medallion to Masolino," says Baldini.

"The young maiden's head is constructed graphically, with clear lines and contours. And this was how Masolino always painted his figures. The contours on the right medallion are not as evident; the figure is achieved with light and color, not with line. The difference between the two medallions is similar to that between a painting and a sculpture."

Baldini's attribution has not been widely accepted. As attribution is never a science but at best an educated opinion, two medallions about the size of a 45-rpm record may not be an ample base for judgment. To further erode Baldini's premise, it must be said that this sort of decorative painting, if not assigned to a *bottega* assistant, was usually dispatched by the *maestro* as quickly and as impersonally as possible. Although it is not impossible to identify the hand of an artist in a perfunctorily rendered cameo, it is certainly much more difficult than in a complete panel or *fresco* where the artist has had sufficient time and space in which to express himself.

However, on close inspection, there is a discernable difference in style between the two medallions. Whether the male figure is sculpted, or whether it is simply not drawn as carefully as the female cameo, there is enough of a discrepancy in style that the prospect of a second artist cannot be ruled out. One could argue that the lack of graphic elements in the second medallion is merely the product of Masolino's haste to finish the job in view of his imminent departure for Hungary. However, it would be difficult to explain why he was able to work in apparent tranquility on the first medallion, which according to a reading of the original scaffolding holes, would have been painted during the same week.

In any discipline as subjective as that of attribution, there is always the danger that the quest define the discovery. Even in an empirical science like subatomic physics, researchers still tend to find the particle whose existence they have hypothesized. Certainly a part of the reticence that has greeted Baldini's attribution is due to the suspicion that Baldini wanted to find traces of Mas-

78 accio's work beneath the altar. The discovery of the Masaccio medallion on the window jamb across from that of Masolino would indicate that Masaccio was also present on the scaffolding during this early phase of the decoration of the chapel. This in turn concords with the hypothesis that the two artists worked as equal partners in the Brancacci Chapel, and that both had participated in the project from the planning stages.

We cannot deny that Baldini's attribution is extremely convenient within the context of his historical interpretation of the Brancacci Chapel. Still, if we accept that the second medallion is not the work of Masolino, Masaccio, who we know was present at some point during the painting of the Brancacci Chapel, remains for now the only viable culprit.

"The first medallion is definitely by Masolino," Ornella Casazza states with unshakable certainty. "It is virtually identical to the Masolino medallion at Santo Stefano in Empoli. The second medallion could well be by Masaccio. From a restorer's point of view," she changes tact, "this is only of relative importance. The heads are much more valuable to us as samples of the quality of the chapel's chromatics before the fire, and before the *beverone*."

Aesthetically, the dismantling of the altar provided an entirely unexpected revision in the reading of Masaccio's *St. Peter Healing with his Shadow*, the lower register panel to the left of the altar. Masaccio had painted a substantial part of the *fresco* along the convex section of the rear wall, the section that sloped inward toward the original gothic window. This section had been concealed from the eyes of artists, historians and scholars since 1748.

Upon removal of the altar, this substantial slice of the *fresco* came into view once more, adding the facade of a church, a belltower, a column capped with a Corinthian capital, and an ample section of sky to Masaccio's composition. These additions drastically redimensioned the distribution of space within the painting, and with that its traditional historical interpretation.

In the panel *St. Peter Healing with His Shadow*, the protagonist of the Brancacci Chapel *fresco* cycle heals a cripple by casting his shadow on him while striding through what had always appeared to scholars as a humble if not miserable quarter of late medieval

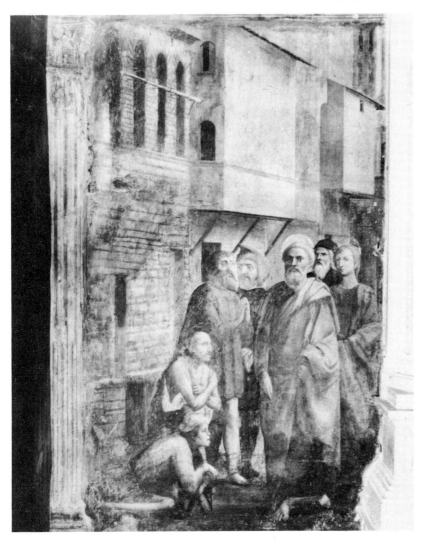

St. Peter Healing with his Shadow by Masaccio.

Florence. When Bigliotti's team removed the altar, Baldini was stunned to discover that the scene in which Masaccio had staged this well-known episode from The Acts of the Apostles was not a poor and decaying urban tenement but a linear alley that opened onto an airy, sunlit, metropolitan square.

The strong classical echoes in the panel's architecture naturally point toward Rome, and toward Masaccio's hypothetical voyage to the eternal city with Masolino. Vasari mentions such a voyage in his *Lives,* writing that while in Rome, Masaccio

> acquired great fame, and worked for the Cardinal of San Cle-
> mente in the church of San Clemente, a chapel where in *fresco*
> he made the passion of Christ with the thieves on the cross
> and the stories of Saint Catherine martyr. He made in *tempera*
> many panels which in the intrigues of Rome have either been
> lost or misplaced.

It has always been tempting for scholars to imagine a young, dumbstruck Masaccio, agape and awed while fumbling for his pencil to sketch the columns in the Roman Forum, or the upper sections of the Pantheon as workmen excavated the tympanum and columns. The trip to Rome would be extremely handy in helping scholars to identify the source of the "classicism" that character- izes the composition of Masaccio's lower Brancacci frescoes and his *Trinity* in Florence's Santa Maria Novella.

Sparked by an unreliable historical source and fanned by an ar- bitrary interpretation of visual evidence, the plot of Masaccio and Masolino's trip to Rome reads far more like a convenient romantic legend than like history. Still, from a reading of the frescoes in the San Clemente Basilica in Rome, Roberto Longhi was convinced that the voyage had indeed taken place, most likely in the year 1425, either before or during the painting of the Brancacci Chapel.

With his usual archival dexterity, Procacci used a series of doc- uments to demonstrate that the fabled Roman sojourn of Masaccio and Masolino, at least in 1425, was most probably an invention of Vasari. Masolino had been in Florence through July 1 of that year, and left for Hungary just two months later, making the logistics of the Roman voyage extremely problematic.

There was another hope that Procacci had long harbored while meditating his Brancacci restoration, a far more ephemeral hope than that of the already tenuous aim of recovering the chapel's original window decorations. Historians had long postulated the existence of a central panel in the Brancacci Chapel. Given the chapel's architecture and the artistic canons of the early Renais- sance, it is unlikely that a space as crucial as the center of the cha-

pel's rear wall had been left undecorated. And as the *fresco* cycle
depicts a series of scenes from the life of St. Peter, it followed that
this central panel had at one time been decorated wtih an episode
from the life of the apostle.

More than one scholar has theorized—perhaps in wishful thinking—that Masaccio himself had frescoed the central panel with the
scene of *The Crucifixion of St. Peter*. The supposition was not illog-
ical, and for a number of reasons. St. Peter's atrocious crucifixion—the founder of the Church of Rome was nailed upside down
onto the cross—was by far the most emblematic episode of St.
Peter's life. The artists of the Brancacci frescoes did choose some
of St. Peter's more obscure moments as the subjects for their painting while omitting many of the more standard scenes. There is,
for instance, no panel in which Christ presents St. Peter with the
keys to his church. Yet, as Baldini says, "In a chapel dedicated to
St. Peter, it's virtually unthinkable that the original plan did not
include a crucifixion scene. And what episode should be glorified
behind the altar if not the scene where Saint Peter leaves the earth
to join his divine maker?"

Aside from completing the chapel's thematic cycle, a hypothetical crucifixion set halfway up the rear wall would have functioned
as a visual anchor for the buoyant geometry of the Brancacci
Chapel. The sublime equilibrium that reigns over the frescoes of
Masolino and Masaccio is far too intricate to have been casual.
Obviously, the optical harmony was carefully plotted by the artists before they started painting. In a sort of geometric counterpoint, the figures in the left wall frescoes are balanced by the figures on the right. As a whole, the chapel draws the eye inward; all
of the frescoes seem to be designed around an axis that used, as its
base, a central point on the rear wall. An inverted cross, with St.
Peter's arms spread perpendicular to the ground, would have
served as a perfect device for providing the horizontal and vertical
coordinates for the complex geometry of the *fresco* cycle.

To further whet the appetites and imaginations of quixotic historians, there was the *predella* panel from Masaccio's dismantled
Pisa Polytich, now at the Staatliche Museum in Berlin. Here Masaccio had painted the selfsame scene of St. Peter's crucifixion in
1426. None of Masolino's surviving works feature a similar episode. And while it is true that a man cannot be incriminated on

82 precedent, it is safe to surmise that if there was a crucifixion scene in the original Brancacci Chapel, it was almost certainly the work of Masaccio.

Historically, the scene does not appear in any of the early descriptions of the famous frescoes. Vasari makes no mention of it; nor do Manetti or *Antonio Billi*. Still, the lack of documentation does not preclude that the crucifixion scene could have existed. The earliest of these sources was written toward the end of the 1400s; Masaccio finished his work in the Brancacci Chapel in 1427 or 1428 at the latest. The panel could have easily been destroyed or removed before Manetti or the authors of *Antonio Billi* and *The Maglibecchiano Code* ever laid eyes on the *fresco* cycle.

There is a *Crucifixion of St. Peter* visible in the chapel today. It is the work of Filippinio Lippi, who completed the *fresco* cycle in the early 1480s. Since it is unlikely that Lippi would have reproduced an already existing episode, we can assume that Masaccio's *Crucifixion,* if it ever existed, had already been removed, destroyed, or covered up by that time.

There are many possible explanations for the disappearance of a panel whose existence had never been proven. The *fresco* could have been removed or destroyed when the Byzantine *Madonna del Popolo* icon was mounted in the Chapel in the 1460s. The *Crucifixion of St. Peter* could also have been hacked or chiselled to pieces during the vandalism that followed the downfall of the Brancacci family in 1436 after their part in the coup d'etat against Cosimo de Medici. This vandalism theory, which while cogent has never been demonstrated as fact, would also provide a convenient explanation for the large gaps that Masaccio left in his *The Resurrection of Teofilo's Son,* gaps that were eventually painted in by Filippino Lippi.

Viewed dispassionately, the theory that argued that *The Crucifixion of St. Peter* had once existed was tenuous at best. And even if the scene had in fact been painted, the chances of its having survived intact were slim. The odds on finding fragments or the preparatory drawing of the crucifixion scene were somewhat better, but still overwhelmingly negative.

Bigliotti and his students at the Opificio did find traces of *fresco* beneath the window when the central section of the *pala d'altare*

had been dismantled. Nearly all of the original painting had been
removed, and apparently all at once, as if whoever had detached
the *fresco* had done so in an attempt to save the image. Only two
fragments still remained, attached on opposite sides of the panel
like mute and enigmatic pieces of a puzzle which in all probability
will never be completed.

A two-foot long fragment in the upper right-hand segment of
the vacant panel is painted with traces of a pastoral landscape and
bordered by a band of blue sky in the background. The second,
left-hand fragment features instead a flesh-colored object that appears to be a piece of a human figure, most likely an arm or a leg.

Although the two surviving segments hardly constitute a solid
basis for judgment, there are some undeniable echoes between the
geometry of the central Brancacci *fresco* and that of *The Martyrdom
of St. Peter,* the *predella* of Masaccio's Pisa Polytich in Berlin. The
human limb featured in the left-hand fragment could very easily
have been the bent elbow of the man who drove the spike through
the hand of St. Peter to affix him to the cross. In the Pisa *predella,*
this elbow appears at a point that corresponds almost exactly with
the location of the flesh-colored fragment in the Brancacci.

Based on a visual analysis, Baldini boldly concluded that the
two fragments were indeed all that had survived of Masaccio's *The
Crucifixion of St. Peter* in the Brancacci Chapel. Like his attribution
of the youth's head in the decorative band along the window, this
declaration was also met with widespread and understandable
skepticism. The discovery of the *fresco* fragments certainly bolsters
the theoretical existence of a Masaccio crucifixion scene in the
Brancacci Chapel. However, the physical evidence that was uncovered during the dismantling of the altar is not nearly complete
enough to transport the painting out of the realm of conjecture
and into that of fact.

From the near-absolute absence of any decoration or plaster
where the central *fresco* would have stood, we can safely infer that
the original chapel decoration did at one point include some sort
of painted scene, and that this scene was subsequently removed.
And from the sophisticated geometry of the Masaccio-Masolino
fresco cycle, it is also more than likely that the missing panel was
also the thematic and optical center of the chapel.

84   For these reasons, the two *fresco* fragments were a tantalizing and important find, perhaps of greater historical significance than the discovery of the original window decoration. But for those who sought a definitive confirmation of the Masaccio crucifixion scene, these two cryptic and disjointed remnants could not possibly have provided the necessary certitude.

CHAPTER SEVEN

The Lost Vault

ENCOURAGED BY THE WEALTH of material, which was brought to light when the altar was removed, Baldini was eager to proceed to the second phase of Procacci's research outline. This phase was to include what would be the definitive search for the four evangelists that Masolino di Panicale frescoed onto the original gothic vault of the Brancacci Chapel, and for the chapel's upper *fresco* register.

In the winter of 1981, a few months after the dismantling of the Brancacci altar, Baldini instructed *fresco* restorer Guido Botticelli to set up a *cantiere* in the chapel with a group of his students from the Opificio Delle Pietre Dure. Botticelli had been on hand in the Brancacci for the three-month altar operation as a *fresco* consultant, and also to insure that the priceless cycle of paintings suffered no damage during the laborious disassembly.

Guido Botticelli is fifty years old. At the age of twenty, along with a friend named Sabino Giovannoni, he entered the Florentine restoration *bottega* of Dino Dini as an apprentice. In 1976, after seventeen years with Dini, Botticelli and Giovannoni both passed a state-sanctioned exam and went to work for Baldini as restorers at the Opificio Delle Pietre Dure.

When I visit Botticelli in January of 1989, he is directing a *cantiere* in the nave of Florence's Santa Maria Novella Cathedral. It is believed that a young Michelangelo Buonarrotti helped his *maestro* Domenico Ghirlandaio in the painting of these brilliantly colored frescoes. I find the veteran restorer in a heavy winter coat, alone on the scaffolding. His students are on vacation, and he has come to examine the zones where his team has effected several different techniques of trial cleaning in order to determine which method will be used on this section of wall.

Botticelli holds out his hand to me as I reach the first level of the scaffolding, but then, at the last instant retracts it. Grinning, he holds up his palm apologetically to explain; the skin is falling off in large, discolored flakes.

"Occupational hazard," he explains. "From all the chemicals we use here. Happens even if you wear gloves. Sometimes I still forget, even after all this time."

Lighting the way with a hand-held electric lamp, he guides me along the frescoed wall toward the end of the platform. Ghirlandaio's colors are warm and hearty: rich violets, deep burgundy reds, sapphire blue. In contrast, the church air is throbbingly cold. "We've experimented with five or six cleaning methods here," he explains, and shines his lamp to illuminate the zones where the trials were effected. "We've tried ammonium carbonate in wood compresses, painted on rice paper, ammonium bicarbonate, distilled water. We even did a trial with the anionic resins that they used in the Brancacci."

He shifts his lamp from one zone to the next to illuminate the various results. "Because in this work, every chapel is different, with different problems which require different solutions. Every *fresco* is different, even if they happen to be in the same chapel." Botticelli pauses; something on the painting before us has caught his eye. He places the lamp flush against the wall and directs the light downward, parallel to the fresco. In this raking light, a thin sprinkling of mineral crystals is suddenly visible across the surface of the painting.

"Mineral salts," he says, shaking his head. "Probably sulfates, but could just as easily be nitrates or carbonates. I wish Matteini were here." Professor Mauro Matteini is the chief chemist at the Opificio's Fortezza Del Basso restoration laboratory which provides the technical support for the city's restorers.

"Last month we were working across the nave." He motions to the wall opposite the one where we are standing, decorated with more panels from the same Ghirlandaio *fresco* cycle. "And in moving fifteen meters, from one wall to another, it's like I've moved fifteen miles. The situation here is entirely different.

"There are no standard cures in this work," he reiterates. "Each

time you approach a new *fresco*, you have to start from scratch. A
technique which might have worked beautifully in the Brancacci
might not work at all here. And another technique which might
provide excellent results here could be totally ineffective at San
Marco."

After having evaluated the cleaning trials, Botticelli suggests
that we go somewhere else for our chat. Climbing down from the
scaffolding, we walk past Masaccio's majestic *Trinity fresco,* out of
the dark Santa Maria Novella Cathedral and cross the wintry, pi-
geon-speckled piazza to have a coffee at Botticelli's habitual bar.

"When we started out at the Brancacci," the restorer says, "we
were all fairly optimistic about finding at least a part of the vault
structure." We are seated at a table in front of a window with an
excellent view of Piazza Santa Maria Novella. Two dog owners
have brought their pets to romp on the small plot of grass. A blue-
eyed husky chases pigeons; on the far side of the piazza, near the
church, a lone vendor sells peanuts.

"Procacci himself was convinced that the vault was still intact,
and that Masolino's frescoes had merely been painted over by
Meucci. He even maintained that as a young man he had been
lowered through a hole in the Carmine roof on a rope and had
seen the vault from above."

Unfortunately, the Opificio team soon discovered Procacci's
recollection to be erroneous. "These chapels were all constructed
according to the same architectural canons," Botticelli explains,
rubbing his hands together to warm them.

"The height of the ceiling, the length of the walls, and the curve
of the entry arch were all dictated by a series of proportions which
were never varied," he continues. "We had hoped to find that the
present ceiling had been erected beneath the original vault. But the
pressent ceiling is much higher than any gothic ceiling would have
been for a chapel of the Brancacci's dimensions. This meant that
the original gothic vault had been completely destroyed when the
present ceiling was constructed in the 1700s. And that Dr. Procacci must have confused the Brancacci with some other chapel.

"After the disappointment with the vault, we turned our attention to the Meucci lunettes above the window." Botticelli stares
blankly out the window at the winter piazza as he speaks. The

88 Brancacci Chapel is somewhat of a delicate subject for him. As senior *fresco* restorer at the Opificio, he directed a team of students through the initial phase of the Brancacci restoration until work was interrupted at the end of 1982. Work resumed in 1984 under the auspices of the Central Institute of Restoration of Rome, of which Baldini had become director, and more significantly with the general sponsorhip of the Olivetti Corporation. This time, however, Giovannoni was selected for the new team, along with a younger colleague named Marcello Chemeri. Botticelli was left off the list.

"What we were looking for were traces of the original Masolino frescoes beneath the Meucci lunettes of the 1700s," he says, at last unbuttoning his heavy coat. A damp and constant chill is another occupational hazard for the *fresco* restorer who spends the greater part of his days working in unheated churches or open cloisters. "At first we cut away a few small sections of the Meucci fresco, sections about five centimeters square, to see what lay underneath.

"And right away we found hints of a red clay drawing," Botticelli remembers, still enthused. "Having found these traces, we removed a larger section and saw that the red-clay *synopia* was intact, and not just fragmentary. As you can imagine, in our work, when this sort of thing happens, when you participate in the discovery of something new, the feeling is indescribable."

Botticelli was not alone in his elation about the find. Having ascertained the existence of two *synopie* (the red-clay preparatory drawings used in *fresco* painting) beneath the eighteenth century lunettes that flanked the baroque window, an excited Baldini authorized Botticelli and his team of students to detach the Meucci work in order to recover the red-clay drawings.

From a historical point of view, the two *synopie,* should they prove to be the work of Masolino or Masaccio, would be of inestimable value. Aside from their inherent intrinsic worth—any fourteenth or fifteenth synopy, even by an unknown master, is of some historical importance—these two preparatory drawings could provide a pivotal hinge for the reconstruction of the lost sections of the Brancacci Chapel.

No copies or drawings of the lost Brancacci vault or upper register exist. None, that is, except for an anonymous eighteenth century painting in the Giovanelli collection at Venice, which histo-

rian Roberto Longhi believed to be a reproduction of Masolino's
The Calling of Saints Andrew and Peter. (Longhi drew this conclusion by comparing the painting with the description of the Masolino fresco in Vasari's *Lives*.) Historians have generally construed
an approximate idea of what the Brancacci Chapel might have
looked like upon completion in 1427 by synthesizing the incomplete descriptions that appear in Vasari, Manetti, and *Antonio Billi*
with the essential design of Masolino's surviving chapels—the
Chapel of the True Cross in Empoli, and the Chapel of Branda
Castiglione in the San Clemente Basilica in Rome. The *synopie,*
which Botticelli and his students had discovered could prove invaluable in piecing together a more realistic image of the vanished
portions of the chapel.

But the newly-located red-earth drawings beneath Meucci's lunettes had a second historical potential that could conceivably
eclipse their already important role as pure archeological evidence.
Should the hand of Masaccio be recognized in one or both of the
red-clay preparatory drawings, this would offer irrefutable testimony that the young genius from Castel San Giovanni was present on the scaffolding with Masolino at least from the time of the
first register decoration, if not from the beginning of the project.
In resolving once and for all one of the most persistent and impen-
etrable mysteries in all of art history, the discovery of the Brancacci synopies would constitute one of the century's most stunning
historical achievements.

It was not at all uncommon for a *fresco* or a painting to be
painted over in a later age. Nor did patrons necessarily wait for
three centuries, as in the case of the Brancacci Chapel, to have their
chapels redecorated according to the latest style.

The late 1480s Domenico Ghirlandaio frescoes in Santa Maria
Novella were painted over a series of frescoes, which Andrea Or-
cagna completed around 1348. In his *Stanze* at the Vatican, Raffaello da Urbino composed several of his superb frescoes over another series of wall paintings believed to have been painted by
Piero Della Francesca just half a century before. And the "divine"
Michelangelo executed his *The Last Judgment* on top of three large
frescoes that his slightly older contemporary Pietro Perugino had
painted on the far Sistine Chapel wall.

Historians and restorers are not generally free to perform random historical excavations on frescoes. A strong professional ethic, and an inculcated respect for all artworks, whether masterpieces or not, usually reins in the scholar's galloping historical curiosity. In the three aforementioned cases, it would almost be absurd to risk damaging a Michelangelo or Raffaello fresco in hopes of finding traces of a work that is at best of equal importance, and whose existence is at best uncertain.

The situation was somewhat different at the Brancacci. Here the truly valuable work had been buried beneath a mediocre decorative solution. And while no historian will ever publicly declare a work of art to be expendable, the risk, albeit minor, of damaging the work of a moderately talented painter like Vicenzo Meucci seemed scant fare to pay for a good shot at retrieving the lost Brancacci *synopie* of Masolino di Panicale, and perhaps of Masaccio.

In order to reach the fifteenth century *synopie,* which Botticelli had discovered beneath the Meucci lunettes on the rear wall, he and his students would first have to detach the Meucci frescoes, and then perform the same operation on the eighteenth century painter's *synopie.* The art of *fresco* detachment is probably not much younger than that of *fresco* painting. Although we cannot know what technique the Romans used, both Pliny the Elder and Vitruvius give accounts of the transportation of Greek wall paintings from Sparta to Rome in the first century B.C.

While it has evolved considerably since Pliny's time, the current technique of fresco detachment—*stacco* or *strappo* in Italian—has changed little since it was perfected in the late 1800s. Botticelli and Giovannoni learned how to perform a successful *stacco* by first observing and then assisting their *maestro* Dino Dini. Dini in turn learned the mechanical skill from his father, who was also a *fresco* restorer.

Historically, the Florentine restorers have been far more adept at successfully executing the *stacco* or the *strappo* than the restorers of any other city. Much of this is due to the diligence of Dini, a diligence that was then transmitted to his students Giovannoni and Botticelli, and through them to their students at the Opificio.

"The *stacchi* of the two Meucci lunettes went fairly smoothly," says restorer Gioia Germani, who as a second-year student at the

Opificio in 1982 assisted Botticelli with the operation. "Because   *91*
the frescoes were in very good condition, they came away quite
easily, without any losses.

"The only difficulty was that the frescoes, having been painted
on a curving wall, were themselves curved," says Germani. "Before the *stacco,* we had to construct a contoured support out of *gesso*
to allow the *fresco* to retain its shape once it was off the wall. Actually, this is something that should be done for all frescoes, because none of them are ever flat."

Gioia is intelligent and articulate and often punctuates her sen-
tences with a mischievous chipmunk smile that belies her twenty-
seven years. We are alone on the second stage of a *cantiere* in the
Church of Santo Stefano at Empoli. It is early February in 1989
and Gioia is restoring the *synopie* and *fresco* fragments of the chapel
that was once believed to have been the site of Masolino's *The
Chapel of the True Cross.* Historians have now attributed the chapel
to Gherardo Starnina and Bicci di Lorenzo. The true Masolino
chapel, which Ugo Procacci discovered in 1956, stands three
niches down from us at the beginning of the aisle.

"This is enough to drive a restorer crazy," she comments, in-
dicating a thin, semi-opaque veil that she has found on several of
the *synopie.* The air about us is sharp with the smell of ammonia;
wood flour from several compresses is scattered about the scaffolding. "My work here was going beautifully until last week, when I
ran into a substance I'd never encountered before. And so far, no
one has been able to identify it. We tried using ultraviolet and infrared analyses, but the substance did not seem to have any particular fluorescence. Sabino was here yesterday, and he was stumped
as well."

As a student at the Opificio, Gioia participated in much of the
early stages of the Brancacci restoration. Aside from assisting Botticelli with the *stacchi* of the Meucci frescoes, she and her class-
mates also cleaned the eighteenth century vault and lunettes. In
1984, when work resumed in the chapel after a pause of nearly a
year, Gioia was hired as an independent collaborator by the Olivetti Corporation to assist Giovannoni and Chemeri in the second
stage of the Brancacci restoration.

"The first step in any *stacco* is always a thorough cleaning of the
surface which will be removed," she explains, removing her plas-

tic helmet and setting it beside her on the platform. "Even the slightest amount of dirt or dust on the *fresco* can prevent the glue from taking hold. You cannot be too careful about this."

After the *fresco* has been satisfactorily cleaned a double-boiler is lit to melt the strong animal glue used in the operation. Restorers usually dilute the adhesive with molasses or glycerine to make the mixture more pliable. When the glue is ready, it is brushed on rectangular strips of calico gauze, which are then laid across the surface of the painting. Working with their hands, the restorers then carefully spread the adhesive so that it permeates into all the spaces in the cloth.

"Each place where the glue doesn't enter is a loss," Germani notes solemnly. "A piece of color which will be left on the wall."

Once this first layer of calico gauze has hardened, the restorers spread a second cloth layer to act as a reinforcement. The cloth used for this second layer is coarser than that used in the first, usually of hemp or linen, and cut into rectangles, which are slightly larger than the calico strips.

"Once everything is in place," Germani continues, "you just have to wait for it to dry. Often the hardening of the glue causes a slight contraction in the fresco, and the fresco literally detaches itself. Other times the restorer has to pull the painting away himself. As you can imagine, this is done very carefully, and very, very slowly."

Depending on their size, frescoes can often be quite heavy, and equally cumbersome. "I once assisted in the *stacco* of 100 square meters of *fresco*," Germani recalls, laughing. "We needed over thirty people just to hold the painting as it came off the wall."

Although Umberto Baldini had far too much experience in art restoration to advance a hypothesis before the fact, he did have some idea of what his restorers would unveil from beneath the two rear-wall Meucci lunettes, namely, the *synpoie* from Masolino's *St. Peter Weeping* and *The Negation of Christ*.

According to the conventional reading of Vasari's very desultory description of Masolino's work in the Brancacci Chapel, the painter from Panicale had decorated the upper register with frescoes depicting *The Shipwreck of the Apostles, The Calling of Saints Peter and Andrew,* and the two scenes mentioned above.

In his subjective but compelling analysis of the painting in the
Giovanelli collection at Venice which he believed to be a copy of
Masolino's *The Calling of Saints Andrew and Peter,* Roberto Longhi
sustained that the copy clearly demonstrated that Masolino had
intended for his original *fresco* panel to be lit from right to left. For
Longhi, this meant that Masolino's destroyed *The Calling of Saints
Andrew and Peter* had been painted on the left-hand wall of the
Brancacci Chapel, above Masaccio's *The Tribute Money.* Both
paintings would have been illuminated from the chapel window
that opened to their right.

If we accept Longhi's deductions, it follows that the other marine scene, *The Shipwreck of the Apostles,* would have stood on the
right wall across from *The Calling of Saints Andrew and Peter.* Aside
from the thematic corrolation between the two vanished frescoes,
these two episodes are usually depicted in large spaces, to best exploit the panoramic potential of the land and seascape. By a process of elimination, *St. Peter Weeping* and *The Negation of Christ*
should have been the scenes that were sketched on the *synopie* beneath the lunettes near the window.

The *sinopia,* which Botticelli detached from the left of the Brancacci window readily confirmed Baldini's intuition. The faded but
still legible drawing shows a robed figure seated in the center of
the scene, his elbow propped against his knee and his head resting
in his hand. Baldini was quite certain that this was the preparatory
drawing for *Saint Peter Weeping.*

Unlike the left-side *synopia,* the preparatory drawing on the
right side of the window did not come close to corresponding
with anyone's preconception. The scene, apparently incomplete
and without a central figure, left both Baldini and Casazza per-
plexed. Initially, the only conclusion they could draw was that this
was *not* the *synopia* for *The Negation of Christ.* The unexpected and
inexplicable presence of four sheep in the lower right-hand corner
of the scene made this impossible.

In addition, the two *synopie* were clearly the work of two distinct
artists. "The right-hand *synopia,* the one with the sheep, was obviously done by Masolino," recalls Botticelli. "When I was in the
Dini *bottega* I helped him detach the Masolino *synopie* in Empoli.
After having had such close contact with an artist's technique, you
tend to recognize it the next time you run across it."

94   Baldini concurred with Botticelli and readily assigned the still-unnamed *synopia* to Masolino di Panicale. As they had done with the second medallion on the window jamb, Baldini cautiously suggested that the *synopia* of *St. Peter Weeping* was painted by Masaccio.

"This is an extremely important historical discovery," Baldini stresses. "The two *synopie* demonstrate, at least in my opinion, that Masaccio and Masolino began work together in the Brancacci."

As a restorer, Botticelli is naturally reluctant to express a judgment here. "It's difficult to say," he observes. "I'd never seen a Masaccio *synopia* before. And besides, attributions are usually left to the historian, not to the restorer. Dr. Baldini is certainly as able as anyone in the field. The work is clearly that of an artist other than Masolino. And if we're talking about another artist in the Brancacci." He pauses to grin, "I mean, who else could it be?"

As far as the episode that Masolino had intended to portray in the sheep-filled *synopia* on the right, Baldini suggested the passage from the Gospel according to St. John in which the resurrected Christ orders St. Peter "Pasce agnes meas," or "Feed my sheep." The vital episode in the life of the Saint is not mentioned in Vasari, although the omission does not in any way prejudice the possibility that it might once have existed in the chapel. The biographer of the artists also neglects to mention Masolino's *Original Sin* and Masaccio's *Adam and Eve Driven from Paradise,* two of the chapel's most celebrated panels.

There is also an excellent possibility that the two surviving *synopie* were once part of a single fresco, or that the two separate scenes were connected by a narrowing band of fresco that bridged the original gothic window. The current baroque window which was opened during the 1748 Brancacci renovation is much higher than the one around which Masolino and Masaccio structured their frescoes. In cutting through the wall to construct their window, the eigtheenth century builders could very well have destroyed the central section of the upper register *fresco,* leaving only the lateral pieces intact.

An attentive reading of Vasari would also appear to second this hypothesis. In describing single frescoes, which contain two episodes, the author of *The Lives* often refers to these episodes as if they were separate panels. He mentions Masaccio's *St. Peter Enthroned* and then cites three other of the painter's Brancacci works before remembering *The Resurrection of Teofilo's Son,* the scene that appears on the same panel as *St. Peter Enthroned.*

Assuming Vasari was at least consistent in his errors, we cannot discard the possibility that *St. Peter Weeping* and *The Negation of Christ* were featured in the same *fresco.* In the "life" of Masolino, the description of the upper register reads: "[he] made his weeping for the sin when he denied Christ and after his preaching to convert the peoples."

This juxtaposition may be just another searing blunder by Vasari, Masolino's *St. Peter Preaching to the Crowd* being still visible today in the Brancacci's second register. But if by chance the description did correspond to what was on the wall, we can surmise that Vasari was describing one continuous *fresco* that spanned the original gothic window and included both St. Peter's remorse at having denied Christ *and* his preaching to convert the peoples.

This would explain the apparent absence of a protagonist in the right-hand *synopia*. The four sheep are somewhat harder to rationalize, although they could arguably have been included in the crowd of people or shepherds who came to listen to St. Peter's sermon.

Baldini's hypothesis is equally cogent, and not incompatible with the idea that both *synopie* originally were part of a single composition. In the left side of the panel, St. Peter sobs in shame after having denied knowing Christ. In the right, the resurrected Christ returns to his apostles, and with the metaphoric command of "Feed my sheep" invests St. Peter as his earthly shepherd. Thematically, the juxtaposition of the two separate episodes in a single panel works very well, forming a collage that takes the observer from the sin of denial to forgiveness and redemption. Vasari, who may not have been familiar with this latter episode might have attempted to gloss over his biblical ignorance by omitting the scene completely. Or the "Feed my sheep" scene might simply have slipped his mind.

The incredible discoveries between the rear-wall frescoes created a rampant optimism among the Brancacci crew. Baldini swiftly gave instructions for Botticelli to begin his exploration on the lateral lunettes. The entire team, perhaps dizzied by its precipitous good fortune, abandoned caution and approached this second search with the full expectation of finding the *synopie* of Masolino's *The Calling of Saints Andrew and Peter* and *The Shipwreck of the Apostles*.

The joyful mood, fruit of a sudden magical moment, was just as summarily dashed. A spot-search and then a full-fledged *stacco* of both lateral frescoes yielded only the tiniest traces of plaster, traces that at best could confirm the existence of a previous *fresco* beneath the current architectonic lunettes. The two marine scenes described in Vasari had been entirely destroyed to make space for the Meucci paintings.

"As you might imagine," Botticelli says as an understatement, "It was a great disappointment."

The disappointment was destined to increase, for Baldini, for the student restorers, and particularly for Botticelli, who had relished his role as head restorer in this historic restoration and who would not be summoned for the team when work resumed in 1984. Toward the end of 1982, a dispute broke out between the Opificio and the Central Institute of Restoration in Rome over which body should have jurisdiction in the Brancacci Chapel restoration. As a result of the dispute, the state funds that had sustained the operation were suspended. In December, with the upper-register frescoes waiting to be remounted, with the two *synopie* lying face-down on a bench at the Fortezza Del Basso, and with the frescoes of Masaccio and Masolino still obscured beneath a dark blanket of grime, work in the Brancacci Chapel came to a halt.

The MATTER ITSELF

CHAPTER EIGHT

A Fresco

Many of our artists excel at other types of work, that is in oil or *tempera,* and in this type have no ability, because it is truly the most virile, most secure, most resolute and durable of all the other methods, and with the passage of time its beauty continually increases to exceed all the other methods infinitely.

GIORGIO VASARI
from The Lives of the Artists *1550*

THE TECHNIQUE OF PAINTING *a fresco* is one of the most ancient and widespread art forms known to man. Translated as "when fresh," *a fresco* painting is a particular method of mural painting in which the artist applies his colors onto a damp section of wall plaster composed of lime and sand. As a consequence of the chemical-physical reactions that occur between the damp wall plaster and the atmosphere, the artist's pigments are inseparably woven into the fabric of the wall as the lime-sand mixture dries. When properly done, the *a fresco* technique allows for a crystalline clarity of color that neither canvas nor panel painting can rival.

Unquestionably one of the most fascinating forms of painting, *a fresco* is also one of the most demanding. In Vasari's words, *a fresco* painting requires

an able hand, resolute and swift, but above all a sound and solid judgment, because colors, when the wall is soft, show a thing in a certain way, which when dry is no longer that. And thus it is that in these works *a fresco* the painter's expertise and design play a greater part, and that he must have as a guide an ability which is greater than grand, in that it is extremely difficult to perform this art to perfection.

100   The art of mural painting was probably man's first form of artistic expression. Homo sapiens sapiens' irrepressible instinct to modify the world around him and to leave a record of his existence found one of its earliest avenues on the walls of his own dwellings. Already in 30,000 B.C., man had discovered a vegetable dye that enabled him to leave the imprint of his hand on stone.

Man's expressive expertise evolved in concert with his ability to exploit the materials that he found about him. The rudimentary handprints gave way to paleolithic cave drawings that narrated episodes of tribal life and also enlivened the environments in which the members of that tribe lived. Most ancient cultures were familiar with the art of mural painting; many produced works of startling beauty.

But none of these early murals were painted *a fresco*. The Egyptian artist who in 220 B.C. painted the graceful *Geese of Medum* panels for the tomb of Itat (now in the National Museum at Cairo) mixed his pigments with an organic binder or *tempera* so they could adhere to the already dry section of wall; *tempera* is a Greek word that means "medium." This technique of applying color onto a dry wall with the aid of *tempera* is known as *a secco* painting, or "painting when dry."

It is unclear where or when the technique of *a fresco* was born; historians believe that the method of painting onto fresh lime-based plaster was known in ancient Greece. Surviving Etruscan wall paintings from as early as the 7th century B.C. demonstrate that the *a fresco* method had been perfected in the Italian peninsula long before the birth of the Roman Empire.

The Romans themselves were quite expert at *a fresco* painting. Aside from its use in painting, the *a fresco* technique was also used to produce an inexpensive alternative to marble. By using a finely-ground marble powder as a pigment, which was applied to the drying wall-plaster, Roman artisans reproduced the lucid, shiny effect of marble for a fraction of the stone's cost.

The Roman frescoes at Pompei and Herculaneum are fine examples of the *a fresco* technique. They are also particularly relevant to the Brancacci Chapel frescoes in that the iron-based earth pigments in the Pompei and Herculaneum paintings underwent the same chromatic shift during the searing heat of the volcanic eruptions as the Brancacci Chapel panels did during the 1771 Carmine fire.

Along with numerous surviving works the Roman *a fresco* technique has also been preserved in several well-known texts including Vitruvius' *De Archittetura* and Pliny's *Historia Naturalis*. In
Book VII of his treatise on architecture, Vitruvius prescribes the
precise proportions, times, and blending techniques required to
obtain a suitably uniform lime plaster. Pliny includes a detailed
recipe for the *a fresco* process, calling for three successive layers of
the lime-sand mixture and the timely application of powdered
marble and/or colors. He even explains the process by which these
pigments are incorporated into the wall's surface.

In thirteenth-century Italy, *a fresco* painting came into fashion as
a practical and above all economical alternative to the more costly
Byzantine mosaic. Limestone, sand, and earth pigments were far
less dear than the precious and semi-precious stones that the Byzantine technique required. *A fresco* painting was also much less
labor-intensive than that of mosaic decoration. Working with a
few assistants or even alone, a painter could decorate a chapel *a
fresco* in a time that for a mosaicist had been unthinkable.
   Like the recipes for all forms of painting or sculpture, the secrets
of the *a fresco* technique were preserved and disseminated in late-
medieval Italy within the nearly monastic network of the *bottega*.
A *maestro*, having religiously absorbed the technique from his
maestro, related it with the same unwavering solemnity to his assistants. In the empirical environment of the thirteenth and fourteenth century *bottega*, there was little room for innovation. An
apprentice was expected not only to duplicate his *maestro*'s choice
of materials, but also to imitate his particular style of painting.
Because of this inflexible structure, the *a fresco* technique was
transmitted virtually unchanged from Giotto to Michelangelo,
and from Michelangelo to our century with only minor modifications.
   The best and most complete description of the Italian *a fresco*
method can be found in Cennino Cennini's *Book of Art or Treatise
of Painting*. Cennini, a relatively unimportant painter who is estimated to have lived between 1372 and 1440, achieved a sort of immortality with this valuable and delightful volume. Far more than
a bland list of recipes, *The Book of Art* is a rich and vibrant tran-
scription of the atmosphere of a typical Florentine *bottega*. Invalu-

able to historians and scientists for its scrupulous descriptions of the various painting techniques, Cennini's *Book of Art* also sculpts a well-wrought relief of the fourteenth-century Florentine artist and his position in society.

Cennini opens his narrative by presenting the reader with his own artistic lineage. Born in Colle Val D'Elsa, a Tuscan hilltown that lies between Florence and Siena, Cennini writes that at the age of twelve he was apprentice to the *bottega* of Agnolo Gaddi. Agnolo Gaddi had learned the art from his father Taddeo Gaddi and Taddeo Gaddi had been the disciple of the great Giotto. This was the most noble peerage to which an Italian artist could lay claim.

It is interesting to note that Cennini's approximate dates of birth and death (1372-1440) more or less coincide with the life of Masolino (1383-1440). The two artists may have had much more in common than their chronology. Gherardo Starnina, whom Vasari cites as Masolino's *maestro,* also worked as an apprentice in the *bottega* of Agnolo Gaddi. Whether or not Masolino knew Cennini personally, their common artistic heritage insures that the curriculum described in *The Book of Art* is that which the genteel painter from Panicale followed during his early years of study.

Having offered his credentials, Cennino Cennini affirms the dignity of art by proclaiming it to be one of the most worthy activities known to man, second only in nobility to the study of science. Then, after an opening chapter in which the author allows himself a brief digression in order to summarize his age's arbitrary scale of values, Cennini jumps right into shoptalk.

In chapter two, entitled "How Some Come to Arte, Who for a Gentle Soul, and Who for Gain," one learns that men choose to become artists for a variety of motives, and that only those inspired by a love of art will succeed in mastering its intricacies.

Chapter three, entitled "Love, Respect, and Perseverence," is Cennini's reiteration of the unequivocal adoration and subjugation that a *maestro* expected of his apprentices. Having laid his philosophical foundation, Cennini uses his fourth chapter to trace his preliminary artistic premises. The essay is entitled "Drawing and Coloring Art, the Foundations of Art" and subtitled "you have to wet, plaster, sand, clean, draw, color in *fresco,* retouch *a secco,* use *tempera,* use gold, finish in wall" for those who may have failed to grasp the subtle and widespread ramifications implicit in Cennini's terse declaration.

Chapters five through eight of *The Book of Art* describe the laborious process by which a wooden panel is prepared for painting.
Chapter nine includes a valuable insider's tip that an artist should
try to raise and lower his figures in relief to take advantage of the
natural light. In chapter fourteen, Cennini describes the best
method to sharpen a quill. Between chapters sixteen and twenty-
two, the reader learns five different techniques for dyeing paper,
that an apprentice should imitate his *maestro* and no other to avoid
caprice, and the most dependable and efficient way to fashion slender charcoal pencils.

The haphazard cocktail of technique, philosophy, and sociology
continues throughout the entire volume. *The Book of Art* contains
instructions for grinding colors, for drawing trees and mountains,
for making glue from sheep, cheese, and fish, for the proper proportions of the human body, on how to mix tin with gold to save
money, and for inserting silver straws into a man's nostrils in order that he continue to breath while you make a wax impression
of his face. In a final touch of Florentine eccentricity, Cennini ends
his treatise with a chapter entitled "Why Women Must Abstain
from Using Medicated Water or Creams for Their Skin."

Cennini is equally eclectic in chapter sixty-seven where he describes "The way and order to work in wall, that is, *a fresco,* and
to color and animate a youth's face." As Vasari would do nearly
two centuries later, the author of *The Book of Art* exalts the art of
fresco painting above all other painting methods. "It is," he writes,
"the sweetest and most expressive mode that is."

Although it contains no surprises, Cennini's recipe for *fresco* is
ample evidence of his age's profound material and technical expertise. While lacking our twentieth-century nomenclature, Cennini
shows that the *bottega maestro* was not only cognizant of the various
chemical and physical reactions involved in *a fresco* painting but
had also achieved a mastery over them.

The plaster mixture, or *malta,* on which the fresco will be
painted, is to be made from one part lime and two parts sand. The
lime, if it is fresh, must be immersed in a fair quantity of water—
Cennini suggests fifteen days worth as a guide—and left to boil
there "until the fire goes out." This is Cennini's way of describing
the caustic reaction that occurs when lime (calcium oxide) comes
into contact with water.

104   The sand, which must be from a river bed or quarry and never from the sea, must also be washed thoroughly to eliminate impurities. When the lime has ceased to boil, it is to be mixed with the sand and spread in a thick, even layer over the brick or stone wall which is to be painted. This first layer of *malta,* on which the artist will execute his preliminary sketches, is known as the *arriccio.* It is usually two inches in thickness. As the *arriccio* will also serve as the support for a subsequent layer of plaster on which the artist will paint, Cennini recommends that the artist leave the surface of the *arriccio* a bit rough to facilitate the grip between the two layers.

The *arriccio* must be left to dry until all the moisture within the plaster has evaporated; depending upon the season, this usually takes three to four months. When the *arriccio* has hardened, Cennini instructs his reader to insert a nail into what will be the focal point of the painting. Using a piece of cord appended to that nail, the artist calculates the horizontal and vertical coordinates through a series of accurate measurements.

After having carefully plotted the geometry of his painting, Cennini instructs his reader to proceed with a preliminary sketch in charcoal. If he has read chapter twenty-two attentively, the aspiring artist will have already prepared a quiver of slender, finely fashioned pencils for this purpose. The charcoal sketch, used as a first draft, is to be brushed away and redone in a red-earth pigment, which is applied onto the *arriccio* with a brush.

This red-clay drawing, known as the *synopia,* will serve as the basis for the artist's eventual painting. The name *synopia* comes from the Turkish town of Sinope on the Black Sea, which was famous for its red iron-based earth pigment. Aside from using the *synopia* as his preparatory drawing, an artist usually submitted this red-earth outline to his patron for approval. If the patron was satisfied, he could begin to paint. If not, he would make the necessary adjustments in the design.

Once an artist had received his patron's permission to proceed with the painting of the *fresco,* he began this second phase by spreading a thin layer of the fresh lime-sand *malta* over a portion of the red-earth *synopia.* It is here that the art gets tricky.

This second layer of *malta,* usually half an inch in thickness, is known as the *intonaco.* Because the artist can achieve the *a fresco* effect by working only when the *intonaco* is fresh, the artist applies the *intonaco* onto the *arriccio* in small portions that are sized according to what he intends to paint in the four to six hours that follow. These portions of *intonaco,* irregular in shape and dimensions, are known as *giornate,* or "days of work."

The *giornate* are plainly visible across the surface of a fresco. Some, as described by Cennini, are no bigger than a man's head. Others are considerably larger. The head of Jesus Christ in Masaccio's *The Tribute Money* in the Brancacci Chapel was done in one *giornata,* while the much larger scene of Saint Peter taking the coin from the mouth of a fish in the same painting was also painted in one work day. By reading the borders, which separate one *giornata* from the next, historians are also able to reconstruct the order in which the various segments of a fresco were completed.

"Then you must consider in yourself just how much you can work," Cennini counsels. "Because whatever you plaster, you must finish in that same day." As a rule of thumb, Cennini advises that "one saint's head" usually constitutes a good day's work.

"It is done by working on lime which is fresh," Vasari would write of the *a fresco* technique in the 1550 version of his *Lives.* "And never leaving more than that which we intend to work on that day. Because extending the workday, the lime acquires a certain crust, for the heat, for the cold, and for the wind and ice, which stain and bring mold onto all the work."

Scientists today have little difficulty in illustrating the process that causes the *intonaco* to harden.

"The *fresco* is a heterogenous mix of spent lime, sand, and water, which is used for its plastic properties," says Professor Enzo Ferroni, chief of the faculty of Physical Chemistry in Florence and the first scientist of international prominence to conduct a thorough scientific study of the *a fresco* technique. Ferroni, who made restoration history with fresco restorer Dino Dini in the cloister of the San Marco convent in Florence, was a valuable consultant to the Baldini team during the restoration of the Brancacci Chapel.

"The colloidal property of the calcium hydroxide, $Ca(OH)_2$, is responsible for the cement-like quality of the mixture," Ferroni explains, scribbling the formula onto a chalkboard in his office. "The *fresco* hardens as the calcium hydroxide migrates towards the surface where it comes into contact with the carbon dioxide, CO_2, present in the atmosphere. The water in the calcium-hydroxide mixture evaporates and is replaced with carbon dioxide to form calcium carbonate, $CaCO_3$. This is the final state of the *intonaco.*"

This process by which the damp *malta* hardens as it absorbs carbon dioxide is known as carbonation. Carbonation takes place first on the surface of the *malta,* which is exposed to the air. In his sixteenth century description of the phenomenon, Vasari notes that the *malta* forms a sort of crust. Gradually, the carbonation extends inward until the entire *intonaco* cements.

The process of carbonation is also the vehicle that causes an artist's pigments to be incorporated into the damp *intonaco* without the use of any *tempera* or binder. The pigments, if applied at the proper moment during the drying phase, are carbonated along with the damp *malta* and inextricably woven into the crystalline surface of the *intonaco.* Colors applied to a wall *a fresco* generally survive as long as that wall remains intact.

Because of their unique physical nature, *a fresco* paintings are far more durable than their panel or canvas cousins. "This [the fresco]," writes Vasari, "in the air purges itself and from water defends itself and resists any adversity."

Both Vasari and Cennini stress that only earth pigments be used when painting *a fresco.* These pigments, usually oxides or sulfides or carbonates, are among the oldest colors known to man. Cennini supplies a list of seven reds, six yellows, and seven greens, all of which may be used in *a fresco* painting.

Through generations of experience, artists had learned that earth pigments were the only colors that were chemically compatible with the drying *malta.* Although unable to articulate the precise reason, the *bottega* masters had observed that the alkaline nature of the calcium-hydroxide *malta* caused copper-based pigments like azurite or lapis lazuli to bleach. *Cinabro,* a mercury mineral used for vermilion red, tends to mute on contact with the *malta; biacca di piombo* or "lead white" often darkens as a result of oxidation.

As certain mineral colors, particularly the sky-blue azurite, were often indispensable in mural painting, these were applied with a *tempera* of egg yolk or animal glue after the *fresco* colors had dried. Gold and gold leaf were applied in the same manner. Colors, which had been applied *a secco* are not nearly as hardy as those

applied *a fresco;* the organic matter used as *tempera* suffers a much
more rapid decay than the minerals used in *fresco.* The azurite
background that Masolino painted *a secco* in his *Original Sin* panel
in the Brancacci Chapel has long since fallen off the wall, leaving
behind the artist's dark-grey preparatory layer. The same is true
for the rays of gold that Masaccio painted with the aid of a *tempera*
in *Adam and Eve Driven from Paradise,* and for the golden halos that
adorn the heads of the saints in *The Tribute Money.*

The most crucial moment an artist faces in *a fresco* painting is in
deciding when to apply his pigments to the surface of the *intonaco.*
Despite its considerable specific knowledge of the carbonation
process, which causes the lime-sand mixture to harden, modern
science has yet to discover a method that can pinpoint this moment or to synthesize a substitute for Cennini's *malta.* An artist
wishing to paint *a fresco* today will use the same materials and encounter the same challenges as Giotto, Masaccio, Raffaello, and
Michelangelo did in their day. If he brushes his colors on too soon,
they will blur and run across the surface of the *malta.* If he waits
too long, they will fall to the floor. As with his illustrious predecessors, today's *a fresco* painter must rely on his own subjective
judgment, or on that of a painter more experienced than he.

The considerable skill required in *a fresco* painting, and the im-
possibility of making corrections without removing an entire *giornata* or "day of work" must certainly have presented a sort of ma-
cho challenge to the artists of the early Renaissance. This perhaps
explains why Vasari chose the word "virile" to describe the
method. Michelangelo himself sustained that it was the only fit-
ting method for a true artist, "much more worthy," he would
write, "than painting in *tempera* or than coloring with oils which
is the work of women or of some hapless monk in the country-
side."

Michelangelo's *a fresco* technique in the Sistine Chapel differs in
only one major respect from the work of Masolino and Masaccio
in the Carmine. Near the end of the fifteenth century, artists discovered that the red-earth *synopia* was no longer a sufficient guide
for them to achieve their increasingly complex spatial constructions in fresco. Toward this end the *cartone* was invented; the *cartone*

108   was a full-sized preparatory sketch done on a sheet of paper. Pressing the *cartone* against the damp *intonaco,* the artist traced his preparatory drawing directly into that day's *intonaco* using a wooden pencil or the blunt end of a brush.

Many historians believe that Masaccio's *La Trinita fresco* in Florence's Santa Maria Novella was the first use of the *cartone* technique by an Italian artist. Although *La Trinita* was painted between 1425 and 1428, it is doubtful that Masaccio could have achieved the astonishing illusion of Brunelleschian space without the control that the *cartone* affords. By the 1500s, the *cartone* device was widely used.

Whether he used the *synopia* or the *cartone,* it was still a matter of honor and pride for an artist to work as much as possible *a fresco* when painting a mural.

"And therefore, those who seek to work in wall painting," concludes Vasari in the introduction to his *Lives,* "work with virility *a fresco* and do not retouch *a secco.* Because from being an extremely vile act, it shortens the life of the painting."

Naturally, very few artists were able to follow Vasari's exhortation to the letter. Most fresco painters inevitably retouched their works *a secco,* either out of a desire to use a certain pigment, or out of a need to correct or elaborate the previous day's work that had been done *a fresco.*

In his *The Last Supper* outside of Milan, the great Leonardo Da Vinci would have drawn Vasari's unmitigated ire for his "extremely vile" practice of constantly retouching his painting *a secco.* Leonardo was literally handcuffed when painting *a fresco;* the sublime modelling and shading effects that he effected in panel painting through *chiaroscuro* could not possibly be achieved within the span of one *giornata.* With his expressive capacity more than halved, Leonardo developed the mural by repeatedly revising *a secco* and also in a technique known as encaustic painting, or *encausto,* in which the colors are bound with wax and baked onto the surface of the *intonaco.* Exquisitely conceived and rendered, Leonardo's *The Last Supper* is also a tragic technical failure. Da Vinci might well have heeded Vasari's admonition, as his unorthodox mural technique has condemned the masterpiece to an irreversible degeneration.

The Thousand Natural Ills the Flesh Is Heir To (Radix Malorum Umiditas Est)

Rain cannot harm the *fresco* except for rain from within the wall.

CENNINO CENNINI
The Book of Art

A S A MEANS OF EXPRESSION, a work of art is inextricably dependent upon the materials that the artist has selected to transmit his image or idea. Whether the medium be marble, panel painting, or poetry, any change in the matter inevitably prejudices our ability to comprehend the work of art. Rearrange the "o" and "i" in the word "savoir" in a Wallace Stevens poem and the passage takes on an entirely different connotation than the one intended by the author. Cancel a few key passages of a Mozart piano concerto and the composer's intricately fashioned structure crumbles in on itself.

In painting, certain material changes can lead to a drastic revision in the transmission and reception of the artist's original image. A painter's sole means of communication are his colors. When these "notes" are modified, his message is blurred, garbled, and in some cases lost. Botticelli's *Primavera* was certainly less springlike when set against a faded browning lawn that it is now after its green background has been recovered.

Modification or degeneration of the materials used in painting
has also misled scholars into some very erroneous interpretations.
Since the 1700s, many of the world's most acclaimed art historians
have lauded the dramatic fiery red sunset in the background of the
extraordinary Beato Angelico 1450 *Crucifixion fresco* in the chapter
room of the San Marco cloister in Florence. These scholars, who
naturally assumed that Angelico had painted his sky red in order
to accent the agony of Christ writhing on the cross, were entirely
unaware that the hematite pigment, which they found so moving
was merely Angelico's preparatory layer for an azurite blue sky,
which he had to apply with *tempera,* and which subsequently had
fallen off the *fresco.*

Although the resilient nature of the *a fresco* painting often gave
its author good reason to hope that his calcium-carbonate composition might conceivably endure to transmit his largely unal-
tered image for centuries, its long-term survival was in no means
assured. Countless frescoes have been damaged or destroyed by
acts of God and man—the first group characterized by floods,
earthquakes, and fire, the second by war, vandalism, renovations,
and above all by misguided and maldextrous restorers. And, like
any other artworks, frescoes have always been subject to a decay
caused by the natural decomposition of the materials used in their
construction.

There are many natural hazards that can contribute to the disintegration of a *fresco,* hazards that range from mold to eruptions
of mineral salts within the fabric of the *fresco* to a shifting vault or
wall support that causes the panel to crumble. Yet this wide band
of assailants that lie dormant both within the *fresco* and in the environment that surrounds it is almost always instigated by a single
culprit: moisture. To alter the ancient adage, in the realm of *fresco,*
humidity (umiditas) has replaced love of money (cupiditas) as the
root of all evil.

Water itself, at least in small quantities, does not constitute a
threat for the calcium-carbonate *intonaco* or for the pigments used
in *a fresco* painting. Once properly carbonated, the materials used
in *fresco* are resistant to moisture. This is what Vasari meant when
he wrote that the *fresco* "in the air purges itself and from water
defends itself from any adversity."

Unfortunately, water is also one of nature's most effective solvents, and as such is a terribly efficient conveyor of mineral salts, which can wreak tremendous damage on these wall paintings. Ground or rainwater that wells up behind a *fresco* after seeping through a fissure in a roof vault or climbing a support wall through capillary action will eventually migrate through the *intonaco* and evaporate. But in doing so it will also leave behind the mineral salts that it has accumulated during its long pilgrimage toward the painting's surface.

"The *fresco* is actually a macro-interface with the environment around it," says Professor Enzo Ferroni. "It is the seat of the processes of condensation and evaporation. Because of this constant exchange of moisture, soluble salts are introduced into the fabric of the *intonaco,* salts which expand in crystal form when solidifying. In the zones where the *intonaco* is strong, these salts appear as a sort of fluorescence across the surface of the painting. In the zones where the *intonaco* is weaker, the salts take form as a solid crystalline mass, which when large enough will displace the colors and cause them to fall off the wall."

Water can choose among a virtual infinity of sources for the mineral salts it so easily assimilates. Often the noxious substance is found in or near the *fresco* itself. The sand used by the artist to mix his *malta* can inadvertently introduce unwanted mineral compounds into the fabric of the *fresco,* compounds that in time recrystallize across the surface of the painting.

The bricks used to construct the wall on which the *fresco* stands often contain sodium, magnesium, or sulfate compounds, all of which are at least partially soluble, and many of which lead to the eruption of a crystalline mass within the *intonaco.* Cement, particularly when improperly washed, is a mother lode of minerals such as potassium, carbon, and nitrites, minerals responsible for the fluorescence that afflicts the ailing murals.

Even when the artist and builder have been scrupulous in their selection of materials, the *fresco* is far from safe. Rainwater can absorb particles of lead or hydrocarbons, which are suspended in the atmosphere, and then deposit them across the painting's surface, darkening the colors. Groundwater is nearly always full of soluble salts, which it encounters in the soil.

Man has certainly not been amiss in contributing to this natural destruction. The vault of Masolino's chapel in the San Clemente

112 Basilica in Rome has suffered a severe color loss due to a series of roof leaks. The roof of the Sistine Chapel, constructed of large irregular blocks of volcanic *tufa,* allowed for countless infiltrations of rainwater, which stained the painting with mineral salts in several zones. The volume of water that accumulated behind the fresco was so large that almost any other *fresco* would have crumbled beneath the weight and fallen to the ground. Michelangelo happened to be as scrupulous about his plaster as he was about his pigments. His extraordinary vault, which is just as much a masterpiece of *malta* as of color and form, was crafted so carefully that it was able to withstand the downward pressure of the water without falling. Although extraordinarily resilient, Michelanegelo's painting did not escape unmarked. Aside from the damage wrought by the saline deposits, the water also caused the *intonaco* to detach from the ceiling vault and sag in several zones. These detachments are clearly visible when viewed from the restoration bridge.

Leaky roofs and capillary action are not the only channels through which mineral-rich water can seep into frescoes. The sulfates and nitrates that broke out in the corner of Masaccio's *The Baptism of the Neophytes* and Masolino's *St. Peter Preaching to the Crowd* were introduced into the rear wall of the Brancacci Chapel when a drainpipe burst.

Even when his roofing and plumbing is foolproof, mankind is an unwitting accomplice in the assault on frescoes. An excellent vessel of water, the average human being produces between fifty and eighty grams of water vapor per hour. While this is a negligible amount, the quantity becomes more significant when multiplied by the hundreds of faithful worshippers who crowd into a frescoed church for mass, or by the thousands of visitors who tramp daily through such major monuments as Michelangelo's Sistine Chapel. At a recent Raffaello exhibit at the Palazzo Pitti in Florence, monitors revealed that visitors introduced an average of one hundred liters of water per day into the rooms where the paintings were on display.

As if its already insidious function as sole conveyor of mineral and organic matter were not sufficient, humidity is also a powerful catalyst for a host of biological and chemical reactions in and

The Baptism of the Neophytes by Masaccio.

around the *fresco,* reactions that would not otherwise occur except at extremely elevated temperatures. These reactions produce substances that play a major role in the disintegration of the materials used in *fresco,* substances that range from mildrew to carbonic acid.

The nature of the ailments that can afflict frescoes is naturally related to the nature of the surrounding environment. Certain *fresco* "diseases" can even be considered regional. In Rome, the most prevalent mural malady consists in the formation of carbonate compounds on the surface of the painting; this is due presumably to the carbonate-rich soil on which the city is built.

In Florence, the primary enemy is calcium sulfate, a common ionic compound better known as *gesso.* Although the process by which the crystals of the calcium-carbonate *intonaco* are transformed into calcium sulfate (*gesso*) is easily explained in chemical terms, the exact causes of this widespread and insidious *fresco* phenomenon are still unclear.

"The sulfate compounds are extremely common in nature," hypothesized Ferroni. "They could be already present in the *intonaco* or in the supporting wall. Or they could be deposited there by groundwater. Another possible cause could be the tio-oxidens bacateria which are often found in the decaying organic matter, the *beverone,* which restorers have slopped across the surface of these frescoes. These bacteria are capable through oxidation of transforming the sulfur dioxide in the atmosphere into sulfur trioxide. And in the presence of water, sulfur trioxide becomes sulfuric acid, which attacks the *intonaco* and can potentially form crystals of *gesso.* A third possible cause of the "sulfatation" of frescoes is the increasingly large quantity of SO_2 (sulfur dioxide) present in the atmosphere due to pollution."

Unlike nitrates and carbonates, which usually recrystallize as fluoresence on the surface of the painting, the calcium-sulfate *gesso* erupts within the *intonaco* like a virulent rash or cancer, which displaces the crystals of calcium carbonate with the invading crystals of gesso. The chemical reaction that spawns the gesso is parasitic in nature, as it generates the compound out of the same molecules that compose the calcium-carbonate *intonaco.*

Like common table salt (NaCl), or bicarbonate of soda (Na-HCo$_3$), calcium-sulfate (CaSO$_4$) is an ionic compound whose single components are stable only in solution or when bonded into a compound with another ion that balances its electromagnetic charge. Sulfate compounds, including *gesso,* are hardly rare. And sulfate ions—along with various ions of sodium, potassium, magnesium, calcium, lithium, and other water-soluble ions—can be found in almost every brand of mineral water on the supermarket shelves.

The calcium carbonate used for the *intonaco* is also an ionic compound and normally very stable. Yet certain ions are fickle, demonstrating an irresistible affinity for other ions, even at the expense of foregoing a current partner. Under certain conditions, the calcium ion has this sort of affinity for his sulfate cousin. When a molecule from a sulfate compound or a sulfate ion in solution comes into contact with a molecule of calcium carbonate (CaCO$_3$), the sulfate ion displaces the carbonate (CO$_3$) in the compound and bonds with the newly freed calcium to form a crystal of *gesso* (CaSO$_4$).

Needless to say, water is usually the catalyst that prompts this ionic exchange in frescoes. The reaction can occur under other circumstances, but rarely at levels that might be considered significant. Sulfates that are found within a *fresco*'s supporting wall are of no threat to the *intonaco* if the construction is sound and there are no signs of humidity. Restorers generally leave these deposits untouched, preferring to intervene in the structure and surrounding environment of the *fresco* to prevent the infiltration and accumulation of moisture. In restoration, as in medicine, the accent is increasingly placed on prevention.

Thanks to the work of Dino Dini and Enzo Ferroni at San Marco, there is now a reliable method that allows restorers to convert the *gesso* back into calcium carbonate and to consolidate the stretched pictorial film onto the underlying *intonaco*. This miraculous technique, which employs an application of ammonium carbonate to transform the *gesso* and a subsequent application of berium hydroxide to reconstitute the pictorial film, is used only as a last resort, and only when the proliferation of *gesso* has reached a point where the *fresco* will be irreparably damaged if the restorer does not act to remove it.

116   *The Damage Wrought by Man*

> If we examine history, if we consult men of art, if we examine the
> few examples which still exist, we must unequivocally confess that
> it has been neither time, nor war, nor fire, nor the iconoclasts, who
> are responsible for the destruction of the majority of our paintings,
> rather the ignorant presumption of those who deigned to clean
> them.
>
> *"Manual of the Mechanical Part of the*
> *Art of the Restoral of Paintings"*
> COUNT GIOVANNI SECCO SUARDO
> *Milan, 1866*

No definitive statistical survey has ever been launched to determine whether Count Secco Suardo's sad affirmation is true. The
survey would require enormous means, and the results would
most likely be enormously depressing. However, it is undeniable
that restorers have been responsible for the alteration and destruction of far too many paintings. It is somewhat ironic that the profound material knowledge transmitted from *bottega* to *bottega* in
the early Renaissance seems to have been completely ignored by
restorers until the 1900s. For centuries, restoration was a craft
practiced for the most part by charlatans, third-rate painters, and
well-meaning but inept art lovers who lacked even a modest com-
prehension of the characteristics of the materials used in panel and
fresco painting.

With no *bottega* rules to guide him, the sixteenth and seventeenth
century restorer used a series of ineffectual panaceas and secret,
homemade remedies to clean and preserve artworks, usually damaging or altering most of the works he tried to save. Secco Suardo,
a gentleman restorer who among other deleterious methods used
amber varnish or extract of walnut to give paintings the golden,
seasoned tone that was so prized by nineteenth century collectors,
is no less culpable than any of his contemporaries or predecessors.

History is full of horror stories about restorers and their tools.
Ulisse Forni, a contemporary of Secco Suardo, regularly used lic-
orice, tobacco water, coffee, and diluted asphalt to give restored
paintings an opaque finish. An account of a 1600s restoration of
the Sistine Chapel under Pope Urban VIII describes how a former
domestic of Michelangelo who was hired as official Vatican paint-

ing cleaner (pulcherrimas picturas,) dusted the famous lunettes and vault with a damp linen cloth, or with the soft center of a loaf of bread. "And thus the figures return to their pristine beauty without receiving any offense."

The author of this Vatican document is not entirely correct, as bread leaves behind a trail of crumbs that in a short time give way to mold. In time, the Sistine Chapel ceiling would endure much more caustic attacks from restorers. Tests performed during the current restoration confirmed the presence of animal glues, fats, hair, powdered horn, nails, hooves, and skin. Traces of Greek wine used by a certain Mazzuola in 1710—scientists are still at a loss to explain the particular attributes that might have caused this restorer to choose the wine of Greece over that of Italy or France—were also found in the analyses.

These proteic substances, generically grouped under the term *beverone,* were initially applied as a varnish to give the *fresco* a finish similar to that of an oil painting. The *beverone* was also intended as a protection against the elements. In the first few years following its application, the *beverone* did bestow a certain lucidity on frescoes, reviving the colors, and apparently increasing the clarity of the work. But like the egg-based *beverone* in the Brancacci, the glue-based Sistine *beverone* trapped suspended particles of dust, pollen, candle and incense smoke, and pollution to form a thick layer of grime, which substantially darkened the paintings. In addition to the aesthetic damage, these organic lacquers constitute an ideal matrix for potentially harmful bacteria when they begin to decompose.

The *beverone* was far from the most deadly arrow in the restorer's quiver. A recipe in the Florentine Palatine manuscript from the year 1500 offers a foolproof potion guaranteed to clean both frescoes and oil paintings. "Take ashes of oak, fresh lime, a pound of black soap, and crushed pine cones, water, and boil the mixture as if it were a broth," the deceptively expert author counsels. "Add three eggs, one ounce of common salt, and a bit of white honey. Mix thoroughly. This blend will surely make your works look as if they were done anew."

This anonymous restorer, whose position in society must have corresponded roughly to that of a country snake-oil salesman ("and leaves your breath alone!") adds that a mixture of egg whites and the milk of figs is effective and reliable in those cases where the owner of a painting wishes to modify the colors.

"Take a bit of ash which is slightly acidic," recommends a seventeenth century recipe furnished by a northern Italian restorer named Giambattista Volpato, "and be sure that there is no charcoal, nor any other large chunks which can abrade the painting. Set it in a pan with spring water and with a sponge spread it over the painting. But be swift in removing this with clear water because it erodes the color. Wash it well with clear water, dry it with a cloth of linen, and when dry, give it the white of egg."

Often the substances that restorers used to patch the intonaco or to fill a gap that had developed between the *fresco* and the supporting wall functioned as booby traps that exploded with the passage of a few decades. Even in the cases where a restorer was conscientious about the contents of his *malta,* the freshly carbonated lime-sand mixture inevitably expanded and contracted with climactic changes at a different rate than the original *intonaco* around it. These patches in the *intonaco* often pressed upward against the fabric of the *fresco,* creating new fissures and cracks in the painting.

In those cases where a part of a panel had detached itself from its supporting *arriccio,* restorers generally dispatched with the problem of injecting cement or *gesso* into the gap, introducing unwanted minerals into the wall along with the moisture necessary to transport them to the painting's surface. The Brancacci Chapel is full of *gesso,* particularly in the Corinthian columns that Masolino and Masaccio painted to divide the panels. The heavy presence of this sulfate compound throughout the *fresco* cycle forced the restoration team to discard any cleaning method that required large quantities of water, as water could have easily induced an outbreak of sulfates.

Today, the idea of injecting cement or *gesso* in the space between the *intonaco* and the *arriccio* or using a substance like wood ash to clean the surface of a painting makes most restorers cringe. Elementary chemistry demonstrates that ash is full of sodium, potassium, calcium, or magnesium alkali—the particular composition varies according to the type of wood—which oxidize with water to become a highly aggressive mixture that can easily eat into a painter's colors. Even the most cautious use of an alkaline solution is hazardous, as some of the alkali inevitably remain in the fabric

of the painting, where they are reactivated each time they come
into contact with moisture.

The thought of these utterly unqualified restorers feigning to preserve both oil and wall paintings with homemade syrups or miracle cures in the seventeenth and eighteenth centuries is, despite the tragic consequences, somewhat amusing. It is much more difficult to laugh when reading that many of these same methods—and methods that were even more destructive—continued to be practiced well into the 1900s.

"The 1800s stretched well into the 20th century as far as restoration is concerned," says Ugo Procacci. "The critics of my time didn't study technique of materials. They had no idea what sort of materials an artist might have used, what type of wood he'd chosen to stretch his canvas, or what pigments might be compatible with *fresco*.

"They treated a panel painting from the 1300s in the same manner as a canvas painting of the 1700s, oblivious that the techniques and materials used were entirely different. Take the 1600s, for example," Procacci points out. "It was a disastrous century for painting. Not because of a lack of talent, but because they didn't know anything about technique. If you look at the paintings from that period, they've all turned black. We don't even try to restore them, because the pigments they used, especially the dark colors, have undergone irreversible chemical changes.

"I had to force a new study of art," Procacci proclaims. "Before that, the study of the technical aspects of art did not exist."

Most of the restorers whom Procacci found in the 1930s were as ignorant as the critics in terms of technique. "The restorers were stuck in the mentality of the previous century, with their secret recipes and magic potions, which at best had no effect and at worst ruined the work of art at hand. When a restorer cleaned a painting in those days, he didn't throw away the grime after it had been removed. He saved it so he could reapply it to the painting after it had been restored, to give it an aged look. It was considered part of the *patina* of time."

Giovanni Poggi, who was the Superintendent of Fine Arts when Procacci began service at the Uffizi, was thrilled when Procacci expressed an interest in restoration. "He said that things certainly couldn't get any worse," Procacci recalls. "And he was right. Restorers in those days followed no method, or took their recipes from the book of Secco Suardo. Paintings were regularly cleaned and ruined with a solution of water and potassium soda. In certain places in Italy, restorers still use bicarbonate of soda, a solution which is not much better. But at least they don't use it here in Tuscany."

Reeducating the restorers was one of the most difficult battles of Procacci's long career. "I remember early on when I visited the Ghirlandaio frescoes in Santa Maria Novella and told the man who was restoring them that he was not to apply any protective coating after he had cleaned the paintings. I was thirty at the time, and he must have been in his fifties. The man said nothing, just nodded in agreement. Years later, when we went back to perform a checkup, I discovered that he'd merely waited until my back was turned to brush on his *beverone*."

Because of the hermetic shroud, which enveloped the restoration trade, Procacci often had to strongarm his way to reform. "I divided the restorers into various categories," the professor narrates. "And I made certain that the second-rate restorers never worked on anything important. I tried to exile those restorers who refused to change, to send them to other provinces where they still might inflict damage, but to a much lesser degree. The mentality was so inflexible that in many cases I had to wait until certain people died—people who were friends, and whom I loved—before their methods could be eliminated."

While Procacci fought to implant a new respect among restorers for the materials that composed a work of art, he also had to overcome the hostile skepticism that restorers and their ineptitude had instilled in the general public. "The widely-held opinion that to restore a painting means to ruin it could and should be discarded," Procacci wrote in the introduction of the catalogue for the 1946 Florence Restores exhibit.

"Or at least we must cease to believe that restorers are people who are absolutely incompetent or worse, nothing better than sadists whose sole ambition in life is that to precipitate onto works of art in order to ruin them with sinful pleasure."

Florence was not the only artistic center whose treasures were being systematically destroyed by charlatan restorers. "I'll never

forget one of the first demonstrations we saw at the Central Institute of Restoration in Rome in the 1940s," says Paolo Mora, who
together with his wife Laura pioneered the restoration techniques
that still form the backbone of the restoration methods used at the
ICR.

"They'd invited an old artisan who was supposed to be an expert restorer to demonstrate his cleaning method. And in front of
a packed lecture hall, this man lay the painting flat out on a table,
sprayed the canvas with alcohol, and then casually tossed a match
onto the work. When the flame went out, he brushed away the
ashes and said 'voila.' This was his method for cleaning canvas
paintings." Mora shakes his head. "I remember turning to my
wife and remarking that we were going to have to start all over
again, from scratch."

Milan. 1988. Tuesday, October 6.

Professor Paolo Parrini sits at his desk in the offices of the Syremont Corporation, of which he is President. The narrow twelfth-

Professor Paolo Parrini, the Brancacci team's scientific coordinator, at his
desk at the Syremont Corporation in Milan.

122 floor room is practical and unpretentious. The furniture, and most of all the order, reflect the personality of a man who clearly favors function over form. Parrini's wide desktop is covered with four large stacks of paperwork, each of them piled neatly and afforded an equal parcel of space.

On the wall over his right shoulder hangs a photograph of one of the gilded bronze panels from Lorenzo Ghiberti's eastern doors of the Florentine baptistry, the doors that Michelangelo once declared worthy of being "the doors of Paradise."

"It's the story of Joseph," Parrini says, pointing not without some pride to the photograph of the splendidly-worked bronze and gold relief. The panel, still in its newly-restored splendor ten years after it left the Opificio Delle Pietre Dure, is currently on display in a plexiglass case in Florence's Museum of the Duomo.

"I worked with Baldini on that restoration in 1979," says the Professor. "From looking at it, you'd think that the relief was in perfect health."

Parrini is right. Ghiberti's delicately-crafted figures have regained nearly all of their original splendor; the gold is malleable, breathing a yellow so rich that it seems to border on red. "Unfortunately," Parrini continues, "appearances can often be deceiving, and especially in art. Our analyses revealed that the state of conservation of the panel is quite precarious."

Parrini sits with his hands folded on the desk in front of him. In his mid-sixties, he is a harmonic hybrid of university professor and high-powered corporate manager. His healthy air is that of a man who has drawn enormous satisfaction from having applied his considerable talents to a wide spectrum of projects. And like most successful businessmen, he is clearly at home with people.

"Ghiberti fashioned his reliefs for the baptistry doors by using an ancient Etruscan fusion technique in which molten gold is applied to the bronze undermold without soldering or injection," the professor explains.

"In the past thirty years, because of the action of pollutants from automobile exhaust and combustible fuels, the gold on the *The Story of Joseph* is now attached to the bronze beneath by a layer of corrosion composed of sulfates and chlorides. This decomposition would continue were the panel to be exposed once more to the atmosphere. And Ghiberti's gold would fall to the ground."

Parrini shrugs decorously, as if accustomed enough to ceding to the inevitable not to protest further. "Ghiberti was one of the finest artisans in history," he observes. "His technique in the baptistry panels is virtually flawless; this is the major reason he is able to achieve the remarkable pictorial effect in the relief. Nevertheless, there was no way he could have anticipated the radical transformation that the atmosphere would undergo in the twentieth century. And how that atmosphere would attack the materials in his panels."

In 1983, Umberto Baldini left the Opificio in Florence to assume the directorship of the Central Institute for Restoration in Rome, the state body that had claimed jurisdiction over the Brancacci restoration. One year later, having resolved the bureaucratic delay that had interrupted the Brancacci restoration in 1982, and having found an ideal sponsor in Olivetti SPA, Umberto Baldini began to assemble his new restoration team.

One of Baldini's first moves as ICR director was to name his wife Ornella Casazza as technical director of the Brancacci project. It was a step that surprised no one.

"We've worked together for so many years," Baldini says, allowing himself a moment of fondness while responding to the question that to him must seem absurd. "And I cannot imagine a better person to wield the baton when I'm not around to direct the orchestra. It's been my great fortune in life to have had a collaborator as able as Ornella."

For his scientific director, Baldini chose Paolo Parrini. Parrini, a Florentine, was both a friend and collaborator. As in any comprehensive restoration, the role of the scientist is essential in procuring the necessary data that then allows the restoration director to determine the team's course of action. By now, at least in Italy, a series of diagnostic tests is a common prelude to all but the most rudimentary restorations.

In the Brancacci, Baldini intended to utilize his scientific support staff to its utmost, not only to the end of preserving the priceless frescoes, but also to the further advancing of the art and techniques of restoration.

Parrini's task in the Brancacci would be multifold. He and his researchers would execute analyses on the materials used in the Masaccio and Masolino panels to ascertain their state of health, and would attempt to identify all the foreign matter that had accumulated on or in them. The scientists would then perform a thorough examination of the climate and atmosphere in the chapel, in the church, and outside in the Piazza Del Carmine to determine what harmful reagents or mechanical actions might attack the frescoes in the future.

A physicist by training, Parrini began his career as a researcher with Montedison SPA, Italy's chemical giant. Like many scientists who participate in restoration, Parrini was first drawn to the profession as a result of the disastrous Florentine flood in 1966. In 1968, Parrini accepted an invitation from Florence's International University of Art to participate in a two-year analysis of the damage suffered by the city's artistic patrimony.

In 1977, Parrini became chief of Montedison's prestigious Guido Donegani Institute, one of Europe's most important centers for pure research. As head of the Donegani, Parrini directed a hand-picked team of top researchers whose superb abilities, experience, and analytical skills were often applied to art. Encouraged by Baldini, Parrini experimented with a slew of science's most sophisticated analytical and diagnostic machinery to determine how they might be useful to restoration.

The bond that linked Baldini and Parrini was constructed of both professional esteem and personal affection. "Aside from considering Umberto Baldini a good friend," says Parrini, "I respect him for his intelligence, and just as much for his humility. He was the first art historian to truly grasp the importance of science. And he has never been afraid to seek the counsel of experts.

"The new analytical technology in art restoration was born with Baldini in the 1960s," Professor Parrini explains, smooth and composed. "Before that, technology had been applied to art mainly to identify fakes and not to assist in restoration."

Since the 1966 flood, Baldini relied continually on Parrini for his technical and material expertise. In the years that followed the disaster, Parrini assisted his friend and colleague in nearly all of his major restorations including the Cimabue *Cross, The Bronzes of Riance,* and Donatello's *Judith and Holofernes.* With a versatile, highly-specialized staff of researchers, Parrini was able to offer scientific support not just for the restoration of paintings and sculpture, but also for architecture, plaster, manuscripts, leather, ceramics, archeology, and metals.

The working relationship between Parrini and Baldini was ideal; the two men never clashed over their respective roles in the restoration team. Each afforded the other a solid autonomy in his own sphere. Parrini performed analyses, experimented with new remedies, and instructed Baldini's restorers how best to utilize the materials he and his researchers had developed. Baldini then determined how these analyses and materials could be incorporated without compromising or modifying the artistic or historical significance of the work at hand.

But in the end, it was Baldini as the historical expert who always charted the course of the restoration.

"The universe of art is unique," explains Parrini. "I believe that the role of the scientist is to analyze and identify the situation, and then to develp new and better products to save as much as possible of the original artwork. The products must then be put at the disposal of the restorer and the historian, who are experts in their fields and know much better than I how best to apply them.

"Pure science can be as dangerous to art as pure ignorance," Parrini cautions. "An unbridled chemical reaction could easily remove much more color or bronze than was intended. In restoration, all decisions regarding color and taste must be left up to the restorer. Science should only serve to verify his results, and to provide material guidelines."

Parrini was not the only scientist qualified or eager to be the scientific director of the Brancacci Chapel team. But for Baldini, any other choice would have been unthinkable.

"Paolo is part of a team which has worked together for many years, a team of exceptional individuals who have grown together through their experiences. Most of all, it is a team which is *affiatato.*" This is an Italiam idiomatic adjective meaning well-integrated, a term which is usually applied to a finely-tuned orchestra or to an expert soccer team. "And a team which has always given excellent results."

As director of the Guido Donegani research institute, Parrini had all of the companies and laboratories belonging to the mammoth Montedison Group at his disposal. One of the first tests that

Parrini ordered was the obligatory search for sulfates, enlisting the help of the Montedison Larac laboratory for applied research.

"In the past," Parrini says, "the only way to obtain a relatively reliable mapping of the sulfates in a *fresco* was by taking a number of samples from various zones of the *intonaco* and analyzing them one by one. Apart from being destructive—even though the samples were quite small, usually no more than a fraction of a milligram, material *was* being removed from the panel—the test method itself was far from one hundred percent reliable.

"For the Brancacci, Baldini wanted a *non-invasive* test for sulfates, a method of measuring the level of SO_4 which could be effected without having to take samples." Parrini gloats here, but without pretension, the way a merchant might beam when showing a fine piece of cloth to a customer. "And *non-invasive* testing just happens to be the specialty of the house here."

Parrini's "specialty of the house" for the testing of sulfates was an anionic resin developed by Montedison that, when applied to the surface of the *fresco,* dissolved the sulfate compounds in the *intonaco* and absorbed the newly-freed SO_4 ion. These resins, about one inch in diameter, were applied to the fresco for a period which varied from thirty minutes to two hours according to the quantity of sulfates in that particular zone. When the ionic-exchange between the resins and the wall had terminated, the resins were tested for SO_4 content.

"The sulfate level in the Brancacci Chapel was quite low," Parrini recalls. "Somewhere around four or five grams per square meter; this is far below the danger level. More importantly, the areas where sulfur was found were all deep within the chapel walls, and these walls are in excellent condition. In short, we found that sulfates were not going to be a problem."

After the sulfate survey, Parrini turned to the *intonaco* itself. "We examined several infinitesimal samples with an electronic scansion microscope," the professor continues.

An electronic scansion microscope (SEM) obtains a highly-detailed and realistic image of an object by projecting a stream of electrons onto the sample. This stream of electrons scans the surface of the sample and elicits the emission of electrons from within the sample itself. These secondary electrons are read by a receptor and then translated into a visual image, allowing for enlargements of up to 100,000 times lifesize.

The SEM technique is not dissimilar to the one that enables the reproduction of visual images onto a common television screen. In the past, Parrini had successfully applied the instrument to perform analyses of paintings, ceramics, marble, and metals.

"The Brancacci *intonaco* was perfect," Parrini says admiringly. "This of course was excellent news, because a healthy *intonaco* is usually the sign of a healthy *fresco*."

From the SEM analysis of the *intonaco*, Parrini's assistants began identifying the various substances trapped in the *beverone* that had been painted across the surface of the frescoes during previous restorations. "We found some dirt, a bit of mold, various pollens, and traces of lead," Parrini remembers.

"The concentration of lead was extremely low, and therefore innocuous. The majority of what we found on the surface of the panels was carbon, which accounted for much of the darkness. As the Carmine Church is located on a large piazza which now functions as a parking lot, we assumed that the carbon originated from automobile exhaust."

In order to select the most appropriate cleaning method, Baldini had to know the exact nature of the materials that he needed to remove. Anyone with the slightest knowledge of the history of *fresco* restoration could see at a glance that the major aesthetic problem in the Brancacci Chapel was that of the *beverone*. But *beverone* was much more a category than a specific, homogenous substance. The restorers who had basted the Masaccio and Masolino frescoes in the Brancacci Chapel with the mixture in hopes of livening up the colors had left no records. And even if they had documented their labors, it is doubtful that they would have given away their recipes. The eighteenth and nineteenth century restorers who used the *beverone* all had their own custom blends for the brew, blends whose ingredients were guarded as valuable trade secrets.

"The ultraviolet photos indicated a large presence of proteic matter on the surface of the paintings," Parrini says, "and it was obvious that this matter was the *beverone,* in various states of decomposition."

The techniques that analytical science uses to identify specific

128 proteins are among its most complicated and most exact. As all proteins are composed of amino acids and therefore very similar, many common analytical examinations like infrared spectrometry are not specific enough to distinguish one protein from another. The Larac team subjected the substance to a process known as pirolosi-gas chromatography.

Gas chromatography is a specific analytic test for organic matter in gaseous form. Through pirolosi—the transformation through a flash of intense heat of a solid or semisolid into a gas—the technique is also applicable to matter in other states. In principle, the sample to be analyzed is channeled into a tube containing an inert solid or liquid absorbent. The various substances contained in the sample are analyzed and identified according to the speed with which they pass through this inert absorbent.

"As suspected," Parrini concludes, "the base of the Brancacci *beverone* turned out to be egg."

Parrini's role in the Brancacci restoration did not end with the conclusion of his ably-executed diagnostics. Technicians from Montedison provided constant scientific support and monitoring during all phases of the restoration. The environmental surveys—including a measurement of the quantity of sulfur dioxide in the air of the chapel—were vital in determining what sort of preventive steps needed to be taken. And Parrini would ultimately supply the Brancacci restorers with a novel cleaning method that would allow them an unprecedented measure of control while they cautiously removed the thick layer of grime that covered the *fresco* cycle.

In 1987, after a year of market research, Parrini founded a new Montedison subsidiary known as Syremont, which seconded the Brancacci team through to the end of the restoration. "Syremont is a company specifically conceived to deal with the problems of conservation and restoration," the president of Syremont explains.

"We are very active in the art field because it is an excellent testing laboratory for our products, and also because it is excellent for our image. Personally, I have drawn great satisfaction from having been able to make a contribution in restoration. But it is certainly not cost effective for us."

As its main source of revenue, the Syremont company applies
its conservational acumen to important structures that are exposed
to an increasingly hostile and increasingly complicated environment. "Cement, stone, and metals," Parrini lists, "the materials
with which we have built our dams and bridges—all of them are
constantly exposed to forces which were not present in the atmosphere when they were created.

"Our work is generally twofold," Parrini says, the dynamic
manager momentarily taking precedence over the more philosophical physicist. "Assess the state of conservation of an object,
and develop a product or a series of products to counteract the
negative impact of the environment and prevent further decay."

As a scientist, Parrini also finds this end of his work extremely
gratifying. "With the incredible variety of materials on which we
intervene," he smiles, a hint of stress momentarily troubling his
otherwise implacable ease, "I am forced to be creative on a daily
basis."

One of Parrini's most interesting challenges was when he was
asked to develop a substance for the 12-meter yacht, Italia-2,
which would allow the ship to better slide through the water.

"We eventually discovered a protective coating which did in fact
reduce the friction between the hull and the water, giving our hull
about a three percent advantage over ships with ordinary hulls,"
Parrini says, tilting his head in amusement. "But during the 1986
America's Cup, the skipper missed a buoy, and one of the crew-
men fell overboard.

"This is merely an illustration that no matter how advanced a
technology might be," the professor pauses, a pedagogue about
to wind up a lesson, "the human factor is still the one which determines the successful outcome of an operation."

CHAPTER TEN

Enzo Ferroni and Dino Dini

O N NOVEMBER 4TH, 1966, the rain-swollen Arno river burst its banks and spilled into the city of Florence, an irrepressible, malignant tide of mud and sludge and gasoline. The damage to the city's streets and buildings was incalculable. The damage to its artworks was unfathomable.

To meet this crisis, the Opificio Delle Pietre Dure hired scores of new restorers, among these a young woman named Ornella Casazza. It would be on the Cimabue cross—the thirteenth century masterpiece that would become the emblem not only of the destruction wrought by the flood, but of the city's proud and genial resilience—where Cassazza would first apply her theory of chromatic selection and abstraction.

Many other professionals—including Brancacci scientific director Paolo Parrini, who would make invaluable contributions to the study of restoration—first came to the field in the period of dire need that followed the flood. But the most productive and prolific partnership forged by the November flood was one that regarded the art of *fresco* restoration, the partnership between Dino Dini and Enzo Ferroni.

Professor Enzo Ferroni is chairman of the department of physical chemistry at the University of Florence. While returning from his laboratory one evening, a few days after the November 1966 disaster, he happened to glance at an article in *La Nazione,* the Florence daily newspaper. The article described the drama of *The Last Supper,* a fourteenth-century *fresco* by Taddeo Gaddi in the Museum of Santa Croce, which had been immersed for several

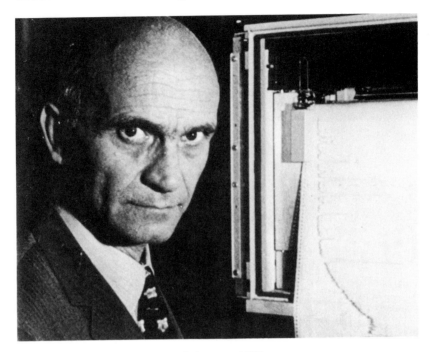

Enzo Ferroni, University of Florence. 1972.

hours in the viscous mass of sludge and gasoline left behind by the flood.

The artworks damaged by the flood were countless. Ferroni's own laboratory was still knee-deep in mud. Fatigued as he was, a simple account of another ailing *fresco* would not have normally captured Ferroni's attention. But his eye was drawn to a detailed description of the wall painting's symptoms; large quantities of saline crystals had erupted like a rash across the surface of the painting when the water began to evaporate. The explosion of these salts was so violent that it displaced the color and caused it to fall onto the floor in large flakes.

It was the description of these salts that fascinated Ferroni. "I looked for the names of the persons involved in the rescue effort," Ferroni says, as an aside, as if he were dispensing with a necessary prologue. Twenty-two years have passed since the flood. We are in his office at the University. It is six-thirty in the morning and he has been at work since five.

"When I returned home that evening I called the laboratory at
the Fortezza and asked 'Have you considered this?' " Ferroni's
voice betrays a hint of emotion as he delves into the story. "The
person replied that he didn't even know what 'this' was, but that
they were willing to consider anything, and could I please come
down in the morning."

Ferroni is a born historian. Although I constitute an audience of
one, he is pacing about the room, concentrated, focused, an actor

Refectory, Santa Croce. November 1966 and the Florentine Flood.
(courtesy of Sabino Giovannoni)

totally immersed in his role. "When I arrived, I saw this exquisite work, in conditions which could not even have been described as pitiful. The colors, consumed by saline crystals. Gaddi's delicate Christ literally illegible. In cases as desperate as these, when there is absolutely no other choice, one proceeds with the *strappo* or the *stacco*. But even this proved impossible, because the animal glue which is used as an adhesive to strip the *intonaco* inexplicably refused to gel."

The sixty-eight year old Ferroni pauses, strides toward my chair, strikes a dramatic, dire pose. "By now," he narrates, "the desperation was total. They had wheeled their ultimate weapon out onto the battlefield. And the weapon had misfired. They were without hope."

The chemical process that causes animal glues used in the *strappo/stacco* process to solidify is known in technical circles as the sol-gel transformation, that is, the transformation of a solvent into a gel. It is the process by which common gelatin hardens. It is also the process to which Ferroni had dedicated eight years of intensive study.

"After reading the article," Ferroni resumes, "I began to think. What are these salts? Where do they come from? To act upon a substance without fully knowing the nature of that substance is inherently irrational. It was obvious that the salts had not been deposited by the floodwaters; the floodwaters had long receded, yet the saline crystals continued to form at a rate which was more than alarming."

He turns away from the window with a start, takes possession of the center of the room. The stage is set. "The waters which had impregnated the Gaddi *fresco* and deposited these salts on the surface had risen from beneath the refectory through the capillary action in the walls. What is beneath the refectory then? Beneath the refectory is the mausoleum where the monks and parishoners of Santa Croce were buried for centuries. The salts then, were those resulting from the decomposition of the cadavers buried there, the salts which form during the degradation of any organic matter: ammonia, nitrogen. Nitrates. The salts were nitrates. And in my eight years of study on the *sol-gel* transformation," he places a marked accent on the words sol-gel, so I will remember them,

"I had discovered that the presence of nitrates can inhibit or even impede the process which turns a solvent into a gel."

No matter how many times Ferroni tells this story—and he tells it often—he never fails to transmit the electric apprehension that characterized his first adventure in art restoration.

"The problem was twofold," he resumes. "The elevated quantity of moisture in the *fresco* precluded any possibility of detaching the painting; animal glues do not harden completely in the pressence of water. And even in the unlikely case of the total evaporation of the moisture, the nitrate salts would prevent the glue from solidifying.

"One of the technicians had proposed the use of a synthetic adhesive which was not soluble in water. But this would mean introducing a foreign substance into the texture of the *fresco* which we could not totally remove after the *strappo*. The solution lay in devising a method which would simultaneously push back the wall of water and isolate these nitrates long enough for the animal gel to harden and for the restorers to detach the panel. I suggested TBP (Tributylphosphate.)"

Ferroni pronounces the name of the compound with the same casual proficiency that a physician might use in prescribing a routine diurectic. TBP is well known in the chemical/industrial field. The dense liquid is used to separate ammonia—a nitrogen compound—from water. Because of its capacity to extract certain ions, TBP is also used in the enrichment of radioactive elements and in the separation of rare earths.

"And I explained the reasons for my choice," Ferroni proceeds, punctuating his momentary pause with a decision turn. "First, TBP is insoluble in water. The substance would not be absorbed or altered by the considerable moisture in the wall. Second, it has an extremely low surface tension which gives it an elevated capillary action. This would allow the liquid to penetrate deep into the wall of the refectory. Third, it has an extremely high boiling point, which means that it does not evaporate quickly. And fourth, it had been proven as an effective reagent for nitrate salts."

Procacci, then Superintendent of Fine Arts, Baldini, director at the Opificio, and the various members of their technical team were nonplused. New products or techniques are always experimented with extreme caution in restoration, given the delicate nature of the work. The anionic resins used in the Brancacci cleaning were tested for several years, first on sections of *intonaco* in the laboratory, and then on frescoes of minor artistic importance before they were judged to be reliable enough to use in the Chapel.

Despite the urgency of the situation, Ferroni's proposal was received with understandable skepticism. "But among this group I met an exceptional man, a restorer named Dino Dini." Ferroni's admiration for Dini is unbounded; the pause during which he searches for the terms with which to laud his colleage is genuine.

"A marvelous man," he says. "Exquisitely timid, incredibly competent, a man who learned the art from his father, who had learned it from his father. Do you know that Dini was capable of distinguishing stones from bricks in the support wall beneath a *fresco* simply by placing his hand on the painting and observing the exchange of heat between his hand and the wall? Dino Dini was not born in the University of *homo sapiens sapiens*. He was born in the *bottega* of *homo faber*. And he taught me more about the nature of *fresco* than all the other restorers and technicians with whom I've had the honor to work."

While the rest of the worried group from the Fine Arts wrung its hands in impotence as Gaddi's *Last Supper* disintegrated, Dini pulled Ferroni aside and asked him to find him some TBP so he could effect a trial. Ferroni didn't even know where to locate the solution in flood-ravaged Florence, and ultimately had to travel to Milan to procure the small quantity, which Dini would need.

For the test, they chose a fragment of a *fresco* in the sacristy adjacent to the refectory in Santa Croce. The fragment—an angel in flight painted by an anonymous hand—was in the same disastrous condition as the Gaddi work. "I cannot sincerely say that I was confident," Ferroni confesses. "In theory the substance should have produced the desired effect. But this was hardly theory. We were working on a *fresco,* a material of which I had virtually no knowledge.

"And even if the solution could perform the function which we'd hoped for," Ferroni specifies, augmenting the already considerable suspense, "there was no way to know whether the effect would be prolonged enough for Dini to perform the *strappo*."

Procacci and his team watched anxiously as Dini applied the TBP to the surface of the *fresco* with a paintbrush. The group ob-

Dino Dini applies TBP onto Gaddi fresco to sequester nitrates and push back wall of water. *(courtesy of Sabino Giovannoni)*

served as the dense liquid penetrated rapidly through the *intonaco* and into the supporting wall. Twenty-four hours later, Dini fabricated the cotton gauze web and applied the animal glue. The glue solidified as if under normal conditions, and Dini executed the *strappo* without any particular difficulty.

For those who had witnessed the first experiment with TBP, the substance suggested by Ferroni seemed to hold some promise, although the successful *strappo* of a small section of *fresco*—in this case two feet by four—was not sufficient evidence of the product's viability on a large expanse of mural like Gaddi's *Last Supper*. After several reunions, during which time the *fresco* continued to deteriorate, the Fine Arts committee decided to enact a second test, this time on a larger painting. A *fresco* by Ligozzi covering fifty square meters of the wall opposite *The Last Supper* was chosen. Dini and Ferroni ably performed the second *strappo*. This was enough to convince the committee to authorize the use of TBP on the Gaddi work.

Between June and August of 1967 Dini detached Gaddi's *Last Supper* from the refectory wall in Santa Croce. Aside from its dimensions—Dini divided the *fresco* into four pieces, which were detached one after another—the expert restorer experienced no unusual difficulties during the operation.

"From that moment on," Ferroni laughs, "I had the sensation of having entered into an enterprise which would require a great deal of my time and energy."

And the sensation was well-founded. Over the next twenty years, Ferroni would provide technical assistance to Ugo Procacci, Umberto Baldini, Paolo Parrini, Maurizio Seracini, Sabino Giovannoni, and Ornella Casazza. He would be the first scientist of international fame to dedicate himself to the study of *fresco*. And the ammonium carbonate–barium hydroxide treatment that he would invent with Dino Dini at San Marco was to be as important to the field of *fresco* restoration as the discovery of penicillin was to medicine.

Given their already-proven expertise, it may seem surprising that Baldini did not select Dini and Ferroni as head restorer and scientific director for the original Brancacci team. Unfortunately, restoration, and particularly an important restoration like the Brancacci Chapel, is often steeped in politics and petty rivalries.

Umberto Baldini is too professional, and much too conscientious to choose a lesser-qualified collaborator over a more competent one. But in the case of having to decide between two or more potential components whose credentials are equally impressive, factors such as compatibility, friendship, and even marketing must of needs influence the decision.

Baldini's preference for Paolo Parrini over Ferroni is fairly easy to comprehend. Apart from the tie of friendship that linked Baldini to the president of Syremont, Parrini also brought with him the weight, expertise, and productive capacity of the Italian chemical giant, Montedison SPA. Parrini's approach to restoration, while no more or less effective than Ferroni's, was certainly more global. Ferroni preferred to work alone, ruminating in his office in the early morning, applying his genially elastic mind until arriving at a solution. Parrini was much more ready to delegate authority, coordinating a team of specialists and at least in theory offering a broader base of scientific support.

The entry of Olivetti SPA as official sponsor also played a role in the drafting of the team. Like any smart businessman, Parrini knew that the Montedison participation in the Brancacci project would reap enormous benefits for the corporation in terms of publicity. And the sponsor could well have felt that the prestige of Parrini and the Montedison Group outweighed that of Ferroni and the University of Florence.

Dini's exclusion from the Brancacci team was certainly not a surprise. It is difficult to imagine the aloof, spiritual, seventy-five year old restorer seeking counsel from Ornella Casazza, or even accepting direction from Baldini. In almost all of his projects, Dini had enjoyed a brand of freedom that far exceeded the confines of the restorer's role within the Baldini restoration module.

"Dini's relations with the superintendency and with the Opificio were always less than idyllic," says one restoration professional. "And it is ironic that under Baldini, the man who generally was acclaimed to be Florence's finest *fresco* restorer usually had to travel outside of the city to find work. On the other hand, it would have been unthinkable for Dini, at seventy-five years old, to have accepted a post at the Opificio at the same rank as his former students Giovannoni and Botticelli. Perhaps there was just no place for a restorer of Dini's caliber and independence in the Baldini restoration scheme."

140   After having made his selections, Baldini did invite Ferroni and
Dini to participate in the Brancacci project as consultants. Showing
an extreme grace, Ferroni overcame his disappointment and accepted his diminished role. With the same consummate dignity,
Dini declined.

In the Brancacci restoration, Ferroni served as a sort of technical
advisor-at-large for each of the members of the team. Parrini con-
sulted him frequently on matters that required a specific material
knowledge of *fresco*. Like Dini had done before him, Brancacci
restorer Sabino Giovannoni sought Ferroni's counsel, meeting
with him in his office at the University as often as twice a week.

"For the big problems, the cleaning method, for the complicated analyses and materials, we have Parrini," Giovannoni explains. "But for the daily difficulties, or even when we just want
to talk over an idea, we turn to Professor Ferroni. He's one of us."

Giovannoni turned to Ferroni when the team discovered a large
gap between the *intonaco* and wall of the lower right-hand register.
Traditionally, gaps like these had been consolidated with injections
of cement or *gesso,* both of which can lead to undesired saline deposits. Cement can produce fluorescence of soda, potassium, and
calcium. *Gesso,* because of its sulfur content, is obviously to be
avoided.

Ideally, the best *fresco* consolidant would be the original mixture
of limestone and sand, which the artists used for both the *arriccio*
and *intonaco*. But limestone needs to interact with carbon dioxide
if it is to carbonate and harden into an *intonaco*. And sealed from
the atmosphere once injected into the Brancacci wall, the calcium-
carbonate *malta* would not be able to carbonate and harden.

"The problem was to invent a way to diffuse carbon dioxide
through the mixture once it was injected into the wall," Ferroni
states. "To make things more difficult, we were operating with
calcium, which is extremely alkaline. Chemical solutions that normally emit carbon dioxide do not work in alkaline conditions.
And in addition, the eventual method could not merely produce
an explosion of carbon dioxide. It had to create a slow, gradual
diffusion lasting several months, to let the *malta* carbonate at the
same pace it carbonates when in contact with the atmosphere."

Needless to say, after more than a year of rumination, experiments, and modifications, Ferroni provided the Brancacci team with a viable method, a chemical compound that created a constant, gradual flow of carbon dioxide through hydrolysis.

In over twenty years of work in art restoration, Ferroni has never accepted payment for his work. "I consider it a civic duty," he says proudly. "For the privilege of having been born in Florence. And I am paid by the marvel in the eyes of all the people who come to see Gaddi at Santa Croce and Angelico at San Marco."

Ferroni visibly downplays his role in the Brancacci operation. "I don't want to appear more important than I am here. I simply put myself at the disposition of the restorers. If they need assistance, they know that I am always here."

It is this availability, and Ferroni's perseverant problem solving, which makes him so valuable as a restoration consultant. Toward the end of the Brancacci cleaning, the ultraviolet photographs showed a series of strange blotches on the robes of the figures in the lower register, stains that had not appeared in the documentation with visible light.

Ferroni identified the substance by seeking its origin.

"You have to always ask, 'What was the use of this chapel? Who came here? What did they do?' The Brancacci Chapel was reconsecrated in honor of the Madonna Del Popolo in the mid-1400s. And what do people do before the Madonna? They light candles, sometimes near the altar, sometimes in candlesticks placed along the walls. And how does one extinguish a candle? Like this." He leans forward and blows out an imaginary flame.

"Naturally, I examined a small sample, and this proved that my hypothesis had been correct. The speckles on the robes were produced by the spray of wax left on the frescoes from centuries and centuries of candles being snuffed out."

The mere identification of the foreign substance did not resolve the problem of the speckles. Ferroni then devised a method of removing the paraffin; he will not tell me what it is, most likely because he is still waiting for a patent.

"I will say this much. It's not a solvent. When you use a solvent, in drycleaning for example, you merely dilute the substance until you no longer see it. But you don't remove it. The substance or

142   stain is still in the fabric. My method was something truly original."

As part of the central committee in the Brancacci restoration, Ferroni met regularly with Baldini, Casazza, and Parrini to evaluate the team's progress and to chart its future course. In November of 1988, with the pictorial restoration nearly complete, the committee met again.

"And we discovered that what I had predicted at the beginning of the operation had come true, that is, that our work was not done." His sails bulging with a new wind, Ferroni tacks toward the bookshelf near the entrance to his office.

"Yes, we were able to remove this layer of meringue (this is Ferroni's rustic appellation for the *beverone*) which had darkened the frescoes. But this same egg layer, although deleterious to the aesthetics of the chapel, had also protected the paintings from the atmosphere. Now that we've exposed them to the air, we must attack the problem of how to protect the chapel. Filters, strict control of temperature and humidity, a constant monitoring of the state of conservation.

"You see, until the Brancacci, the entire attitude towards restoration was flawed. A problem was defined, the labor was performed, and the work of art was proclaimed healthy because it had a healthy look. The historian would then travel to a convention, where he would show before and after photos from the restoration to attest that the situation was under control. Can you imagine a physician at a medical convention who shows a picture of his patient's worried face before surgery and his smiling face after the operation as proof of the validity of his method? Of course not. The physician will present the results of the patient's EKG, or his blood pressure. And he will also monitor his patient's condition on a monthly or yearly basis, depending on the case, after the operation."

"The Brancacci is a historic restoration for precisely this reason, that the sponsor has also provided funds for periodic checkups. The filtration system, the lighting, the atmospheric controls; these are the elements which transform restoration into conservation, which preserve the chapel's well-being after the team has restored its beauty. And should the case arise, we are ready to reintervene at a moment's notice."

Masaccio: *Adam and Eve Driven from Paradise*. An early cleaning trial.

Masaccio: *Adam and Eve Driven from Paradise* after restoration.

Masaccio: Central group of *The Tribute Money* after restoration.

Masaccio: Saint Thomas from *The Tribute Money*. Believed to be a portrait of Felice Brancacci. Note the golden halo repainted with the technique of chromatic selection.

◄ Masolino: *Original Sin* after restoration. The grey background is the artist's preparatory layer.

Masaccio: *St. Peter Healing with his Shadow*. The scene was transformed from an urban lane into a cosmopolitan square when restorers removed the baroque altar to reveal a classical cathedral on the far right of the panel.

The red-capped figure to the left of St. Peter is believed to be Masolino. The man with the white beard over St. Peter's left shoulder is supposedly a portrait of Donatello, while the blond-haired Saint John to the right of St. Peter is most likely "La Scheggia," Masaccio's younger brother.

Masaccio: *The Alms Giving*. Ornella Casazza discovered that the mountains in the background were covered with snow.

Masolino: detail from *The Resurrection of Tabita*. Roberto Longhi once called this *loggia* "a rickety shack." With its colors restored, Masolino's use of shading and *chiaroscuro* are plainly evident. The structure occupies real space and has weight.

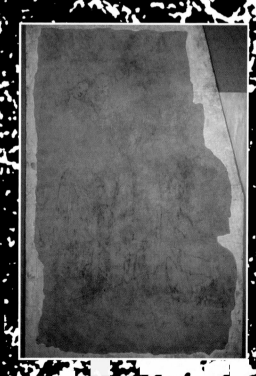

Masolino?: Synopia for *Feed My Sheep* discovered on the rear wall beneath the first register fresco of Vincenzo Meucci.

Masaccio: detail from *St. Peter Enthroned*. The black-hooded figure on the right of the scene is Filippo Brunelleschi. To his left Masaccio has painted the architect Leon Batista Alberti, while the hulking, red-robed figure that stares out at the viewer is the artist himself.

Filippino Lippi: detail from *St. Paul Visiting St. Peter in Prison*. The discovery of Lippi's sublime narrative gift was another fortunate consequence of the restoration.

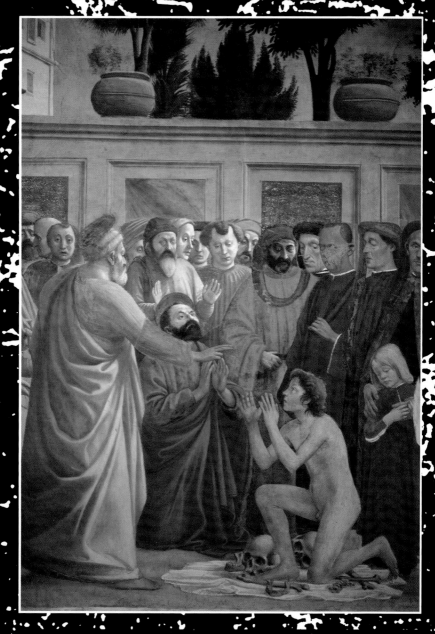

Masaccio and Fillipino Lippi: central group in *The Resurrection of Teofilo's Son*. The recent cleaning confirmed the traditional historical opinion on the division between the two artists. Here we see Lippi's skillful integration in the newly-resurrected boy and in the first four figures from the right. The remaining figures and the architecture are Masaccio's.

CHAPTER ELEVEN

Infrared and Ultraviolet

W HILE DINO DINI and Enzo Ferroni may have ushered in a new era of *fresco* restoration with their ammonium carbonate—barium hydroxide method, the craft's evolution hardly stopped at San Marco. Many of the chemists, physicists, biologists, and engineers who first participated in restoration in the aftermath of the 1966 Florence flood would use their respective expertise to dramatically transform the field.

One of the most important advances which the flood would generate was in diagnostics, in the widely-expanded array of sophisticated analytical and diagnostic techniques which could be applied to art. These techniques, when properly applied, afforded the restorer a level of intimacy with an artwork that would have been impossible through a more traditional visual or microscopic examination.

Many of these techniques were based on highly-specialized forms of photography. The phenomenon of sight is actuated by a type of electromagnetic radiation known as visible light. We could not view the Brancacci Chapel frescoes or any other painting for that matter without this light. When an object is lit by electromagnetic radiation in the visible range, the human eye can perceive and measure characteristics such as size, shape, movement, and color, according to the radiation that that object reflects.

Photography, too, is entirely dependent on electromagnetic radiation, and the ability of certain objects to reflect that radiation. A photograph is literally a drawing made with light (the word itself comes from the Greek *photos* meaning light and *graphos* meaning writing or drawing.)

144   The band of visible light is but a small, central window in the wide spectrum of electromagnetic radiation. Our sight is sensitive only to those wavelengths that fall between violet and red, while the entire spectrum of light ranges from gamma rays to radio-waves. Although the vast majority of electromagnetic waves cannot be received by the sophisticated seeing apparatus with which nature has equipped us, science has devised a series of instruments that are capable of perceiving them.

In many ways, this mechanical perception is parallel to the phe-nomenon of human sight. When an object is lit or excited by these non-visible rays, the rays that bounce back can be photographed or converted into a graph or a visual image. Just as certain charac-teristics of an object come to light when they are excited by wave-lengths in the visible range, the non-visible wavelengths can reveal other types of information about the object that they illuminate.

This second sight, or the technology of using electromagnetic waves to investigate the nature of matter, has been used success-fully in many fields, particularly in medical diagnostics. Since the late 1970s, it has also played an important role in restoration.

A Surface Reading

Ultraviolet fluorescence reflectography is usually the first anal-ysis prescribed in the series of diagnostic examinations that im-mediately precede the restoration of a *fresco* or of a panel or canvas painting. A complicated technique requiring highly selective op-tical filters and an able operator, the ultraviolet reflectograph is essentially a photograph taken while the subject is radiated with ultraviolet light. The test provides a primary reading of the paint-ing's surface and enables restorers to distinguish between the ar-tist's original materials and the foreign substances that have sub-sequently been added to the artwork—substances including lacquers, varnishes, and pigments used in repaintings.

The reflectograph technique works by using ultraviolet light to induce fluorescence in a substance. Fluorescence can be defined as the optical phenomenon that occurs when a certain wavelength of light stimulates an object to emit a reflection of light in greater wavelengths. When fluorescence occurs in the range of visible light, the secondary wavelengths usually appear as an off-color glow. In the ultraviolet range, these wavelengths of light are imperceptible to the naked eye but can easily be recorded on film.

As the nature of the ultraviolet fluorescence is dependent upon the material composition of the object and not its color, the technique is extremely useful in discerning between two pigments that in visible light appear identical. An iron-based blue will have an entirely different fluorescence than a blue obtained from sodium-silicate. In the state of excitation brought on by the ultraviolet

Engineer Maurizio Seracini of E.Di.Tech executing a reflectograph analysis on *The Annunciation* by Leonardo Da Vinci at the Uffizi Gallery in Florence.

waves, even whites can appear as two distinct colors in the reflectograph.

Maurizio Seracini, a friendly, forty-year-old engineer, executed the ultraviolet fluorescence reflectography in the Brancacci Chapel. Commissioned by the Olivetti Corporation, Seracini shot two sets of reflectographs in the Brancacci Chapel, one in 1984 to serve as a guide before the cleaning, and one in early 1988 to verify that all the proteic matter had been removed from the frescoes.

Paolo Parrini and his assistants used the 1984 reflectograph series as a map, which they followed to isolate and analyze the various stains of proteic matter, and the areas that were repainted during the restoration that followed the disastrous 1771 Carmine fire. The second set of reflectographs revealed the wax stains that had escaped the close scrutiny of the restorers, and for which Ferroni would later devise a method to export from the surface of the paintings.

Unlike many of the technicians involved in the Brancacci and in other art projects, Seracini is a full-time restoration professional. Trained as a medical diagnostics engineer at the University of California at San Diego, he returned to Italy and used his acumen to assist a California art historian and restorer in their search for Leonardo Da Vinci's lost *The Battle of Anghiers* fresco in Florence's Palazzo Vecchio. The search, which was part of a nationwide project known as Project Leonardo and sponsored by the Kress Foundation, yielded only fragmentary evidence of the lost fresco. But during his two years at the Palazzo Vecchio, Seracini and his colleagues developed and perfected the instruments and techniques that would become the basis for restoration diagnostics in the 1980s.

After Project Leonardo, Seracini decided to take a gamble and see if he could make a living in art diagnostics. The engineer relied heavily on Enzo Ferroni, who was a family friend and who had also participated in Project Leonardo.

"I must confess that for the first three or four years I survived solely on account of Professor Ferroni's expertise," Seracini says. "Professor Ferroni is a man of enormous means, and enormous capabilities. Beside him I feel like an apprentice, like a schoolboy. Most of all, I feel fortunate."

As president of E.Di.Tech of Florence, Seracini now works twelve-hour days performing diagnostic examinations on works of art for restorers and also for would-be art buyers who are wise enough to request a clean bill of health for an artwork or antique before writing a five or six figure check.

It is eight in the evening and we are in Seracini's high-ceilinged office in Via Dei Bardi, on the south side of the Arno. The street is named for the Bardi family, a powerful banking clan that once owned all of the houses on it in the 1300s. In its heyday, the family was banker to the monarchs of Europe, and commissioned the painter Giotto to decorate the family chapel in Santa Croce. It is believed that the young Masaccio rented a house on this street between 1417 and 1421 from Piera dei Bardi. "The Brancacci Chapel restoration may not be remembered as the be-all and the end-all of restorations but it will be remembered as a restoration in which intelligence and sensibility were the protagonists. The difficulty in the Brancacci was in divining the ideal chromatic equilibrium which could do justice to this artistic creation without being offensive," Seracini philosophizes, staring up at the frescoed ceiling. He is a very tall man, with a square jaw and a ready smile. His floppy hair is a youthful grey.

"This restoration is a success due to the splendid teamwork between Sabino Giovannoni and Marcello Chemeri, who followed the equally splendid direction of Umberto Baldini and Ornella Casazza. In essence, it was a success because the frescoes were understood."

Like the rest of the professionals involved in the Brancacci project, Seracini has collaborated on a number of important restorations, many of them with Umberto Baldini. His x-ray and ultraviolet analyses of Botticelli's *La Primavera* were instrumental in the successful cleaning of the painting. Seracini also performed the diagnostics for the Piero della Francesca *fresco* cycle at the church of San Francisco at Arezzo.

"As a profession, although we've taken some giant steps, we're still not where we ought to be," the engineer observes. "Fortunately, in Florence, and in Rome, people understand the need for diagnostics, and for a scientific approach. A few years ago, the only question historians used to ask was whether to restore or not to restore. Today we are starting to comprehend the forces which

148   cause our artworks to decay, and to take steps to retard this disintegration."

"And no matter how sophisticated our techniques become, it will never be possible to dictate a series of systematic rules which can be applied indiscriminately to all works of art," Seracini's blue eyes pulse sharply, full of bold faith.

"Restoration is and will remain a manual art, dependent above all on the hands of the restorer. And the degree of subjectivity in his work will increase along with the degree of difficulty of the particular restoration."

And They Saw that They Were Naked

The infrared band of the electromagnetic spectrum comes after the band of visible light, which itself succeeds the ultraviolet zone. Of the three, ultraviolet waves are the shortest, while the wavelength increases as it passes through the visible range, and continues to expand into the infrared.

As in the band of visible light, which contains a variety of different wavelengths that we perceive as colors, the infrared band is also composed of several different grades of radiation, each of which provokes a separate optical effect.

The first sector in the infrared band—the sector that borders on that of visible light—can be used to as a lightsource for a reflectograph. This is useful in performing analyses on paintings whose colors are cloudy or hazy. These first infrared wavelengths suppress or eliminate the random diffusion or scattering effect of visible light and restore a transparent legibility to the photographic image of the artwork.

The superior infrared wavelengths—those radiations at the far end of the infrared band that border on thermal waves—tend to produce heat when directed onto a subject. These wavelengths are used in thermovision, the diagnostic apparatus that by absorbing the thermal waves emitted by an object is capable of "seeing" through frescoes and walls. Although these wavelengths cannot be captured on film, the information obtained through a thermovision analysis is easily and immediately transformed into a black and white image on a modified television monitor.

Piero Della Francesca:
The Madonna of Birth
in Monterchi, Italy.

Piero Della Francesca:
detail of *The Madonna
of Birth* in visible light.

Same detail in
infrared reflectograph.

150   Like the superior infrared wavelengths, the medium-range wavelengths are also visible to the eye, although they do not induce a thermal reaction in the objects that they radiate. These medium-range wavelengths, when aimed at a painting or *fresco* and observed with an apparatus similar to that used in thermovision, penetrate the first stratum of the painting and allow restorers to "see" through the paint layer and through to the material immediately beneath the colors.

This technique, known as the infrared reflectograph, is extremely valuable to both restorers and historians. The sub-surface image provides restorers with a reliable reading of what they should expect to find beneath layers of grime and repaintings. And as the technique offers the unprecedented opportunity to view the artist's preparatory drawings and any eventual corrections or *pentimenti*—the word can be translated literally as repentances—his-

The thermovision machine and monitor which revealed the absence of the leaves in Masaccio's underlying *synopia*. *(photo by Torrini, Florence)*

torians can often reconstruct the process by which the painting
was conceived, modified, and terminated.

One of the most publicized and least significant aspects of the
Brancacci restoration was the issue of the leaves that covered the
genitals of the two Adam and Eve panels. No one knows exactly
when these leafy branches were painted. For many years, historians believed that the still unidentifiable vegetable matter was added
as an awkward nod to modesty sometime during the puritanical
eighteenth century. Naturally, as is to be expected with the Brancacci Chapel, there is no record of the censorship.

The nude figures in Michelangelo's *Last Judgment* on the Sistine
Chapel wall were also victims of a similarly conservative climate.
In the late 1500s, after a reunion of the Council of Trent, the car-
dinals opined that the unclothed figures on the Sistine Wall were a
bit too indecorous. A former domestic of Michelangelo named
Daniele di Volterra was commissioned to paint a series of *braqhe* or
"bloomers" over the loins of those figures considered unduly las-
civious. Strangely, the nude figures on the ceiling remained unclothed, including Adam and Eve.

Although it was only a minor mechanical problem, the removal
of these branches was the most debated and publicized aspect of
the Brancacci Chapel restoration. In lieu of more serious problems
that the public either could not or did not care to investigate, and
with the muted but never subdued schoolboy excitement that discussions on genitalia never fail to arouse, the issue of the return of
Adam and Eve to their "natural" state became a misunderstood
emblem of the Baldini project.

"One Florence radio station even staged a referendum," Baldini
remembers, jamming his fingers into his hair, "encouraging its
listeners to phone in and say whether or not the leaves should be
removed. As if we should base our actions purely on hearsay and
ignorant parlor talk, or as if a piece of an artwork like the Brancacci Chapel should be changed because someone decides he
might like it better without the leaves."

There was even a small faction of scholars who were convinced
that the leaves were painted by Masolino or Masaccio during the
decoration of the chapel. Although there was no evidence to support their conclusion, and although the branches clearly clashed

with the body of the painting, no historian or technician had ever been able to demonstrate that it was untrue.

An agile historian and an astute restoration director, Baldini provided bombproof testimony that neither Masolino nor Masaccio had ever intended that Adam and Eve be anything but nude. From the Florence archives, Baldini extracted a treatise on painting and sculpture written in 1652 that made clear reference to the state of undress of the Carmine figures.

"Masaccio was a valiant man," the essay reads. "And after Giotto he worked more liberally, as can be seen in the figures of Adam and Eve painted in fact nude in a chapel in a principal church in Florence."

According to Baldini's deductive reasoning, our progenitors' sex organs were concealed sometime between 1652 and 1775. "We know that the leaves were already present in 1775 because they appear in the prints of the *fresco* which Tommaso Piroli made in that year," the professor states. "Although we cannot be certain, the coverup is most likely the work of either Antonio Pillori in 1736 or Vincenzio Meucci in 1746."

It was conceivable that a plausible argument could be constructed to counter Baldini's historically-based assertion. An enterprising scholar could take issue with the fact that no overt reference is made to Adam and Eve's sexual apparatus in the treatise. He could also argue, improbably, that Masolino or Masaccio had painted their own branches *a secco,* branches that subsequently had fallen off the wall and were still not repainted in 1652. But with the help of Seracini's infrared thermovision machine, the director of the Brancacci restoration definitively closed the case.

"The thermovision reflectograph which we took of the two Adam and Eve panels revealed that neither Masaccio nor Masolino had planned to cover his figures' genitals," Baldini says. "There was no hint of the branches in the underlying drawings, while the figures on the surface corresponded perfectly with the lines sketched beneath them. This left no doubt that the leaves were strictly a superficial phenomenon, and that as such they could be removed without modifying the whole of the work. In fact, the removal of the leaves was a method of restoring the paintings to their original states."

As with any major step in restoration, Baldini had to obtain   *153*
permission from the Superior National Council of Fine Arts before the counterfeit branches could be erased from the *fresco.*

"Bureaucratically, it was surprisingly simple," recalls Casazza,
grinning faintly. "The council is formed of twenty people, including historians, writers, and critics. We requested a reunion, presented a short paper outlining the physical and historical evidence.
The council debated briefly, and then gave us its wholehearted
consent. This sort of issue usually is resolved quickly. It's only the
questions of finances and the division of funds which tends to
make for lengthy meetings in Rome."

CHAPTER TWELVE

Showtime

T HERE IS A STORY that toward the end of the 1970s, Umberto Baldini invited Dino Dini to the Brancacci Chapel to assess the situation, and to seek advice on an eventual restoration. In his usual meticulous and unsuspecting manner, Dini performed a preliminary survey of the frescoes, first in plain sight, then in raking light, and then with his magnifying lens. After a quarter of an hour, the expert restorer had formulated his opinion.

"Doctor Baldini," Dini said cheerfully, incapable of being anything but honest. "This should be easy. Look." Dini licked his thumb, rubbed it across the surface of one of the paintings, then displayed the dirty digit to Baldini. "Look how easily the grime comes off!"

It is not known whether the anecdote is based on fact. Dini would never respond to what was for him a trivial and undignified question, and no one has ever had the courage to ask Baldini. It is true that aside from the sulfates and nitrates in the upper corners of the rear wall, the Brancacci restoration presented neither the technical challenges of a San Marco or Santa Croce, nor the dire urgency of the many restorations that followed the 1966 Florence flood.

As Parrini's detailed analyses would show, Masaccio and Masolino's *intonaco* was in excellent condition; the Syremont president had even ventured to use the word "perfect" to describe the panels. The major problems in the Brancacci Chapel were the aesthetics: the repaintings during the long restoration after the 1771 fire; the damage left by the fire; and most of all the thick layer of grime that shrouded the sublime artwork of Masaccio, Masolino, and Filippino Lippi.

Despite its excellent bill of health, Baldini had always intended to use the Brancacci restoration as a laboratory for a series of diagnostic techniques that were not usually applied to *fresco* in an attempt to determine their potential utility. Many of Baldini's critics accused him of exploiting the well-publicized restoration for personal gain. The historian's autocratic style and the homogenous hierarchy that he imposed on Florentine restoration stirred up hostility in the restoration community, particularly among those professionals and restorers who have seen their own autonomy severely reduced.

"Let's be honest and admit what all restoration directors will say in private," says one Italian art historian. "At the beginning of any restoration, you order as many tests as you can imagine, fully aware that only about five percent of them will be of any use during the project. The rest of the analyses are merely window dressing."

This competition among historians to link their names to a specific method or restoration is both inevitable and understandable. With the meager monetary remuneration usually afforded to historians and restorers, restoration professionals are usually left to vie for the various badges of merit and prestige. The Brancacci Chapel was the most prestigious jewel on the block—perhaps even more prestigious than the concurrent Sistine Chapel restoration because of the mystery surrounding the Brancacci and its history—and Baldini had it in his pocket. There were many interests involved here—the enormous artistic importance of the work, the contention between Florence and Rome, the jostling among scientists, industry, and government officials for the honor of participating in the project, and Baldini's own noted ambition. Given all these, it was unthinkable that Baldini would allow the long-awaited restoration to deteriorate in the public eye into what might appear an unglamorous, methodical, albeit thoroughly effective cleaning.

Because of the unwavering goodwill of his sponsor, Baldini had the means to experiment with a series of techniques, which never could have been employed had the project been funded by the state. Aside from the analyses performed by Parrini, Baldini prescribed a microbiological examination to identify potential sources of organic pollution and a fotogram relief to provide a topographical map of the frescoes. This second technique had been used effectively during the restoration of the bronze panels from Gioberti's Baptistry doors. Baldini also requested a thermograph survey, which can locate minimal gaps between the *intonaco* and the *arriccio* by measuring the rate at which heat is exchanged between the *fresco* and the atmosphere.

One of the techniques that was used in the Brancacci as pure experiment was the holograph. A holograph is a three-dimensional photographic image obtained through a superimposition of two exposures taken of the same object at different times. By recording the changes in the distribution of light and dark across the surface of the object, the holograph image is capable of perceiving minute movements that over time can constitute a source of stress for the material in question. Any movement, even a shift of one micron, will appear in the final double-image as a series of ridges that radiate outward like ripples in a pond. The technique, which uses a laser as its light source, has proven invaluable in anticipating metal fatigue in aircraft, and in the preservation of delicate objects such as musical instruments.

Professors Guiseppe Molesini and Franco Quercioli of the National Optical Institute in Florence conducted the holograph experiment in the Brancacci Chapel. Although it was the first time anyone had attempted to apply the holograph to *fresco,* the two scientists had collaborated with Baldini in the past.

"We first experimented with this technique on the Ghiberti *Story of Joseph* panel," says Molesini, a somber and static man who speaks in a profound and powerful monotone.

"We used an electric heater to simulate the thermal effect the sun might have on the panel, and to identify zones of dilation," Molesini recalls. "It was obvious that as the metal plate expanded with the heat, minute folds broke out in certain zones, folds that in time would become fissures."

The holograph is an extremely delicate and precise technique that is best utilized in the laboratory. "You need an almost absolute stability," Quercioli says. "When dealing in a realm of microns, even the slightest vibration can completely ruin the image. Whenever you take the instruments out of the laboratory and onto location, the image you might have hoped for is never quite like the image which you bring home."

158   The Brancacci Chapel was hardly an ideal location for the delicate holograph operation. "The chapel floor is very thin, as there is another chapel directly below," Molesini explains. "And the type of laser we use requires an exposure of ten to thirty seconds. Footsteps, traffic outside the chapel, even certain sounds are enough to invalidate the results. If we had an impulse laser, which only requires nanoseconds for an exposure, the technique would be more feasible. Unfortunately, the laser which we use needs at least ten seconds, and sometimes up to half a minute to record the image."

The two scientists eventually constructed a platform, which rested on the marble shelf beneath the bottom *fresco* register and whose legs were set in sand to reduce vibrations to a minimum. "In theory, we were trying to determine whether the holograph could be used to identify the forces which caused the frescoes to crack in certain places," Molesini continues. "Normally, the cracks have always been attributed to a shifting in the walls or vault. Baldini wanted to see whether it was possible that the *fresco* itself had its own dynamic routine or motion.

"We selected a square of ten centimeters (four inches) for our experiment. The first exposure was taken at six in the evening, the time when the church closes its doors and all visitors are asked to leave. The second exposure was taken ten minutes later."

When the holograph image was developed, the scientists discovered that there was a slight but significant thermal motion in the *fresco* section that they had examined. "Effectively, the section folded towards the middle, where a crack was already visible," sayd Molesini. "In all, the holograph had singled out a movement of about two microns. We hypothesized that this movement was due to the drop in temperature which occurred each night when the church cooled after closing. In fact, we repeated the experiment at seven o'clock, and the movement was far less evident."

Molesini and Quercioli are not convinced that the holograph can be successfully applied to *fresco,* although they are quick to point out the utility of the technique in other branches of restoration. "In order to obtain reliable results, one would have to photograph the entire *fresco* cycle," Molesini observes, almost sadly. "Even with more powerful machinery capable of reproducing a larger image, this would constitute an enormous project, and would provide results which probably could be obtained through other, less costly analyses.

"The holograph is certainly not exploited to its full potential in art," Quercioli points out. "But much of the reason is the cost of the machinery. The laser alone sells for more than a million dollars, and restorers generally do not have that kind of money to spend on tests. Technically, I see enormous potential for the holograph in examining panel and canvas paintings, statues, reliefs, ceramics, in short; any object which can be transported to the laboratory."

Far more satisfactory than the holograph experiment were the results of the spectrophotometry examinations performed under the supervision of Professor Vito Capellini, director of the National Research Center's (CNR) laboratory for the study of electromagnetic waves in Florence.

In 1932, when Ugo Procacci removed the two marble "ears" from the Brancacci altar to discover the stunning colors beneath, he had a *fresco* copy made to preserve a record of those colors for future reference.

Baldini, too, wished to record his Brancacci colors, first to measure the contrast between the pigments before and after the cleaning, and second to provide information which could be used as a reference point by future restorers. Fortunately for Baldini, in the fifty years that separated the Procacci discovery from the beginning of the restoration, science had evolved considerably and had developed several methods or recording and reproducing the chromatic values of an artwork. All of these methods were more precise and more durable than Procacci's *fresco* copy.

"A color is visible to the human eye because the pigment absorbs certain wavelengths of light and reflects others," says Doctor Mauro Bacci, chemist, and spectrophotometry specialist at the Florence CNR. "When we perceive something as red, it is because the pigment is reflecting red and absorbing all the other colors which are contained in light.

"In spectrophotometry," Bacci continues, cheerfully reciting the necessary elementary prologue that enables an inexpert audience to comprehend his analytical technique, "the reflex of a particular color—the band of visible light which the color reflects—is

160   measured and transformed into a graph or spectrum. Every color
or tone has its own spectrum, a graph which indicates exactly
which wavelengths of visible light were absorbed and which were
reflected.

"In the Brancacci Chapel, we wanted an objective record for
every area of color in the chapel, a record which would be far more
exact than one which could be obtained through photographs.
The spectrophotometer is much more sensible, and much more
impartial than the human eye in discerning visible light," Bacci
proceeds, almost finished with the pouring of his theoretical foundation. "The human eye, for example, is more responsive to yellow than it is to red or blue, and often blends or distorts colors.
Our apparatus, if used correctly, produces an entirely reliable and
objective measurement of the color value."

In November of 1984, Bacci took his apparatus to the Brancacci
Chapel. "We wanted to produce a spectrum for every color in the
chapel, before and after cleaning," the scientist explains. "Normally, the technique requires that a sample be taken. But since we
were dealing with a work of art, we wanted to develop a non-
invasive method. And we discovered that through the use of
fiberoptics, we would be able to take our readings right off the
fresco without removing the slightest bit of *intonaco*."

Bacci crosses his laboratory toward the spectrophotometer and
takes the sensor in hand. The body of the apparatus is about the
size and shape of a standard household television if laid flat on its
back. The sensor is roughly the size and shape of a shower massage
head, and is connected to the body of the apparatus by two metal
cables. There is an aperture of 0.8 centimeters (approximately 1/4
of one inch) on the flat surface of the sensor.

"The reading is obtained by placing this sensor against the color
you wish to measure," Bacci says, illustrating the process by
pressing the sensor against the white wall behind him. "The machine emits a flash of white light, which is transported through
these two cables into the sensor. The first cable channels the light
into the aperture and onto the subject, in this case a color on a
fresco. The light hits the surface, and is either absorbed or reflected
according to the pigment. Whatever light is reflected travels back
through the cable and into the machine where the wavelengths are
measured and recorded on a graph.

"The second cable channels the original light onto a sample of titanium white within the sensor," Bacci continues. "Titanium white is the purest white we possess and reflects all wavelengths of visible light. The machine uses the spectrum of titanium white as a constant control against which it can measure the reflex of a particular color."

In all, Bacci took one hundred spectra from the colors in the Brancacci Chapel. "Naturally, it would be impossible to record every inch of color in the *fresco* cycle," Bacci laughs, "at least using this apparatus. And since the machinery is very heavy, we didn't want to risk carrying it up the stairs on the scaffolding. We ended up taking our samples from the scene of *The Resurrection of Teofilo's Son,* choosing to measure significant color zones of the painting, such as the flesh tones, which are usually a blend of several pigments. That particular painting was chosen because it also gave us a chance to compare Masaccio's pigments with the pigments used by Filippino Lippi when he completed the painting fifty years later."

In November of 1987, Bracci returned to take the readings of the same zones that he'd examined three years earlier. The two series of graphs were superimposed to create a before and after spectrum of each color. "The graphs obtained after the cleaning will serve as an inalterable catalogue for future historians and restorers," Bacci says proudly. "If someone wants to know what the colors were in the Brancacci Chapel in November of 1987, those colors are indelibly recorded in these spectra."

The spectra obtained after the cleaning also had a second function, that of verifying and validating the work of the restorers. "In comparing the second test results with the first," Bacci explains, "we confirmed that the original pigments had not been altered during the restoration, and that no chromatic material had been removed. The cleaning had only removed the thick film of grime which had caused the colors to appear muted or darker. We know this is true because the second spectra reflect the exact same wavelengths as the first spectra. They simply reflect them more intensely, as the grime was no longer there to filter out the incoming light, and to trap the reflecting light. The second series of graphs rises and falls much more steeply than the first, but always from and to the same coordinates along the horizontal axis. Had the pigments been altered, the spectrum would have shifted."

In the true scientific spirit, Bacci was curious to explore several other possible applications of the spectrophotometric technique to art and restoration. "Having observed that the grime generally altered all the spectra in the same manner, I tried to see whether the grime itself had its own spectral identity, and whether its effects on the colors beneath could be deducted before the cleaning," Bacci says, returning to his desk.

"If there proved to be a standard deviation in all the spectra caused by grime, we could easily obtain the spectra of the colors beneath by adjusting the graph to compensate for the distortion of the grime. This would allow us to furnish a guide to restorers, to give them an approximate idea of what color should emerge after the cleaning."

Bacci also attempted to use his apparatus as a means to identify the pigments used in the Brancacci frescoes. "Unfortunately," the chemist says, "the spectrum obtained with visible light is far from a reliable test. An infrared spectrophotometer would be much more precise, but the fiberoptics which we possess here is not capable of transmitting that wavelength of light."

The infrared spectrophotometer is a test that is similar to the spectrophotometric analysis except that the device operates in the infrared band of lightwaves and records those frequencies of infrared light that are absorbed by the sample. As each element absorbs a different band or frequency of infrared light, the spectrum obtained is a virtually infallible fingerprint of the composition of the sample.

In oversimplified terms, imagine if one had to determine whether the person sealed inside a windowless house was Little Miss Muffet, Jack Sprat, or Mrs. Jack Sprat. As the only communicating door with the house is a dumbwaiter, one might think to prepare a plate with three items: curds and whey, fat, and lean. After the plate has been sent into the house, it is analyzed upon its return. If the fat is missing, it is clear that the person inside the house is Mrs. Sprat. If the curds and whey are gone, we can assume that Little Miss Muffet has abandoned her tuffet to take refuge behind closed doors.

Like the sample plate, the infrared band of light is also divided into various dishes or frequencies. When the light is analyzed after having passed through a sample, the substance in question can be easily identified according to which infrared frequencies it absorbed or ate. Extremely reliable, the now common analytical technique has been of great assistance in helping restorers identify an extremely wide range of substances including varnishes, glazes, pigments, mineral salts, and binders.

"Visible light can give you a general idea of the composition of the pigment," Bacci concludes, "but it is far from foolproof. It helps if you know what sort of pigment you are looking for. We used Cennino Cennini's *The Book of Art* as a guide, and found it to be almost ninety percent accurate in terms of its description of minerals."

The CNR also conducted a series of analyses to determine whether the substances which eighteenth and nineteenth century restorers had painted over frescoes could have induced a colorshift in the artists' original pigments. "The Brancacci restorers prepared several samples of *fresco* painted over bricks," Bacci says, lifting two of these samples out of a cardboard box in his office. The blocks of *fresco* are about one foot in length and painted with a dozen vertical bands, each of a different color.

"These pigments are all taken from Cennini's book, and are similar if not identical to the pigments used in the Brancacci, and in most frescoes of the Renaissance," Bacci says, setting the block on his desk. I have seen identical objects at Enzo Ferroni's office in Florence, and at Paolo Parrini's office in Milan.

"As a control, we took the spectra of each color on the sample. Then we applied various foreign matter to the colors, substances which might have been used in previous Brancacci restorations: beeswax, egg, animal glue, wine, and let them sit for several months. After removing the organic material, we took the spectra again. Surprisingly, we found that there was some alteration in the colors, particularly in black. In *fresco,* the color cannot change unless the crystal structure of the *intonaco* somehow changes, as it does, for example, in the cases where *gesso* enters into the fabric. What this meant was that these substances, aside from darkening

164   the *fresco,* can potentially alter the chromatics of the painting if left to decay."

For Bacci, the opportunity to collaborate in the Brancacci Chapel restoration was an extremely gratifying experience. "I'd followed a program of classical studies in high school," he says, his tone undisguisedly warm. "But the chemistry curriculum at the University was so demanding that in a sense I was forced to abandon a certain sensibility which I'd very much enjoyed. I rediscovered this sensibility when I performed the analyses in the Brancacci Chapel. It made me feel more human. Of course, there is also the enormous satisfaction of seeing one's analyses applied successfully, all the more so when the analyses regard a work as important as the Brancacci Chapel."

Bacci also admits to having felt a bit of anxiety the first time he applied the sensor from his spectrograph onto a *fresco* in the chapel. "I was ninety-nine percent sure that nothing would happen," he recalls, chuckling now at the insistent uncertainty that accompanied him and which now, in hindsight, appears totally unfounded. "I'd even covered the face of the device with tape, partly to seal out any extraneous light which could spoil the reading, but also to avoid any contact between the metal sensor and the surface of the *fresco.* It was a rather emotional moment, not unlike what I imagine a surgeon must feel the first time he performs an operation."

The PRESERVATION OF THE VISIBLE

CHAPTER THIRTEEN

The Restorers of Florence

T OWARD THE END of 1984, with the majority of the diagnostics already completed, restorers Sabino Giovannoni and Marcello Chemeri returned to the Brancacci Chapel to begin the most delicate part of the operation, that of the cleaning of the frescoes. Four years would pass before the restorers would finish their meticulous labor; it was the same amount of time that Masolino and Masaccio spent painting the panels.

The city of Florence has the most able and dedicated *fresco* restorers in Italy, and probably in all the world. "Florence has a sensibility towards art which is unparalleled," says Umberto Baldini.

"For a Florentine, a work of art is not an object to be observed in a museum. It is a part of his daily existence. Had the 1966 flood occurred in any other city, the results would have been devastating. In Florence, a city of artisans and craftsmen, we had the resources to contain the damage."

In *fresco,* one man was singly responsible for shaping a generation of restorers. Although he did not participate in the Brancacci project, he formed the minds and hearts of the restorers who would lift the murky *beverone* from the surface of Masaccio's and Masolino's frescoes. The man's name was Dino Dini, and he was, in Procacci's words, "the finest restorer with whom I've had the privilege of working."

When Dino Dini began his career as a restorer in the 1930s, his colleagues in Florence used the soft inside of bread to clean the wall paintings. A few restorers dusted the frescoes with brushes. In his fifty years of work, Dini did more than any man to drag the

Dino Dini, San Marco. 1972

craft out of the hermetic, superstitious world of Secco Suardo and into the twentieth century.

"People tend to point to the flood as the beginning of the scientific approach to restoration," says Sabino Giovannoni, Brancacci restorer and alumnus of the Dini *bottega*. "What they might not realize was that Dini had already developed this approach years before."

As early as 1945, on the Domenico Ghirlandaio frescoes in Sala Dei Gigli in Florence's Palazzo Vecchio, Dini had devised a technique for removing the proteic *beverone* without eroding the artist's colors. Dini's miracle drug was ammonium carbonate, a slightly alkaline solution, which was brushed directly onto the *fresco* and caused the proteic material to congeal while having absolutely no effect on the inorganic *intonaco* or pigments beneath. Once transformed into a gel, the *beverone* and any remaining ammonium carbonate could be easily removed with a sponge and distilled water.

In itself, the discovery of an effective and innocuous method of
removing the most common form of grime from frescoes was a
vital contribution to the craft of *fresco* restoration. But Dini's ultimate ambition was to one day discover a means to regenerate calcium carbonate out of the rashes of mineral salts that erupted from
within the *intonaco*.

None of his colleagues, not even the scientists whom Procacci
had gradually enlisted into his restoration army, thought this re-
motely possible. To many, Dini's quest appeared as vain as the
search for the philosopher's stone.

"How I wish we could find a way to turn this *gesso* back into
intonaco," Dini once exclaimed while surveying the sulfate damage
in the Ghirlandaio frescoes in Santa Maria Novella with a chemist
from the university.

"We'd all like to be young again," the chemist replied.

In December of 1967, a few short months after their Santa
Croce adventure, Dino Dini and Enzo Ferroni found themselves
once more in front of a *fresco* in a dramatic state of disintegration.
The Beato Angelico *Crucifixion* at San Marco was beset by the
advanced decay of the egg, vinegar, oil, and glue that had been

Beato Angelico *The Crucifixion* in chapter room of San Marco, Florence.

applied during previous restorations. But much more alarming was the protruding mass of mineral crystals that had run rampant like a cancer within the *intonaco,* displacing the pigments and leaving a series of pockmarks and craters where the pigments had fallen to the floor.

Ugo Procacci suggested that the situation was dire enough to warrant the detachment of the *fresco,* but Dini refused to perform the *strappo.* Given the disastrous conditions of the *fresco,* Dini was certain that the operation would entail a substantial loss of color without resolving the principal cause of its disintegration.

Through an x-ray diffraction analysis—a technique that identifies the specific crystal structure of a mineral by projecting a band of x-rays through the sample and "reading" the spectrum that emerges—Ferroni confirmed that the salts that had invaded the body of the *fresco* were calcium sulfate, or *gesso.*

Examining the surface of the Angelico *fresco* with a microscope, Dini showed Ferroni that the *gesso* crystal seemed to dissolve on contact with a solution of ammonium carbonate, shrinking in size and returning into the fabric of the *intonaco.* Ferroni raced back to his laboratory where he repeated the experiment in order to obtain the formula that correctly explained the reaction.

"When the calcium sulfate compound comes into contact with the ammonium carbonate, the sulfate ion immediately bonds with the ammonium ion, freeing the calcium ion from the *gesso* to bond with the carbon trioxide ion left behind by the ammonium," explains Ferroni. "The products of the reaction are ammonium sulfate and calcium carbonate."

He rises to write the chemical formula on his blackboard: $CaSO_4 + [(NH_4)_2(CO_3)] = CaCO_3 + (NH_4)_2SO_4$.

Although the Dini-Ferroni discovery was promising, the Angelico *Crucifixion* was far from saved. The solution did produce the desired transformation of *gesso* into calcium carbonate. Unfortunately, the reaction took place on the surface of the painting causing the reagents to crystallize into an opaque calcium carbonate veil over the artist's colors. The effect would be similar to that of spreading a fresh layer of *intonaco* over the painting and allowing it to harden.

If the *gesso*-ravaged *intonaco* of Angelico's splendid chapter room *Crucifixion* was to be preserved, the chemical reaction which converted *gesso* back into calcium carbonate had to take place within the *intonaco* and not on the surface of the painting. Toward this end, Dini proposed the use of a purified wood-flour compress as a support for the ammonium carbonate solution.

Dini's wood-flour compress transferred the seat of the evaporation and crystallization process from the surface of the *fresco* to the surface of the compress that was in contact with the atmosphere. The white *patina* that had previously formed on the surface of the *fresco* now took form on the external surface of the compress. In addition, Dini's compress also facilitated the diffusion of the reagents within the *intonaco,* insuring that the reaction occured beneath and not across the color layer.

Ferroni's laboratory analyses of the conversion process and Dini's onsite experiments permitted the two men to determine the proper dosage of the ammonium carbonate solution, and the length of time that the compress should remain in contact with the *fresco* before the reaction was complete.

Both Dini and Ferroni were aware that their experiments under controlled laboratory conditions might not produce identical results when repeated in the unstable environment of the San Marco cloister. Changes in temperature and humidity, and the levels of sulfates that varied from one zone of the *fresco* to another required that the treatment be constantly modified.

And there were other potential hazards. From experience, Dini knew that the ammonium carbonate solution could not be used indiscriminately. Alkaline in nature, the compound would cause a violent color shift in copper-based pigments like azurite and malachite. A restorer also had to be extremely cautious when using ammonium carbonate in zones where the artist had painted primarily *a secco*. The animal glue or egg *tempera* that the artist had used to apply his colors to the dry *fresco,* being organic in nature, was easily congealed by the solution. Any brisk mechanical action—sometimes the mere passage of a water-filled sponge was sufficient—could cause the colors to slide off the painting.

Working with consummate skill and patience, Dini prepared his compresses and applied them to the surface of the mural. As had been expected, the eruptions of *gesso* slowly withdrew as they were transformed back into the calcium-carbonate *intonaco*.

There was another problem, though. Soon after the ammo-

Detail of *gesso* explosion
on Beato Angelico
chapter room *Crucifixion*.

Same figure after ammonium
carbonate treatment.

nium-carbonate treatment, Dini noticed an incoherency between
the pictorial film and the *intonaco* beneath it. After discussing the
phenomenon with Ferroni, the two men realized that the color
layer had been stretched during the eruption of *gesso* crystals. Now

that the *gesso* had shrunk back into *intonaco,* the color layer hung
limply, like a skin that somehow had been stretched.

After a week of intense thought, Ferroni showed up early one morning at San Marco and without even saying good morning announced, "I like the idea of barium."

Ferroni's fondness for barium was founded in the material's already demonstrated utility as a marble and stone consolidant. A concentrated solution of barium hydroxide reacts with the atmosphere very much the same way calcium hydroxide does; both compounds bond with carbon dioxide to form carbonates as the water evaporates. Barium carbonate ($BaCO_3$) can be considered a close chemical cousin of calcium carbonate, with an identical crystalline structure.

As with the first experiments with ammonium carbonate, the application of barium hydroxide presented several practical obstacles, not the least of which was Procacci's understandable reticence in using an untried substance on a work like Angelico's *Crucifixion*, particularly a substance like barium, which would be impossible to remove once it was introduced into the body of the painting.

Technically, it was essential that the carbonation of the barium hydroxide occur beneath the pictorial film and not across it. Should the solution come into contact with the atmosphere on the surface of the painting, a thin white film would solidify across the colors, masking them forever.

Once again, Dini proposed the compress of purified wood-flour as a vehicle for the application, and for identical reasons. Working with the utmost care, and with the close supervision of Ferroni, Dini applied the wood-flour compress which had been impregnated with the barium-hydroxide compound. When the compress was removed, Dini saw immediately that the operation had had the desired effect; Angelico's pictorial layer was once more coherent with the supporting *intonaco* beneath it.

Florence. 1988. Tuesday, November 15
The San Marco cloister

The San Marco Museum, while one of the city's most stirring and significant artistic landmarks, is certainly not one of its most visited sites, particularly on a cold Tuesday morning like this one. The sun just barely slices through the hazy morning piazza and the air within the open cloister is damp and prickly. My hands are jammed into my jacket pockets in an attempt to keep them from freezing.

Virtually alone, I am at leisure to view the splendid *Crucifixion* and the various altarpieces and panel paintings. Upstairs are the forty-four monks' cells that Fra Giovanni di Fiesole, better known as Fra Beato Angelico, frescoed for his fellow Dominicans at San Marco between 1440 and 1450.

A small two-stage restoration scaffold stands against the eastern cloister wall. Two men work on the upper platform, patiently filling in blank spaces in a seventeenth century *fresco* lunette with minute dabs of neutral color. The restorers, one elderly, and one very young, are so finely attuned to their work that they seem to blend in with their surroundings. Although the scaffolding is not concealed, they are barely noticeable. The men, particularly the older one, seem oblivious to the cold, to the few people in the cloister, to everything but the section of *fresco* before them.

One hour later, after a visit to the cells upstairs, I return to the cloister and see that the elderly man has climbed down from the platform and is walking, curved and swiftly, toward the northern door. Something about him, seen from behind with the restorer's magnifying lens still strapped onto his head, reminds me of a photograph I have seen. Apologizing for the interruption, I ask the younger man still on the platform if he could please tell me the name of his colleague.

"His name is Dino Dini," the boy replies.

The following morning I find the restorers once more at work. Apologizing again, I introduce myself to the grey-haired man and ask if it would be possible for us to speak when he had finished.

"I can't understand you," Dini replies, whimsical and benevolent. "I'm deaf. If you'll wait a moment I'll come down."

His lean, aged body moves like a marionette as he climbs down the scaffolding, his stiff limbs carrying him downward as if they remembered the steps themselves after so many years of work. The seventy-seven-year-old restorer appears to have no weight. When both his feet are on the ground, I explain who I am, and that I would like to talk about his work in San Marco.

"It seems to me that everything about the restoration has already been written down," he says, not hostile, but surprised, amused that someone could still wish to speak to him. His eyes are azure, deepset, abstract but poised to flash into focus at an instant. "Perhaps we could speak inside my office. There are a couple of chairs."

Dini's office is a room in the first floor of what once was the monastery. The room is full of vats containing *malta* and of sections of *intonaco*. A young woman sits in the corner retouching a section of *fresco*, which she has mounted on an easel. She is Dini's daughter Daniela. The young man on the scaffolding with him was Massimo, the restorer's grandson.

"The important thing is for the restorer to enter into the whole of the work," Dini begins, after having made a place for us near the portable electric heater. His manner is disarmingly meek. Not timid, as Ferroni had described him, but courteous, with a humility that could easily be mistaken for an insincere servility.

"Because there are tones, and there are halftones," he says, his eyes a distant glow. "The work of art contains as much information as a page of music. In fact, I think it is even more complicated than music. And if we as restorers cannot immerse ourselves in the work, then we are nothing better than gap-fillers."

Dino Dini was *maestro* to a generation of *fresco* restorers. Sabino Giovannoni and Guido Botticelli spent seventeen years in his *bottega*. Marcello Chemeri worked there for three. Along with the demanding technical studies that Dini imposed on his students, the restorer imbued his pupils with his own implacable, spiritual commitment to art and excellence.

"The work of art is the torch which holds the flame of civilization," Dini says. "It is the highest expression of the human mind and soul. Without art, we have nothing. We are nothing, no different than animals. This is why it must be preserved at all costs."

"He always told us that restoring a work of art was akin to executing a divine mission," says Branacci restorer Marcello Chemeri. "And that we shouldn't think that it was a way to make easy money."

Despite having redefined the craft, Dini never would have taken on assistants had he been given the choice. Before the Second World War, Dini had always worked alone. When he returned to Florence in 1945 after two years in a German prisoner-of-war camp—and after dropping from one hundred-sixty to one hundred pounds—he met Fine Arts Superintendent Giovanno Poggi on the street.

"Poggi was not a man who liked to talk," Dini recalls; his impassive face begins to glow, a radiance from within that comes and goes like a breeze. "We hadn't seen each other for several years. He said hello, and asked what my intentions were. I told him that I intended to start working again. And he replied, 'Go talk to Procacci.' "

It was Procacci who insisted that Dini take on help. "There was just too much work to be done," Dini remembers. "In Florence, in Pistoia, in Pisa and Arezzo. The war had caused incredible damage to the region, and to its art. I would have liked to refuse. I had no desire to teach, or to run a *bottega*. All I wanted to do was work. I just wanted to work.

"There were some very difficult moments with Giovannoni and Botticelli at the beginning," he recalls, his face effervescent with affectionate laughter. "They were two boys, just out of art school, who didn't know how to do anything. Botticelli told me that for the first year he used to go home after work and cry every night. Because when I came to inspect their work at the end of the day, if I didn't like what they'd done, I'd wash it off with my brush. I think I was a very severe *maestro*. Severe, but fair. I had no choice. Otherwise, we could have ruined a work of art."

Flaubert would have loved a man like Dino Dini, loved the absent, tolerant, deferential smile of a man who has measured out his days by work and work alone. A man who has defined himself through his dedication to a craft. Even now — Dini is gravely ill with cancer — on a relatively unimportant wall painting on a cold November morning, he forges patiently ahead, matching each day's sun step for step as it inches across the winter sky.

"I like to work alone," he admits. "I like to interpret the work before me in my own way. I don't like discussions, round tables. They've always seemed a waste of time to me. I've never seen any advantage in them.

"I'm often invited to conventions, or to visit other restoration sites. I've been invited to visit the Sistine Chapel. It just seems so futile. I tell them that we already know we disagree on certain techniques. And we know that we will never agree. What's the use of wasting even more time reiterating our positions. For the most part, these so-called meetings are just an excuse for people to get together and not to work."

In 1977, commissioned by Baron Frederick Von Thyssen, Dini returned to San Marco and began work on the forty-four cells that Fra Beato Angelico had frescoed on the second floor of the convent. In total solitude, the restorer spent eight years on the project.

"I was never distracted," he recalls. "I was never bored. I loved every minute of my work. And there were times with Angelico, while staring at his paintings, that I swore I could smell the daisies in the scene."

There are many practices in current restoration that Dini does not agree with. "I don't see how restorers can work in a team and expect the result to be uniform," he says frankly. "The work of my daughter Daniela is as close to mine as possible, but even between us there is a difference."

Nor does Dini approve of the current method of sending young stu- dents to school to learn the restoration trade. "You don't form a restorer in two or three years," he explains, with complete conviction. "There are so many things to learn, how to approach a work, the cleaning, re-plastering, the pictorial touch-up—this is the most subjective part of the work. A person isn't a restorer because he's received a diploma from a school. He needs at least six years of supervision. Many need even more time."

It may seem incongruous that a man so strongly cemented in the *bottega* tradition was also responsible for the introduction of the scientific method in *fresco* restoration. Yet there is a solid agreement between the two seemingly contrasting poses; both are manifestations of Dini's in-transigent and unyielding crusade toward the betterment of his art.

"I had the good fortune of meeting the right people at the right time," he says with genuine modesty. "And during the war, I spent two years working in a chemistry laboratory in Florence. It was there where I began my experiments with various cleaning techniques and solutions. If I must be honest, I will say that I am responsible for the amalgam of science and restoration. Not because of any great insight on my part. I merely understood that the situation as it stood when I began working was not the proper one."

Dini is confident that his contribution to the craft will be a lasting one, and that future restorers will develop techniques which are superior to his. "Tomorrow's restorer should be much more able than I am," he explains. "If only for the simple reason that he will have better methods of analysis at his disposition."

To his former students, Dini's figure looms like a paternal but men-acing storm on the horizon. "He was a tyrant," recalls Giovannoni. "Ter-rible. Demanding, precise, unforgiving. But loving, too. He wasn't only my boss. I was nineteen when I came to his *bottega*. And I was thirty-five when I left. He was a father to me. And more than a father."

"The *bottega* was like a family," Guido Botticelli says fondly. "And Professor Dini treated us all like his children, severely, but fairly."

Although the source of lingering nightmares for his former stu-dents, Dino Dini's wordless, unwavering, at times fanatical devotion have proven as invaluable to the craft as his many astounding technical inno-vations. His spirit survives him in Botticelli and Giovannoni, who have in turn transmitted it to their students.

"They were wonderful as teachers," says Gioia Germani, who along with her Brancacci colleague Lydia Cinelli Bianchi learned her trade from Giovannoni, Botticelli, and Marcello Chemeri at the Opificio Delle Pietre Dure. "But ever so often, when one of us did something really stupid, Sabino would say, 'I ought to send you to Dini for this! I ought to call Dini! He'd know what to do with the likes of you!' "

Like their *maestro,* both Giovannoni and Botticelli believe in teaching by example. "When I give lessons to students I tell them that they don't learn the craft by listening to what I say but by watching what I do," Giovannoni illustrates. "Especially with my hands. A deaf-mute could do this work quite well, I tell them. But if they don't have the right hands, they can study and read for their entire lives and still not become restorers."

"I try to get my students to immerse themselves in the work of art, and in the materials," explains Botticelli. "When I travel abroad, most young people ask me about the pictorial intervention, which is probably the least significant aspect of our work. I try to get them interested in the materials, and curious about the techniques which the artist used. When we encounter a problem, I try to establish a dialogue.

" 'What would you do here?' I ask. Because these students should learn that in our work there are no solutions, but there are always possibilities. The only indispensable quality that a restorer must possess is love for the object before him. When there is love, almost any obstacle can be overcome."

Brancacci restorers Gioia Germani and Lydia Cinelli Bianchi could be considered Dini's grandchildren, having studied with Dini's disciples. "The *fresco* sector was a world apart from the other departments in the school," Gioia affirms. (The Opificio also trains restorers for panel painting, marble, bronze, wood, paper, and semi-precious stones.)

"We had our own laboratory in the museum of San Salvi. And our instructors all came from the private sector; they were all students of Dino Dini, and all used to working hard. Together, we learned the technique of *fresco.*" The blond restorer's clear blue eyes glow as she recites her Opificio curriculum.

"How to boil the lime, how to mix the *malta,* how to carbonate colors, how to calculate a *giornata.* We learned to love *fresco,* not merely as a vehicle for art, but for itself, for the materials, the minerals, the calcium and sand. And I know that this may sound foolish, but I honestly believe I could restore a blank wall with the same passion I feel when I restore a mural."

"It may be that my work is negative, and that I have done more harm than good," Dini observes from his chair in his workshop in San Marco. His voice is a myriad of tones, ranging in a breath from the simple Tuscan to that of a professor of chemistry. Light seems to breathe in him, like sound surging from an organ.

"Until now, a restorer could almost always remove the materials that a previous restorer had added to a *fresco*. Today, with products like barium, and with synthetic substances, this is no longer possible. In a sense, yesterday's restorer could do less damage. Not because he was better than today's restorer. But he was more innocent."

"So far, we've had no other problems with the *Crucifixion* in the chapter room," he shrugs. "But only twenty-two years have passed, too little time to judge. Everything is temporary, even art, and ourselves as well. One day all our frescoes will disintegrate, San Marco, the Brancacci, all of them. One day the tower of Pisa and the cupola of the Duomo will tumble to the ground. And there is nothing that we can do. Nothing."

CHAPTER FOURTEEN

The Colors Beneath the Grime

THE CLEANING OF A PAINTING or a *fresco* is generally considered to be the most demanding and the most interesting phase of a restorer's work. By carefully sifting through the various layers of dust, grime, lacquers, repaintings, and *beverone* that have accumulated over the surface of the painting, the restorer can read the history of that painting by reconstructing the various interventions that it has suffered. If he works judiciously in discarding these superfluous materials, he can recover all that remains of the true face of the painting, and of its soul.

"A picture is at the height of its beauty the moment the cleaning has ended," says eighty-one-year-old Florentine restorer Leonetto Tintori. "When it has been stripped of all extraneous matter, and before any of the gaps have been filled in."

In addition to its restorative effect on the aesthetics of a painting, an attentive cleaning can often lead to important historical discoveries or revisions. Roberto Longhi discovered the hand of Masolino in the upper regions of the Uffizi's *Sant'Anna Mettterza* after the meticulous cleaning to which the panel painting was subject between 1934 and 1953. Longhi's discovery became a vital component in his revolutionary theory regarding the relationship between Masolio and Masaccio.

The recent and highly publicized cleaning of the vault of the Sistine Chapel has revealed a vivid, lively, colorful *fresco*, far brighter than the muted, somber tones to which most observers and historians had grown accustomed. The stunningly beautiful

182   sight of Michelangelo's pigments receiving and reflecting light no
longer smothered by a thick and cloudy layer of dust and horse
glue has spawned one of the decade's most heated and most ill-
founded controversies.

Despite the enormous evolution of diagnostic and analytical science that the restorers have at their disposition, the cleaning of a
painting remains a highly subjective and much-debated art. If
cleaning a painting was merely a question of identifying the materials, which in time have been appended to the artist's pigments
or preparatory layers, a restorer could work with relative tranquility. With the proper scientific support and instrumentation, almost any substance can be removed from the surface of a *fresco* or
a painting without damaging the artist's original materials.

Unfortunately, these original materials, while often astoundingly resistant, inevitably suffer some degree of mutation through
contact with even the most innocuous of environments.

"For a painting to be preserved exactly as the artist painted it,
the work would have to be taken at the precise moment of completion and closed in a container which sealed out both air and
light," says Ugo Procacci. "Given the fact that most paintings have
been created with the intention of their being seen, I'd say that this
solution is hardly satisfactory or practical."

An artist's colors change or shift depending upon the chemical
composition of the pigments, and on the external forces that surround them. The iron-based pigments in the Brancacci Chapel
took on a reddish hue when exposed to the searing heat of the
1771 Carmine fire. The white that Cimabue used to color an ox-
en's horns in his Assisi *fresco* has muted to a murky brown due to
the oxidation of the lead-based pigment. These chromatic changes
are common in *fresco* and even more frequent in panel and canvas
paintings.

In many cases, the visible effects of these color shifts is diminished or even concealed beneath the diaphanous drapery of *beverone*
or grime. Lacquers and dirt can also gloss over the repaintings of
previous restorers, allowing them to blend in with the original
work. The revisions that Gaetano Bianchi painted into the Giotto
frescoes in Santa Croce's Bardi Chapel in the late 1800s were only
discovered when Baldini's restorers began to clean the murals in
the 1960s. After the grime was removed, the difference between

Bianchi's artificially aged *fresco* inserts and the body of Giotto's
work had grown so dramatic that Baldini was forced to order the
removal of the restorer's work.

Even in the rare cases in which a painting has not undergone a
subsequent repainting, an indiscriminate cleaning often unveils an
artwork whose colors are disastrously out of tune. "The act of
cleaning does not bring the artist's original colors back into view,
as those colors have long ceased to exist," explains Umberto Baldini. "The cleaning of a painting simply exposes that painting's
colors in their current condition."

Of all the phrases that have become associated with the craft of
restoration, none has been so ambiguous and so profusely misunderstood as the word *patina*. In theory, the *patina* of a panel painting or a *fresco* is the seasoned, aged aspect that the work takes on
naturally after the passage of a certain amount of time. During the
eighteenth and nineteenth centuries, this *patina* was considered an
indispensable embellishment; collectors were known to refuse to
take delivery of paintings whose appearance was too fresh or new.
In theory, the *patina* should be respected by restorers.

In practice, the issue is still very much open, particularly because there is no consensus as to a precise definition of this vital
patina. Accepted as a real phenomenon in panel and canvas paintings—artists often covered their finished paintings with a layer of
varnish or lacquer to protect the painting and to promote a seasoned appearance—there is some discussion as to whether the *patina* even exists in *fresco*. Varnishes were rarely applied to frescoes,
except by restorers who usually did so at the request of a patron
who wished to confer an oil-like texture on the wall painting.

Professor Mauro Matteini of the Fortezza Del Basso in Florence
points out that what had often been considered in the past to be
the *patina* of *fresco* was in reality a veil of calcium oxalate, a hard,
translucent calcium compound that often formed over decaying
proteic matter, and that absorbed suspended particles or dust,
soot, and smoke while solidifying. This veil of calcium oxalate
resulted from the incomplete carbonation of the *intonaco,* and the
subsequent migration of moisture to the surface of the painting
where it hardened. It did give the wall paintings an aged look—
masking, muting, and dulling the colors.

Matteini's opinion is not universally accepted. Ornella Casazza believes that the *patina* is merely the natural aging of the pigments in a *fresco*. "The *patina* is not equivalent to the *beverone*, as the *beverone* was an arbitrary addition, which therefore can be removed. *Patina* equals history," she recites by rote; this is one of the central concepts of the Baldini restoration theory. "And as history it should remain. You cannot erase history from a painting except by falsifying. It would be the equivalent of a woman trying to erase twenty years of life by having a facelift."

Much of the discussion revolving around the *patina* arises from the fact that until recently, most art critics and historians knew very little about the techniques of *fresco* and *fresco* restoration. The *patina* became an aesthetic issue; paintings and frescoes just did not look right without the mandatory veil of modesty, regardless of its nature or origin.

Despite the advances made in restoration diagnostics, the *patina* issue still is largely unresolved; the debate has merely shifted in focus from aesthetics to ethics. Like any object that is exposed to air, dust, smoke, changes in temperature, and moisture, the materials used in *fresco* inevitably undergo certain transformations. In certain clear-cut cases, like those of repaintings or the *beverone,* almost all historians recognize the casuality of the act and sanction their removal. In other cases, such as a layer of dust and smoke particles, which have formed "naturally" across the surface of the painting, restorers are deeply divided. Some argue, and not without foundation, that even phenomena such as the calcium-oxalate veil, a compound that is a natural although involuntary consequence of the artist and his technique, should be considered part of the mural's *patina,* and as such should remain untouched.

Critics of the current Sistine Chapel restoration complain that the restorers have cleaned the vault too thoroughly and in doing so have also removed the *patina* of time, thereby ruining the original chromatic balance that Michelangelo had devised.

"I don't know how these people can draw certain conclusions if they don't know anything about the techniques of *fresco* and *fresco* restoration," says Gianluigi Colalucci, chief restorer of the Vatican. We are standing on the ingenious restoration bridge that spans

the width of the Sistine Chapel, and where Colalucci and his colleagues have been working for the past eight years. Michelangelo's
imposing vault looms over our heads, within arm's reach.

"From reading some of the protests, you'd think that Michelangelo had wanted to paint this ceiling dark. And that we were up
here scraping his work off with sandpaper."

Colalucci and his restorers have cleaned the Sistine vault with
the standard Roman *fresco* cleaning solution known as B-57. Developed by restorers Paolo and Laura Mora at the Central Institute
for Restoration, the mixture is composed of ammonium carbonate, sodium carbonate, and dexogen, an antibiotic used to combat
mold and bacteria. These three active elements are blended into an
inert base of liquid cellulose, which the restorers apply directly
onto the surface of the *fresco* with a paintbrush and leave there for
three minutes. When the chemical reactions are finished, the B-57
mixture and all proteic matter is removed with a sponge and distilled water. If necessary, the treatment can be repeated after
twenty-four hours.

"This technique cannot harm the materials used in *fresco,* as the
chemicals in the B-57 solution only react with organic matter,"
Colalucci explains wearily, and with tolerance. "All we are removing are the layers of glue and wine and dust which have accumulated over the centuries."

Some opponents of the Sistine project claim that Michelangelo
had used black smoke to add relief to his figures, and that in their
over-zealous cleaning of the *fresco* Colalucci and his colleagues
were erasing an element of the original work. "It is extremely
doubtful that Michelangelo shaded his figures with black smoke,"
the Vatican's chief restorer says. "And if you look above you,
you'll see why."

Colalucci indicates a twelve-foot male nude directly over my
head. "This zone has already been cleaned," he says. "You will
notice that Michelangelo did use black to shade the figure, and to
give it depth when viewed from below. And you will also notice
that he shaded the figure in *fresco,* adding these streaks of black
while the *intonaco* was still fresh. Look at this work. It's perfect.
Now why would an artist need to use a torch to shade his figures
with smoke, which he knew was only temporary when he could
achieve the same effect permanently in *fresco?*"

A third criticism of the much-publicized restoration maintains that Michelangelo often returned to sections of his *fresco* after they had dried and retouched them *a secco*. These critics claim that many of the repaintings that the restorers were removing had actually been painted by Michelangelo.

"Any historian worth his salt should know better than that," pronounces Ugo Procacci. "Vasari, who worshipped Michelangelo like a god, said that retouching a *fresco* after it was finished was a horrid act, *vilissima*."

"The truth is that Michelangelo did make corrections in his *fresco*," admits Colalucci. "But they are minimal. He shortens a thumb by half a centimeter. He adds a centimeter to an elbow. Evidently, he occasionally found an imperfection in his creation when viewing it from below. The interesting thing is that these corrections are never more than ten or twelve centimeters long; the flaws which he discovered were probably so minor that no one would have ever noticed them.

"The corrections are easy to identify, because Michelangelo has scraped off his own pigments." He points to one such correction; the abrasion marks are plainly evident. "And then paints over the blank sliver of *intonaco*. We know that these are the work of Michelangelo and not of a restorer, because a restorer doesn't make these microscopic adjustments. If anything, he repaints a hand, an arm, or an entire scene. There is an abyss between Michelangelo's corrections and the repaintings done by other restorers. And we have respected and preserved all of Michelangelo's work, including the corrections he performed *a secco*."

In practical terms, the heart of the debate over the ethics of cleaning beats in the choice between an absolute loyalty to the original materials of a painting and a subjective preservation of the original chromatic harmony. As it is an aesthetic matter, and inherently subjective, diagnostic science cannot resolve the issue.

Some schools, like that of the English restorers, favor the complete removal of all foreign substances from the painting's surface, regardless of the visual cacophony which may result. Other philosophies, like the one to which the Florentine restorers adhere, support a gradual, "interpretive" cleaning designed to preserve the chromatic harmony of the work. Even countries are divided into

separate factions over cleaning. Restorers in Rome are more in-
clined to side with the English. Baldini, a Florentine, has always
pitched his tent firmly in the interpretive camp.

"If a restorer forges blindly ahead, removing everything in his
path without respecting the integrity of the artwork, that artwork
does not benefit at all from the cleaning, except perhaps in that it
has become more transparent," Italy's most respected restoration
director expounds. "It is a choice between trying to save the notes
written on a piece of music or trying to save the music itself."

Except for the few stray notes that trickled through when Ugo
Procacci removed the two ovals from the marble altar in 1932, the
music in the Brancacci Chapel had not been heard for decades or
perhaps for centuries. This was the real challenge of the Brancacci
restoration. The unprecedented thickness of the grime that muffled the melodies of Masaccio and Masolino suggested an extraordinary circumspection. And the absolute lack of information regarding Filippino Lippi's Brancacci technique gave Baldini good
reason to fear that Lippi's work—like the work of restorer Gaetano
Bianchi in Giotto's Bardi Chapel—would prove chromatically incompatible with the work of Masaccio and Masolino once the *beverone* had been removed.

The Brancacci team had to be aware of the surprisingly bitter
debate that the Sistine Chapel restoration had inspired, regardless
of how inaccurate or unfounded. But Baldini, Casazza, and their
collaborators knew that they were risking much more than just a
hostile press as they drafted their strategy for the cleaning of the
Brancacci Chapel frescoes.

*July 19, 1988. 9:00 am. The Carmine Church,
just outside the Brancacci Chapel.*

It is a typicaly unbearable summer day in Florence. Although still
cool from the night before, the air in the narrow, shadowed streets of San
Frediano tastes stale and unsanitary, like that of a house that has been
sealed for months. A stagnant stillness reigns here. Nothing seems to
move; children's clothes and tableclothes hang stiff on clotheslines over-
head like mocking wooden effigies.

In Via D'Ardiglione, the shifting rows of houses and the choppy
pavement seriously tax the equilibrium of even the most settled inhabi-

tant. About halfway down the street, on the side that borders on the wall of the Carmine Church, there is an unobtrusive plaque in *pietra serena* that marks the slanting second-story room where the painter Fra Lippo Lippi was born in 1406. Lippi, who was raised by the Carmelite friars within the convent walls and took his monastic vows at the age of fifteen, was most likely the first artist to be dazzled by the genius of Masaccio. It is more than probable that as a young novice, Lippi spent long hours observing the father of modern painting plying his miracles in the Brancacci Chapel. In the early 1480s, Lippi's son Filippino would be called to the Carmine to complete the famous *fresco* cycle.

Stepping from Via D'Ardiglione into the wide-open Piazza Del Carmine is almost like discovering the ocean. From a world of hazy monochrome one suddenly emerges into a world clear with color. A scattering of cars adorns the still dormant square like a bed of tulips. The early morning sun and the vestiges of a dawn breeze remind one that July, too, can be a glorious month. Yet even this relative comfort is ephemeral; already, in the light, it is uncomfortably hot.

The climate inside the church is decidedly more pleasant than that outside. Even the damp ecclesiastical darkness is welcome. Having just concluded their early morning mass, two priests in coarse brown cotton robes with hemp belts tied around their waists are shuffling from the central altar to the sacristy. A handful of worshippers, nearly all of them old and heavy women, remain kneeling at their benches.

Ornella Casazza in the Brancacci Chapel.

In the far-right nave, a group of tourists drifts toward the barrier that seals the Brancacci Chapel from view. Some of them are disappointed that they cannot enter and vainly try to peek through the planks. Some of them are relieved and happy to be spared the duty of having to cram the picture of yet another masterpiece into a mind already gorged with images.

Three Florentines knock on the door to ask Ornella Casazza when she hopes to finish.

"I can't really say," she says, stepping out of the chapel and closing the temporary door behind her. It is clear that Casazza does not know these people.

"For Christmas?" one of the Florentine women asks.

"We do hope to reopen the chapel before the end of the year," she answers graciously.

"It would be nice to have the Brancacci open for Christmas," the woman's husband observes. "We would very much like to have it open for Christmas."

The group lingers, perhaps hoping for an invitation to climb onto the scaffolding, but without conviction. In another minute they are gone. Casazza motions for me to follow her inside.

"I just arrived myself," she says, fanning herself with a leaflet she is holding. "I rode over from my office at the Uffizi on my bicycle. My God, it's hot. I hadn't realized."

We climb past where her restorers are working up onto the second level of the scaffolding. She leans against the support rail and scrutinizes Masaccio's *The Tribute Money,* her eye scanning diagonally, from upper right to lower left.

"It's funny," she says, a gentle, fresh smile. "I was just thinking that when I first came here I really didn't understand anything. It seemed so foreign. It wasn't that I felt intimidated, or that I had doubts about being able to do my work. But you always feel this way when you take on a new job. Timid, curious, reverent, a feeling of excitement which makes you want to understand the object before you, to know it better and better."

To the unaccustomed eye, there seems to be very little motion in the chapel. Casazza's four restorers seem less busy than phlegmatic. But gradually, almost as if growing acclimated to the dark, one begins to perceive the precise, rhythmic, watch-like movement of the restorers at their work.

"You can never fully know a work of art," Casazza opines, turning to face me. "It renews itself each day. It does not satiate. It escapes us, always, what the artist wanted to say, his language, his symbols. In a way, you come to know it the same way you come to know a person. At first you shake hands. You speak. Perhaps you have a drink together. You can always get to know a person better. But you will never know everything about him. It is the same with art.

"One might expect a restoration like this one to be a sort of artistic adventure. But I have no spirit of adventure. Only a spirit of caution." She gazes, serene, at *The Tribute Money,* and then leans over the railing to look at *The Resurrection of Teofilo's Son.* Apparently satisfied, she turns once more toward me.

"Here everything has been examined, analyzed, and planned. Virtually nothing has been left to chance. Nothing. We have eliminated the element of subjectivity to an absolute minimum."

She chuckles, softly, to herself. "Don't misunderstand me. It's not that I have nightmares of Masaccio coming at night to strangle me in my bed for having ruined his frescoes. But I would like to think that he would have approved of what I've done here. And above all, I sincerely hope that I *haven't* interpreted this chapel. This is not my job.

"The original fresco which Masaccio painted is gone," she says peremptorily. "Finished. It doesn't exist. The restorer works only with what time has left him. And what we do is only of minor importance. The restorer of the Brancacci Chapel doesn't count. He must shed this presumption before he steps inside. What counts is the artist. I as restorer am at his service. I work to preserve the value of his work, in the hope of allowing others to appreciate it. This," she pauses, expertly, "if anything, is my presumption."

CHAPTER FIFTEEN

Anionic Resins

I N HISTORY, at least in the way that history is usually told, it is not particularly uncommon for an expedition or experiment to obtain a result that was not at all anticipated at the outset of the quest. Columbus discovered the American continent while trying to plot a short route to the Indies. Alexander Graham Bell supposedly invented the telephone while working on a device intended to aid the hard of hearing. The mold that would eventually yield the antibiotic penicillin was first discovered in a culture dish that Alexander Fleming inadvertently left uncovered for a week while he was away on vacation, and that he nearly threw out on his return.

According to Paolo Parrini, the discovery of the cleaning technique that was used in the Brancacci Chapel was also a fortuitous coincidence. "Umberto Baldini had asked us to furnish him with a cleaning method which could be applied gradually," says the Syremont president and the Brancacci restoration's scientific coordinator. "Given the eighty years which separated the work of Masaccio and Masolino from that of Filippino Lippi, and given the centuries of touchups and repaintings, it was an operation which suggested an exaggerated prudence."

When Parrini's technicians performed the survey for sulfates in the Brancacci Chapel, they used anionic resins, which the Montedison company had developed specifically for the purpose of absorbing sulfate ions that were buried in *fresco* or in marble. Tinted in a solution of ammonium carbonate to slow down the rate of the ionic exchange, these resins were applied directly to the surface of the *fresco* and removed when all the sulfates had been absorbed.

"In observing the three or four centimeter zones where the resins had been applied," Parrini happily proceeds, "the restorers who were on hand pointed out that the resins seemed to have a cleansing effect, and that the survey zones were much cleaner than the remainder of the paintings. Aside from the intended ionic exchange, we discovered that these resins also demolished any proteins on the surface of the paintings. This occurs because over time, proteins decay to form certain groups of atoms which have many of the characteristics of sulfates. The resins have no effect on earth and mineral matter, and therefore cannot dissolve the pigments or the artist's *intonaco*."

Having witnessed the unexpected grime-busting prowess of his anionic resins, Parrini brought the product back into the Montedison laboratory for modifications that would better adapt them to their new function.

"Naturally," Parrini adds, "these modified resins were thoroughly tested, first on sections of *intonaco* which we had prepared, and then on other frescoes. When we were satisfied that the product was both effective and safe, we proposed that it be used as the cleaning agent in the Brancacci Chapel. It seemed an ideal solution. With this method, a restorer can perform a gradual cleaning, and can leave some signs of age in a work if he desires, the so-called *patina* of time. Man is used to viewing the work of art in a certain condition. Sometimes a cleaning can appear too abrupt or shocking; this is the complaint which many people voice over the Sistine Chapel restoration, that too much was removed. The anionic resin provides the restorer with a greater degree of control than other traditional cleaning methods."

It is somewhat difficult to believe that two experienced *fresco* restorers like Sabino Giovannoni and Marcello Chemeri were actually surprised to discover that Parrini's resins, tinted with ammonium carbonate, caused the organic grime to congeal. Both restorers had used the ammonium-carbonate solution to obtain the identical result since their apprenticeships with Dino Dini.

Parrini's version of the discovery must also be viewed with an indulgent cynicism; the Syremont president is far too accomplished a scientist not to have at least considered the possibility that the anionic resins would cause the proteic *beverone* to gel. As both ammonium carbonate and the Montedison resins adduce an ionic exchange with sulfate compounds, it should not have been entirely unexpected that the anionic resins also produce a similar secondary effect, that is, the gelification of the organic matter found on the painting's surface.

Not all scientists are convinced that the anionic resin provides any greater efficiency or control in *fresco* cleaning than the wood-flour compress.

"The mechanics of the reaction are identical both in the case of the compress and in that of the resin," says one Italian chemist. "The only difference is that if you use a wood-flour compress as a support for ammonium carbonate in your restoration you're going to pay very little, and if you use the Montedison resins as a support, you're going to pay a lot."

Viewed dispassionately, the Montedison resins were much more a successful modification of an existing cleaning technique rather than an entirely new method in itself. Along with the evolution of its diagnostic techniques, art restoration had made similar progress in its cleaning methods since the 1940s. The archaic, empirical recipes of Secco Suardo were gradually replaced by more effective techniques that did much less damage to the artworks. Thanks to Dino Dini, *fresco* restorers began to treat frescoes exclusively with inorganic substances that were compatible with the materials in the wall paintings.

While each restoration inevitably poses a unique series of problems including mineral salts, mold, abrasions, and repaintings, there are some conditions like the egg-based *beverone* that are so widespread as to be considered standard, and that as such can usually be treated with standard cures. Because of its proven ability to congeal any proteic matter on the surface of a *fresco* without altering the pigments of *intonaco,* Dini's ammonium carbonate became the most widely accepted and most successful method of *fresco* cleaning. Since the Dini-Ferroni restoration at San Marco in 1967, Dini's wood-flour compress was almost always used as a support for the solution. And in cases of extended sulfatation, the ammonium carbonate treatment was complemented with an application of barium hydroxide to neutralize the sulfates and consolidate the stretched pictorial film.

Because the barium method had produced such splendid results, many people, including several of the Brancacci restorers, expected that the Dini-Ferroni technique would be adopted for the Carmine frescoes.

"We didn't use the barium method because there wasn't a high percentage of sulfates," responds an incredulous Umberto Baldini. "Barium is a medicine. It isn't the grated *parmaggiana* cheese which you put on your spaghetti. And besides, it isn't the medicine which counts. It's the cure."

"The barium method is an all-or-nothing proposition," says Parrini. "Once the barium is introduced into the fabric of the *fresco,* it is impossible to remove. There is no turning back. Then again, there is also no reason why a material should not be used in art if it has been successfully tested in the laboratory."

Baldini and Casazza still could have elected to use ammonium carbonate applied in wood-flour compresses to cure the Brancacci frescoes of the grime that afflicted them.

"To be honest, there was some disagreement about Baldini's and Casazza's decision to use the resins," admits Gioia Germani, the young restorer who assisted Guido Botticelli in the early phases of the Brancacci restoration and who was subsequently hired to assist Giovannoni and Chemeri in 1984 by Olivetti SPA.

"At the beginning, it seemed that we were to use these resins simply because the restoration directors had their minds set on it," Germani recalls. "And while we all agreed that in theory it was an excellent material, we were also skeptical about using such a new method on a work as important as the Brancacci Chapel."

The canons of modern *fresco* restoration had always dictated that any organic substance or grime be removed from the surface of the painting in a single operation. The mixture of proteins, soot, and smoke tends to solidify after a treatment of ammonium carbonate, making its removal extremely difficult and in some cases impossible. Knowing that there was no second chance, the restorer had to determine the dosage and time of contact of the ammonium carbonate tinted wood-flour compress in order that the congealant penetrate through the entire layer of *beverone.* As the ionic exchange provoked by the Montedison resins was much more superficial, the consequent post-treatment hardening did not occur. This allowed the Brancacci restorers to remove the grime in layers, and to return to perform a second or third treatment on zones that had already been cleaned.

Germani and her colleagues gradually came to appreciate the increased control that the resins afforded them, and also to comprehend Baldini's insistence.

"The ammonium-carbonate solution applied in the wood-flour compress produces a deeper and more immediate reaction," the blond-haired Germani explains. "The action of the resin is very similar, except that when it is tinted with ammonium carbonate, the reaction is retarded. Because ammonium carbonate is an anion

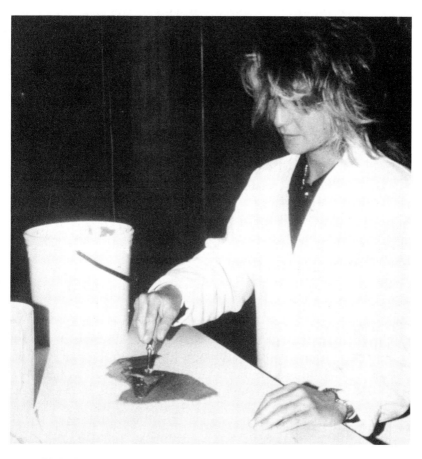

Gioia Germani, Brancacci Chapel, preparing the anionic resins for application.

(a negatively-charged ion), it partially satisfies the ionic pull of the resin. Because of this, the action of the resin is less abrupt. And the times of exposure are much shorter.

"There were also several valid reasons for using the resins in the Brancacci," Germani continues. "First and foremost, although all artworks require caution, important works require extreme caution. In the Brancacci, the quantity of grime was so intense that we really couldn't see where we were heading. With paintings by three different authors, there was a serious risk of creating a chromatic imbalance."

In addition to the increased control over the cleaning reaction, the fact that the resins required much less water than the wood-flour compress also proved to be a valuable advantage. "The restorers who worked in the Brancacci in the late 1800s injected a substantial quantity of *gesso* into the wall to fill gaps which had opened between the *intonaco* and the *arriccio*," Germani says plainly.

"The pilasters which divide the scenes are full of *gesso*; you can see the holes in the wall where the substance was injected. A wood-flour compress with water could conceivably dissolve this *gesso* and bring the salts out onto the surface of the painting."

"There is another advantage of these resins over the traditional wood-flour compress," says Dr. Giuseppe Pizzigoni, Parrini's colleague at Syremont. "Given that they require much less water than the compress, and that the material exerts an ionic pull without the addition of ammonium carbonate, they can be used to clean copper-based pigments like azurite with no danger to the color. Ammonium carbonate causes copper-based pigments to shift dramatically."

The Brancacci Chapel frescoes were cleaned centimeter by centimeter with a microscopic attention to detail and a macroscopic attention to equilibrium. Each piece of cotton that was used to remove the congealed *beverone* after the application of the anionic resins was conserved and sent to the Syremont laboratory in Milan for analysis.

"We wanted to be absolutely certain of the materials which we were exporting from the surface of the frescoes," says Pizzigoni. "The cotton samples were analyzed through infrared spectrometry and identified according to the wavelengths which the substances absorbed. We found that the restorers were removing organic material and also a small quantity of sulfates. In the scene of *The Alms Giving,* which is amply repainted, some of the pigments which were applied with *tempera* were also removed."

As the anionic resins cause all proteic material to swell, the egg- or glue-based *tempera* that restorers had used to make their colors adhere to the wall while repainting was also subject to an identical effect. Once the organic binder has swelled by the action of the resins, the pigments that they have been supporting can be removed quite easily, either by rubbing with a wet sponge or piece of cotton, or with steam. In addition to many of the abundant repaintings in *The Alms Giving* and *St. Peter Enthroned,* the resins were also used to remove the celebrated leaves that concealed the genitals of Adam and Eve, and which had been applied with *tempera.*

Given the unprecedented opportunity of being able to return to further clean a zone that had already been treated, Casazza and her team of restorers exploited the new material to its fullest potential. "There was very much a parliamentary atmosphere in the chapel," Casazza recalls. "An *esprit du corps.* Every morning, every afternoon, we would discuss that day's work. Sabino or Marcello would call me twice, three times a day. Should we continue here? Should we stop there? What effect will this have on the whole of the painting?"

The cleaning phase of the Brancacci Chapel restoration lasted nearly three years; in comparison, the pictorial touchup took just twelve months. The frescoes in the upper register were cleaned in one year, while the lower register required twice that time. "The restorer is a person who works out of passion, because he feels drawn to the profession," says Ornella Casazza, expanding on the type of patience that a *fresco* restorer needs to practice his craft.

"These people certainly aren't in it to get wealthy, because the restorer's salary is barely enough to feed a family." Casazza, who began her career as a restorer of panel and canvas paintings, has firsthand experience here. "They work because they feel a passion for these artworks. They work with discipline. On the other hand, if a restorer does not work with every bit of energy at his disposition, his results will never be satisfactory. The level of energy which an artist devotes to the creation of an artwork requires that the restorer devote the same quantity of energy to its restoration."

As so often occurs during the cleaning of a painting, the removal of the Brancacci *beverone* led to several significant historical revisions. In Masaccio's *The Alms Giving,* Casazza and her team discovered that the mountains which form the background of the scene were covered with snow, a snow that had been masked beneath the thick layer of grime. The protagonists who donate their earthly goods to St. Peter do so in the midst of winter, making their sacrifice all the more meaningful.

In addition, a *giornata* by Filippino Lippi was discerned in the upper right-hand corner of the scene. The restorers also discovered that a healthy part of the lower section of the panel—a section that even after the cleaning is still illegible—had been repainted. The crescent-shaped contour that divided the repainted section from the *fresco* work of Masaccio inspired several of Casazza's team to surmise that the original panel had been frescoed above a door that led out of the chapel, and that was subsequently closed. A discernable concavity in the panel also supported that hypothesis.

The cleaning of the panel featuring the stories of *The Resurrection of Teofilo's Son* and *St. Peter Enthroned* facilitated an accurate reading of the *giornate,* and also allowed the restorers to distinguish the work of Masaccio from that of Filippino Lippi. Historians had traditionally assigned the *St. Peter Enthroned* scene, the classic Roman architecture in the background, and the figures in the left-hand side of the semicircle of onlookers who witness the miracle of *The Resurrection of Teofilo's Son* to Masaccio. The remainder of the work was attributed to Lippi. In examining the use of color, the painting style, and most of all the texture of the *intonaco,* Casazza and her team were able to confirm this view. Unfortunately, the cleaning has not and could not provide any new clue that might help historians decide whether Masaccio left the panel unfinished when he left Florence in 1428, or whether, as Baldini believes, the *fresco* was vandalized after the fall of the Brancacci in 1436.

In his 1977 address given at Harvard's I Tatti villa in Florence, Professor A. Molho furnished what must still be considered the most plausible solution to the riddle. Having located Felice Brancacci's 1432 will in the Florentine archives, Molho notes that the patron of the Brancacci Chapel expresses his desire to be buried in his family's chapel in the Carmine. Felice Brancacci also requests his heirs to finish the decoration of the chapel—*dicta cappela in totam pingatur e ornetur*—should the chapel not be totally painted and decorated at the time of his death—*in quantum tempore mortis dicti testatoris suprascipta cappella non esset in totum picta et ornata prout decet.* As the will is written two years prior to the Albizzi plot and the subsequent banishment of the Brancacci, there is no reason to believe that the frescoes had been vandalized or destroyed at that time. And as the will is written four years after the death of Masaccio, it is most likely that Masaccio had left the *fresco* cycle unfinished when he departed for Rome in the spring of 1428.

Probably the most important interpretation afforded by the Brancacci cleaning regarded Masolino's *Tabita* and Masaccio's *The Tribute Money.* In concert with his revolutionary theory that asserted that Masaccio was much more a *maestro* than an apprentice in his relationship with Masolino, Roberto Longhi was convinced that Masaccio was the author of the architecture in the *Tabita* panel. Given his modest assessment of Masolino's mastery of space and perspective, Longhi believed it inconceivable that the painter from Panicale might have been capable of creating the sophisticated spatial illusions in *Tabita.*

Consequently, Longhi also believed that the head of Christ in Masaccio's *The Tribute Money* was executed by Masolino. The head and face of the redeemer, which is painted in one *giornata,* is noticeably softer than the marble-like visages of the apostles who surround him. Because of an undeniable similarity with the Christ in Masolino's Empoli *Pieta,* and because Longhi found it improbable that Masaccio would have deliberately allowed his Christ to be overshadowed not only by St. Peter but by the rest of his heroic retinue, he suggested that Masolino had begun the panel, getting as far as this one central *giornata* before abandoning the *fresco* and most likely the Brancacci Chapel.

Based on her close contact with the two panels during the four-year restoration, Ornella Casazza believes Longhi was wrong in both cases. "While it is true that attribution can never be absolute, it is also true that each artist has his own particular way of painting," she explains. "The same way each of us has his own handwriting, or his own tone of voice. The *Tabita* scene was painted by Masolino; now more than ever, this is evident, just by following the *giornata*. This is certainly an atypical painting for Masolino. Undoubtedly, Masaccio did participate in the preparatory sketches, as the two artists obviously collaborated with the planning of the chapel from the beginning. Masaccio could very well have been instrumental in drafting the architecture in the background. But there is nothing on that panel which was painted by Masaccio."

"Insofar as *The Tribute Money,* we believe that the *giornata* featuring the head of Christ was painted by Masaccio, perhaps in a Masolino-like moment," Casazza recites with a placid certainty. "You have to remember that these two artists worked very closely together. There had to be a reciprocal influence between them."

The cleaning of the Brancacci panels has certainly bolstered the reputations of the three artists who painted them. Although Masaccio was already a legend, the restoration has brought to light his splendid use of color, a gift that had been concealed for centuries. Filippino Lippi's frescoes have taken on an entirely new appearance. No longer the "poor cousin" of Masaccio and Masolino, Lippi has emerged from beneath the *beverone* as a powerfully expressive painter. No longer the pupil of Sandro Botticelli, Lippi becomes himself while finishing the Brancacci Chapel. And his greatness is now evident in the newly-restored frescoes.

Yet of all the Brancacci frescoes, Masolino's *Tabita* has drawn the most benefits from the cleaning. While Masaccio's Brancacci panels were equally obscured before the restoration, his preeminence among fifteenth-century painters had never been questioned. Masolino, who enjoyed much more popularity during his lifetime than did his collaborator from Castel San Giovanni, lost much of his esteem in the centuries that followed his death.

With the cleaning of *Tabita,* Masolino's stature must now be reassessed. Unlike Masaccio, who created a skeletal structure in his paintings by following precise rules of optics and perspective, Masolino achieved his spatial effects through his use of color and shading. Masaccio's sculpted figures and geometric staging, while muted, still pulsed perceptibly beneath the murky *beverone;* Masolino's more subtle chromatics were entirely suppressed.

Because of its exclusive dependency on color, Masolino's Brancacci work suffered far more than Masaccio's beneath the thick layer of grime. Unmasked, Masolino's architecture acquires a new integrity, and his figures a new character. We see a *Tabita* in which Masolino used *chiaroscura* to fashion a spatial reality, which is far more convincing and realistic than previously believed.

"I'm old, I'm tired, and I've still got to get through these three volumes of the 1427 *catasto,*" says Ugo Procacci, motioning behind him to three loose-leaf notebooks stuffed with odd-sized sheets of handwritten *catasto* declarations. "But before I die, I'd like to make one more statement. And I'd like that statement to be about Masolino. I'd like to say that most of us were wrong. I, too, at the beginning, thought he was just a painter of rosy colors, dazzled and blinded by Masaccio. But if you look at the *Tabita,* or at the *synopie* at Empoli, you see that he was a lot more aware of the novelties of the 1400s than any of us believed."

Procacci's labored, saintly smile usurps the better part of his kindly face. His narrow eyes are nearly shut. "Now more than ever, after the restoration, we see a Masolino who already had turned the page on the late-Gothic period, who knew about spacing and *chiaroscuro,* who had already begun experimenting with modelling his figures. Masolino was an artist who could do whatever he wanted to with a brush. He is not Masaccio," Procacci pronounces, shaking his head, "because Masaccio is unearthly, a genius which was repeated only in Michelangelo, and only because Michelangelo had a Masaccio before him to study. But Masolino is far greater than history had made him out to be."

Marcello Chemeri

Brancacci restorer Marcello Chemeri has sidled off into a corner of the scaffolding while a group of fur-wrapped women from high Florentine society coos before the transparent, pastel tones of Masolino's newly-cleaned *Tabita*. It is a few minutes before noon in November of 1988.

"There's too much publicity about all this already," Chemeri mutters. "We're not superhuman. We're not geniuses. We just try to work as best we can. That's all."

Chemeri tries to suppress his annoyance at this latest interruption. He does not appreciate company. He does not enjoy conversation and has already informed me that he would prefer not to be interviewed. Each phrase, each word, is spoken in a fitful, dark-voiced spurt. Each pause appears to mark the end of his acquiescence.

"Our main concern revolved around the Filippino Lippi intervention. Lippi painted his frescoes nearly sixty years after the bulk of the chapel was completed." The thirty-nine-year-old restorer draws nervously on his cigarette, his dark, rodent's eyes trained at a spot on the platform beneath his feet. He looks as if he had just come in out of a cold rain.

"We knew that there would be no problem with Masaccio and Masolino; since they worked together, it was obvious that they had used the same materials for the *intonaco* and the same colors. We had no similar guarantee about Lippi."

The Brancacci Chapel frescoes presented a much greater challenge to the restorers than they did to the technicians who collaborated in the Baldini restoration. "The frescoes were badly blackened," recalls Chemeri, obviously ill at ease. "In many places, for example the lower part of the *Baptism* scene, you couldn't even make out the figures or the shapes. We were aware of the historial and artistic importance of this chapel, and how it would reflect on the profession as a whole. For this, we began very slowly." He pauses again to pull on the cigarette. "With feet of lead, trying to understand precisely what technique the author had used."

Chemeri exhales, lifts his right hand, and uses the cigarette as a pointer to indicate the chapel's rear wall. "The work was so badly obscured that we didn't know whether it was *a fresco,* or whether it had been repainted *a secco,* or whether it was a sort of table painting like Leonardo Da Vinci's *Last Supper* in Milan. You can imagine our relief when we discovered that Lippi had used the same technique as was used by Masaccio and Masolino, that is, the *a fresco* technique, which is found in Cennino Cennino's *The Book of Art.*"

From his early teens, Marcello Chemeri had hoped to become a painter. He still paints now, in his spare time, when his work allows him spare time. "I think that a restorer needs a certain predisposition towards art," he suggests. "As a boy, I was always drawing, or experimenting with colors. I went into restoration because I needed a job after I finished art school."

Like his colleagues Sabino Giovannoni and Guido Botticelli, Marcello Chemeri first learned the art of *fresco* restoration in the *bottega* of Dino Dini and later moved on to the Opificio Delle Pietre Dure. "From

Dini I learned to have the utmost respect for the materials which one finds before him. The atmosphere in his workshop was very similar to the atmosphere of the *bottega* of the 1400s. I remember that on my first day of work he had me carrying pails of water to the other restorers on the scaffolding. After a few weeks, I was allowed to work at removing a light crust from two plaster angels with a pair of tweezers. It was obvious that he was a very demanding man, demanding, precise, and very reserved."

In 1977, after four years with Dini, Chemeri passed the state exam to qualify for a place at the Opificio. Together with Giovannoni, he has worked on numerous *fresco* sites in Florence, Filippino Lippi's Cappella Strozzi in Santa Maria Novella, the Taddeo Gaddi frescoes in the Church of Ognissanti; Giotto's Peruzzi Chapel in Santa Croce and Andrea Del Sarto's *The Last Supper* in the museum of San Salvi. Like his two colleagues, he also instructed students at the Opificio in the art of *fresco* restoration, and later at the International University of Art.

"I try to give my all on every job," Chemeri continues, taking one last bitter pull on his cigarette, spreading his fingers and letting the butt drop to the platform, crushing it maliciously with his foot. "Whether it is a *fresco* by Masaccio or a so-called unimportant wall painting by an anonymous sixteenth-century master. It is a profession which requires an absolute tranquility. In a six-hour morning, you usually clean a zone of twenty square centimeters. You have to learn patience, and you have to learn to block out all problems which are not related to work. If you have an illness in the family, if money is tight, the cleaning does not come out well. Write that down. That a restorer needs an absolute tranquility in order to do his job."

The visiting women are trundling down the scaffolding stairs. A short, drawn, silver-haired matron who appears to be the leader of the group stops between levels to point out a detail to her friends. They almost seem like the chorus in a Greek tragedy, speaking in unison, marvelling on cue, repeating the last few words that Ornella Casazza pronounces. Against their slightly comic background, Chemeri's cloudy reticence is a somber contrast. He seems a tragically flawed protagonist, a character who wishes to be anywhere but on stage.

"This has been four years of enormous satisfaction," the restorer says in a gust. "And four years of torture." Chemeri's hand is still posed on the railing as if it still held a lit cigarette.

"Write that down," he instructs me. "Because people should know. Four years of satisfaction, not for what we did or didn't do, but for what we were able to see, to be the first people to discover that beneath this layer of filth there was still a healthy *fresco,* and that the colors hadn't been damaged. To have been the first ones to see the work of Masaccio in *fresco*. And to have had the privilege of liberating his paintings."

Chemeri glances quickly as the visiting ladies finally make their way to the door. The faint ray of emotion that had momentarily seeped into his narrow brown eyes is gone. His face is newly turbid.

"And four years of torture and torment from the tremendous responsibility, from the problems of the group falling into its rhythm. Write that down, too. That today, any large project is done in a group and not alone.

"There are many times when you don't sleep at night," Chemeri asserts, still staring away, still avoiding the slightest chance of contact. "Problems that come up daily, problems which you resolve when the group is in tune, and that appear insurmountable when the team falls out of step.

"It isn't hard to worry if you want to. Working here, with the eyes of the entire world upon us. The history of restoration clearly shows that with the passage of time, nearly all restorations have proven to be negative."

He pauses to scan the frescoes in the upper register where we are standing, gesturing faintly with his forehead. "We cannot be certain that the work we've done here has been positive."

CHAPTER SIXTEEN

Filling in the Gaps

A LTHOUGH IT USUALLY accounts for only ten percent of the total restoration, the pictorial intervention is perhaps the most important phase of all, as it determines what will be seen when the painting is returned to view. In restoration jargon, the expression "pictorial intervention" or "touchup" generally refers to the final phase of the restoration, where the restorers, after having stripped the painting of all superfluous materials, attempt to stitch the isolated or interrupted segments of the original colors back into a comprehensive whole. Depending on the history of the painting, the condition of its pigments, and the quantity of repaintings that have been removed, the pictorial intervention can be either relatively insignificant or particularly laborious.

The purpose of the pictorial intervention or touchup is to erase or eliminate the gaps that are left in the fabric of the painting after the previous repaintings have been removed, and which presumably disturb the ability of the artist's materials to transmit their message. While almost all restorers concur on the necessity to perform some sort of pictorial touchup, there are, as can be expected, many different and contrary solutions to the problem.

Historically, restorers have nearly always tried to fill in pictorial gaps by repainting, in a style that resembles that of the author as closely as possible, the missing section of the painting. Obviously, this tactic is laden with shortcomings. As any repainting, even a religiously scrupulous imitation, is inherently interpretive, the appearance of the original work of art is inevitably modified. Gaetano Bianchi's revisions on Giotto are a prime example, as are the series of repaintings suffered by Leonardo Da Vinci's *The Last Supper* in Milan.

Restorers who are light-years away from Raffaello or Fra Angelico or Botticelli in ability have set about to imitate those masters, fully expecting that their revisions go unnoticed, or in some cases, convinced that their contributions have actually improved the painting. After three or four pictorial interventions, much of the original work has been replaced or submerged; the painting is transformed into a sort of layered collage that loses most of the character with which it had been invested at creation.

Toward the middle of the current century, Italian restorers began experimenting with an alternative technique in which pictorial gaps were no longer repainted, but masked by a neutral tint that in theory reduced their visibility and caused them to blend into the whole of the painting. This, too, had its drawbacks.

"The problem of the neutral tint is rooted in the term itself," says Laura Mora of the Central Institute for Restoration in Rome. "We have an oxymoron. If it's a tint, then how can it be neutral?"

Since the 1950s, Roman restorers have used a method called *tratteggio* to eliminate pictoral gaps. *Tratteggio* is a repainting system in which the restorer recreates the missing sections of a painting by applying his colors in a series of minute vertical brushstrokes that can only be distinguished from the original work on very close inspection.

"*Tratteggio* is not THE solution," says Mrs. Mora. "It's a solution, one of many, and for our purposes usually the most convenient. We cannot afford to sit for days agonizing over a choice of color while all over the country frescoes are falling to pieces. The pictorial intervention should be barely noticeable. The best compliment my husband and I can receive after restoring a painting is when someone asks us, 'Why, Mr. and Mrs. Mora, did you do anything at all here?' "

Ornella Casazza began her career as a restorer of panel and canvas paintings. In 1972, after a rigorous ten-day audition in Rome, an audition that included oral, written, and practical trials, she became a state restorer. Five years later, after taking a degree in art history at the age of thirty-four, she passed another state examination to become a restoration historian at the Opificio Delle Pietre Dure.

"Ironically," she says dryly from behind her desk at the Uffizi

Gallery where she has worked as an inspector of art history since 1982, "in the written section of the 1977 art history exam, I was assigned to write a theme about Masolino. Sometimes I think it was my fate to end up directing this restoration."

The touchup method currently practiced by the Opificio Delle Pietre Dure and in all state-sanctioned restorations in the Florentine province is known as chromatic abstraction. It is Casazza's invention; she first applied the technique in 1968 to the Cimabue cross, the most illustrious victim of the 1966 Florentine flood and the most stirring symbol of the city's proud reaction.

"The pictorial intervention must conform with three specific criteria," Casazza intones. She is reciting, in a tired, hackneyed tone, the cornerstone phrase of the Baldini restoration philosophy. It is clear that this is the two-hundred-thousandth time she has been called on to reiterate.

"First, it cannot be competitive. Second, it cannot be imitative. And third, it cannot be a falsification. We needed to devise a system of repainting which did not infringe on any of the three cardinal rules," Casazza elaborates, "and which could be taught to all restorers.

"You cannot teach someone to paint," she sustains. "Of course, you can teach him how to mix his colors, or how to create certain effects. But how could you say to someone 'this is the way you paint a cloud' or 'this is how you paint a castle.' It would be like saying 'this is how you write a poem.' We needed to discover a method which was easily transmitted and which would allow for a certain uniformity from one restorer to the next. I thought about it day and night, for weeks on end."

"It's entirely her discovery," says Baldini proudly. "Ornella developed the method on her own. I merely pointed out the need for a more rational, standardized system of closing pictorial gaps."

Chromatic abstraction is based on the assumption that pictorial gaps interrupt the natural flow of a painting, and therefore must be closed or bridged. Baldini's anathema on any intervention that is imitative or falsifying immediately excludes all attempts at reproducing the style and technique of a particular artist, leaving the neutral tint method as the only practical alternative.

Casazza's pictorial technique is an intriguing hybrid of the neutral tint and the Rome *tratteggio* method. Instead of filling the gaps in a painting with a monochrome hue, chromatic abstraction uses a weave of three colors, each of which is applied separately, in a series of short, slender brushstrokes. Theoretically, the three colors, which are obtained through a summation of the color values in the whole of the work and applied according to the rules of complementary colors, combine to reproduce the effect of the original color without reproducing the color itself. As the three colors continue to exist separately, the final mixture takes place in the eye of the observer, and not on the surface of the painting.

In order for it to function properly, the three-color weave of chromatic abstraction must be identical throughout the whole painting. The elements of the chromatic weave are obtained through a careful chromatic reading of the entire work, and not just the zone contiguous to the pictorial gap.

If performed correctly, chromatic abstraction should endow all of the pictorial gaps with the same chromatic vibration as the whole painting; in short, the restored sections will dance to the same beat as the original work. These formerly blank spaces will no longer attract the eye of the viewer because they reflect too much light. Nor will they fade into the background because they are too dark. As they possess the same dynamics as the rest of the painting, they should be assimilated into the whole of the work.

Because of the texture of its tricolor weave, Casazza's chromatic abstraction can be distinguished from the artist's original work from a distance of two or three meters. In this way, the chromatic abstraction method conforms with Baldini's third prerequisite, which excludes any intervention that might compete for attention with the original work. Chromatic abstraction is also much more noticeable than the Rome *tratteggio,* which can only be discerned at extremely close range.

As a complement to chromatic abstraction, Casazza has also developed a corollary technique known as chromatic selection. The technical director of the Brancacci Chapel believes that pictorial gaps can be divided into two groups: gaps that can be reconstructed, and gaps whose total absence of any graphic elements render reconstruction impossible.

In the case where the original work leaves no clue as to what the artist had intended for a certain space, that gap is eliminated with chromatic abstraction. But in the case where the artist's preliminary drawing is still intact beneath the color layer—in *fresco* this would be the *sinopia,* the red-clay sketch done on the *arriccio* beneath the *intonaco*—or when the surviving graphic elements suggest a probable solution, restorers usually opt for selection.

Chromatic selection is virtually identical to chromatic abstraction except that this second method draws the colors for its polychrome weave from the chromatic values in the vicinity of the gap and not from the painting as a whole. With selection, restorers can complete an elbow or a hand, or patch a garment using a tricolor weave whose sum equals the chromatics of that garment.

Selection is the closest the Casazza method comes to reconstruction, as the method allows the restorers to restore a missing finger or hood or section of wall. As in abstraction, selection is still applied in a three-color weave, and with the same short and slender brushstrokes. It is up to the restoration director to decide whether a gap should be closed with abstraction or selection.

As with most techniques in the intensely subjective and fractious field of restoration, chromatic abstraction and selection have their share of detractors.

"They can do it if they want to," Dino Dini once commented sardonically. "I don't care for it."

Dini's pictorial touchup method consisted in painting gaps with a hue that was similar to the surrounding colors without duplicating that color; it was designed to allow gaps to fade into the background and highlight the original work. "What I do is an abstraction as well," Dini admitted. "But the abstraction takes place here on my palette and not on the *fresco* itself."

Laura Mora feels that the high visibility of the chromatic abstraction is self-defeating, in that the coarse chromatic weave tends to attract the eye of the viewer, inviting it to pause at the repaintings instead of at the original work. Still other restorers argue that all pictorial interventions are inherently flawed, and that the best way to show one's fidelity to the original work is not to repaint at all.

Both abstraction and selection were used in the Brancacci Chapel frescoes. As in the cleaning, Casazza directed her quartet of restorers—in 1987, Lydia Cinelli Bianchi joined Giovannoni, Chemeri and Germani for the touchup phase—from one passage

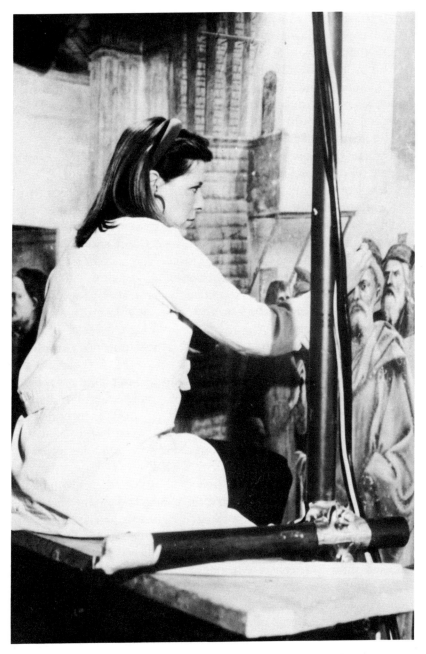

Lydia Cinelli Bianchi, Brancacci Chapel, "filling in the gaps" with chromatic selection on Masaccio's *St. Peter Healing with his Shadow*.

through the next as they patiently filled the various pictorial gaps in the panels of Masolino, Masaccio, and Filippino Lippi. The work of each restorer was reviewed and evaluated at the end of the workday, and the team met frequently to discuss its progress and its strategy.

"Essentially, I did what seemed right to me," comments Lydia Cinelli Bianchi. "Casazza provided the day-to-day direction. And she and Baldini would decide whether a gap could be integrated back into the whole of the panel with selection, or whether it should be filled in with abstraction. Much is left up to the restorer."

"It was obviously very important that the restorers share our ideology," Casazza explains. "There are so many different philosophies of restoration today. Sabino and Marcello have been at the Opificio for over ten years. And Gioia and Lydia are our students. There had to be a good agreement within the group if the end result was to be satisfactory. Imagine an orchestra in which every member feels free to interpret the score in his own way. What comes out isn't Beethoven or Brahms but pure chaos."

The team did perform several reconstructions that are destined to incite discussions among historians and critics. Casazza's restorers used selection to repaint the gold halos over the heads of the four apostles at the right of the central scene in Masaccio's *The Tribute Money*. In the lower right corner of the same panel, beside the tax collector who avidly accepts payment from a stolid St. Peter, the team reconstructed three stairs and a walking bridge.

"The section had been repainted previously; we removed both the colors and the *intonaco*," says Casazza. "During the cleaning of the *fresco*, we discovered some of the original lines, and used them to structure the missing segment. The current reading of the painting is much more valid than what was seen before."

Chromatic selection was also used to repaint the pink robe of the worshipper kneeling at the feet of St. Peter in Masaccio's *St. Peter Enthroned*, and in the prostrate body of Anania in Masaccio's *The Alms Giving*. Casazza also chose to repaint many of the Corinthian columns that divide the scenes, and whose colors were badly eroded.

"The Brancacci Chapel was a confusion of repaintings and losses," states the restoration's technical director. "Many of the mantles, the robes in *The Tribute Money* or in *The Resurrection of Teofilo's Son* had suffered abrasions, and had been repainted. We removed these repaintings during the cleaning—they are falsifying, and do not comprise a part of the chapel's history—and left them as they are. It's very difficult to intervene on an abrasion; the abrasion is more or less the erosion of time."

Casazza is strangely detached from her work; there is none of Baldini's fiery passion, or Dino Dini's profoundly silent spirituality. She paces through the record of the many difficult decisions she made during the four-year project like an athlete walking dispiritedly through a drill, showing less enthusiasm than most homemakers display when renovating a playroom. Even now, at the end of the restoration, there is virtually no emotion in her voice.

"Certainly I consider it a privilege to have been able to direct the restoration of the Brancacci Chapel," she opines. "The same way a surgeon might consider it an honor to perform an operation on the Pope. But in the end, the actual operation is still the same, whether on the Pope, or on a postman. For me, it's the same sensation."

Casazza's tone is just a shade too nonchalant to be entirely convincing. Yet she insists. "And when a job is finished," she continues, "I feel no great regret.

"There is an extended period in which you do live with the work, and this period can be intense. But it's like having a friend. At the beginning, you might miss him. Then, you replace him. And anyway, around here, we tend more than anything else to heave a sigh of relief when we finish a job. You would, too, if you saw the list of paintings that are awaiting our attention."

Sabino Giovannoni

"You've got to wake up every morning and kick yourself in the butt and say, 'YOU'RE NOBODY! YOU'RE NOBODY!' " Sabino Giovannoni speaks with his back to me, his emphatic, slightly nasal tenor resounding through the chapel. It is a Saturday morning in December of 1988. He has come to the Brancacci to finish repainting a seemingly unimportant section of Masaccio's *St. Peter Healing with His Shadow*.

Sabino Giovannoni in workshop in basement of the Carmine. Here he is removing the gauze from one of the lateral lunettes that were detached during the search for remnants of Masolino's *The Shipwreck of the Apostles* and *The Calling of Sts. Peter and Andrew*.

Giovannoni is a big man, with big features, big hands, and a big voice. Despite the grey hair that now and then falls across his forehead, despite his nearly fifty years, he still radiates the sincerity and courtesy of a teenager at his first job, eager, willing, almost desperate to please. Physically, he hardly meets the standard preconception of the patient, introverted, tenebrous restorer.

Dressed in a white, one-piece overall that if anything accents his substantial but well-proportioned frame, he perches forward, snapping down the magnifying glass that he wears in a band around his head to take a careful look at a one-square centimeter section of *fresco*. It seems almost ridiculous that a man of his power be focused on so fine a detail.

"Otherwise a restorer might get the idea that he's somebody," Giovannoni admonishes. "That he's a painter, too. He might start to think he's good. And the moment he says to himself that he's good, he's finished as a restorer."

At forty-nine years of age, Giovannoni has worked with frescoes since he was hired as an apprentice by Dino Dini in 1958. He is far more outgoing than his former *maestro,* less cryptic, and less reflective. But ironically, of all of Dini's former students, Giovannoni is the one who has best learned his lessons.

"A restorer must work with the utmost humility," he avows. "This is what we learned from Dini. An absolute respect for the work of art before us. An absolute respect in his choice of materials. But above all with an absolute humility."

As an apprentice, Giovannoni was on hand for all of Dini's most significant restorations, from Santa Croce to San Marco. "It has been my extreme good fortune to have been present during the historic collaboration between Dini and Professor Ferroni," he exclaims with unadulterated gratitude. "The perfection of the *stacco* and the *strappo*. The discovery of the barium method. I could not have asked for a better school, or for a better pair of teachers."

Giovannoni worked in the Dini *bottega* for sixteen years. "The Dini method of instruction was strictly personal," he explains, flipping up his magnifying lens, dipping his fine-tipped brush first in a solution of water and ammonium caseinate, then in a powdered pigment.

Setting his palette down on the chapel's marble shelf, he braces an elbow against the Brancacci wall to apply three minute dabs of color. He pauses, draws back, then returns to add another three strokes.

"The apprentice had to observe every phase of the work," he says, "from the cleaning to replastering to repainting. And there was no timetable. Professor Dini was the one who decided when the student was ready to perform certain tasks."

Like his friend and colleague Guido Botticelli, Giovannoni affords Dini the title of professor even though the *maestro* did not possess a university degree. "Dini taught by example, by working with respect and precision," Giovannoni continues, pausing for an instant in his work. "He also believed in forming character in his *bottega,* and in a rigid discipline. He could not accept the slightest deviation."

In 1977, at Baldini's invitation, Giovannoni took and passed the state restorer's exam and was hired at the Opificio Delle Pietre Dure. From student in the Dini *bottega,* Giovannoni has evolved into an instructor. At the Opificio, and at the International University of Art, he teaches courses in *fresco* restoration, in the *stacco* and *strappo* techniques, and in the construction of new supports for the detached *fresco* or *synopia.*

Giovannoni's first task when the Brancacci Chapel restoration resumed in 1984 was to construct the supports for the two *synopie* that had been removed from the chapel's rear wall.

"The *synopie* were placed facedown on a grid of stainless steel in order to steam off any animal glue which may have remained from the *stacco.* This is of extreme importance," Giovannoni underlines. "The *fresco* in itself is porous, and a *fresco* which has been detached is almost always full of cracks and fissures. Any infiltration of water in the future can melt the glue and transport it into these gaps, causing serious conservation problems when the animal matter begins to decay."

After steaming off the glue from the surface of the detached *fresco* or *synopia,* Giovannoni and Chemeri filed the *malta* on the backside of the panel to obtain a relatively even surface, filling any gaps with a calcium-caseinate solution. The calcium "mortar" has a double function, serving as both filler and as the adhesive for the skeleton that will eventually support the panel.

Still working from the rear, a hard support was set into the calcium mortar while it solidified. Essentially, there are two brands of hard support for frescoes, a lighter one, which is fashioned for the *fresco* that will be remounted onto its original wall, and a more sturdy brace for the *fresco* that will stand alone. A historian's indecision can often be costly here; the restorers who eventually remounted the Masolino *synopie* that Dino Dini had detached in the San Stefano Church in Empoli had a very difficult time. Ugo Procacci, who supervised the operation, had intended for the *synopie* to be displayed permanently in a museum, and had instructed Dini to fit them with freestanding supports. These rigid supports complicated their reinsertion into the chapel walls.

The hard support for frescoes that are to be returned to their original sites is usually made of fiberglass and resin. In the Brancacci, where Giovannoni and Chemeri did not have to worry about staying within the narrow budget usually afforded to restorers, the *synopie* were fitted with a support made of two layers of carbon fiber with a slice of polyvinyl-chloride in between.

"Behind the polyvinylchloride sandwich," Giovannoni concludes, pronouncing the word "sandwich" in an aggressive English, "we insert what is known as an intervention layer." The intervention layer is Giovannoni's contribution; a layer of cork that is fitted to the back of the support, it allows for an easy *stacco* in the future should the condition of the remounted *fresco* deteriorate and require further attention.

"There are many different techniques to choose from," says Giovannoni, flipping down his lens once more, dabbing on more color. "Each one suited to a particular situation. I remember just after the war, when they were detaching the frescoes in the Campo Santo at Pisa, they couldn't find the right cloth. They had to use the mosquito netting which the American soldiers gave them from their tents. If you look closely at those frescoes, you can still see the gridmarks. And now we have dozens of techniques to choose from if we have to perform a *stacco*.

"We also have dozens of techniques to choose from for the cleaning," Giovannoni continues. "This controversy over the Sistine Chapel. It makes no sense. Poor Gianluigi." Giovannoni's tone turns hostile as he mentions Gianluigi Collaluci, chief Vatican restorer and a personal friend. "You Americans. You almost caused him to have a heart attack, and all because you don't understand that he chose the best technique available to him. Today, the restorer has a wide selection of cures. And all of them are good. The choice depends on the particular case."

In his thirty years as a restorer, Giovannoni has seen and lived many changes. In terms of method, the greatest adaptation he has had to make has been in learning to work as part of a team. "Today, all major projects are performed in a team," he says dogmatically; Giovannoni has a talent for maintaining his intransigent sincerity while still espousing the party line. This talent and willingness to conform was probably decisive in his being selected for the Brancacci team. Giovannoni is a team player and also a man who respects the differences of rank. Many restorers with Giovannoni's thirty years of experience in *fresco* might have resented taking direction from Ornella Casazza, who despite her university degree and her background as a restorer had virtually no experience in *fresco*. Giovannoni accepted his subalternate rank without questioning. Like a true Florentine, if he has any personal ambition, he keeps it well concealed.

"There are no two ways about it," he reiterates. "This is the way the work is done. I am the oldest one here in the Brancacci, and also the restorer with the most experience. But the job is too big for one man to do alone. And too important for each restorer to act independently. We have to communicate. If this were a film, Baldini would be the producer, and the *Dottoressa* would be the director. When a problem comes up, we discuss it among ourselves. If it regards aesthetics, we make the decision. If it's a scientific matter, we consult the specialist in that particular field.

"Technology has allowed us certain types of information which weren't available ten years ago," Giovannoni continues, backing up slowly to view his work in perspective. He sets his palette down on the marble shelf that juts out from beneath the first *fresco* register, pulls a lighter out of his breast pocket to relight his sawed off *toscano* cigar. "With the infrared reflectograph, we could see through the grime, beneath the colors. We saw what we were heading for. We saw beneath the leaves. But with this, there is also a greater responsibility. It's no longer enough to envision what was on the surface of a *fresco*. Today, we also have to know what was beneath the colors if we want to do our job correctly."

Giovannoni heaves a sigh; smoke swirls out the side of his mouth, "And most of all, we had these zones here," He plucks the *toscano* from his lips and uses it to point, with a sort of rustic reverence, at the sections on the rear wall that had been hidden beneath the baroque altar. "They became our objective. They were our goal. We knew that if things went well, these would be the colors we'd arrive at when we were done."

With the *toscano* back in the corner of his mouth, he picks up his plastic palette and returns to the Masaccio *fresco*. The same section, the same minute attention. The same insistence on seeking perfection while all the time aware that perfection cannot be reached. "Our pictorial intervention here," he says after a long pause. "It's done with a reversible *tempera*." He points to his own day's work, and quickly to the many other repaintings in the adjacent panels. A year's work for Giovannoni and his companions. "This means that if someone decides he doesn't like it, say in fifteen or twenty years, he can remove it and redo it his own way. Our plaster will still be good."

Earlier in the week, Giovannoni was notified that he had been chosen as head restorer for the restoration of the frescoes on the interior of the Brunelleschi *cupola* atop the Florence *duoma*. The project, which had been delayed for nearly ten years, involved the restoration of over three thousand square meters of mural. To further complicate an already overwhelming situation, the *cupola* paintings were executed by two different artists who employed two different techniques. Giorgio Vasari began the decorations in 1573, painting almost exclusively *a fresco*. On Vasari's death in June of 1574, Frederico Zuccari completed the work *a secco*, applying his colors to the dry *intonaco* with a calcium-based *tempera*.

Giovannoni will direct a team of over twenty restorers in an immense and very difficult project. Naturally, and almost thankfully, he admits to a certain measure of apprehension.

"I'll have to affront this restoration with as much humility as I possess," he says, almost in a chant. "And try to do the best job possible. The *intonaco* on the *cupola* is in terrible shape. And the two different painting techniques will require two different cleaning methods, and two different methods of consolidation. Humility. Humility. One must always work with the utmost of humility."

Unlike Ornella Casazza, Giovannoni speaks frankly about the emotions lived during a project like the Brancacci restoration, and the regrets he feels on leaving. "After four years working with the same people, and here with Masaccio, you can't help growing attached to the situation, sometimes to the point of obsession. I often ask myself, 'Have I left anything undone here? Have I given the best of myself?' "

The amiable restorer turns to face me, somber as he interrogates himself once more; his wide eyes are a bright, transparent blue, as if to afford both of us a view into his own heart. "And in truth, I feel I've done everything possible in the Brancacci. That, and only that allows me to leave my work at the end of the day and sleep through the night."

CHAPTER SEVENTEEN

An Unexpected Snarl

T HE BRANCACCI CHAPEL. February 1990. More than a year has passed since the Brancacci team completed its work on the priceless *fresco* cycle. The air filtration system and strict humidity control designed to protect the newly-restored frescoes have been in function since last Spring. Macroclimatic exams conducted by Paolo Parrini's technicians from Syremont—the first in a series of regularly scheduled checkups that the Olivetti Corporation will sponsor—have shown the levels of sulfur dioxide and other potentially noxious elements inside the chapel to be well within acceptable levels.

The quantities of dust, lead, and carbon in the Carmine air—substances that while not immediately harmful to the wall paintings will darken them over time—are also considerably lower than they were at the outset of the restoration. With the installation of double doors at the entrance of the church, and in raising the interior air pressure slightly above atmospheric levels, dust and grime now blow out instead of in when the doors are opened.

"This will be remembered as the start of a new cra in restoration," says Professor Enzo Ferroni in his office at the University of Florence. "The climate in the Brancacci Chapel will be as stable and controlled as that of a sophisticated electronics laboratory."

By any standard, the Brancacci project is an unequivocal success. Unlike the mixed and frequently violent reactions to the Sistine Chapel project, critics have been overwhelmingly positive in their reviews of the long-awaited Brancacci restoration.

"The work of Umberto Baldini and Ornella Casazza has afforded us the good fortune of rediscovering Masaccio," writes art

220 historian Luciano Berti in the introduction to his recent monograph on Masaccio.

"That is to say, the way Vasari saw him, the Masaccio who was studied reverently by all of the *maestri* of the Florentine Renaissance. . . .The effect of the restoration on the chapel could be compared to the difference between listening to a symphony on a phonograph record and then on a stereophonic compact disk."

"This is an exceedingly important restoration, and exceedingly well done," commented Federico Zeri, Italy's most prominent art historian.

"[It] has brought out extraordinary colors, not to mention the true monumental measure of Filippino Lippi. Insofar as the relationship between Masaccio and Masolino, the cleaning has done nothing other than to clarify and accentuate the differences of vision, of temperament, and quality."

The prime components of the Brancacci team have long ago left the chapel to begin new projects. Ornella Casazza is busy with her responsibilities as an inspector at the Uffizi Gallery, responsibilities that include the supervision of the technical examinations currently being performed on the museum's collection of Leonardo Da Vinci paintings.

Sabino Giovannoni has worked since last February as head restorer at the cupola of the Florence Duomo, directing a team of twenty collaborators across the immense expanse of fresco. Marcelle Chemeri can be found on the scaffolding in Florence's Santa Trinita Church, cleaning a chapel frescoed at the beginning of the fifteenth century by Lorenzo Monaco. Gioia Germani and Lydia Cinelli Bianchi have also moved on to other jobs.

And the Brancacci Chapel has yet to reopen to the public.

The inauguration that should have been the happy ending to a splendid operation has been delayed, adapted, and ultimately rewritten by a last-minute disagreement that no one could have possibly anticipated at the outset of the restoration. The Superior Council of Fine Arts in Rome, after an interminable series of debates that kept the fate of the Brancacci in limbo for over a year, has voted to remount the marble baroque altar on the rear wall of the chapel.

It is both ironic and telling that a project as important as the Brancacci Chapel restoration should end in such blatant discord.

Since obtaining approval for the restoration in 1979, Baldini had managed to maintain personal control of the operation, despite the interruption between 1982 and 1984. And now, at the end of his most ambitious project, his will had been checked.

As the decision was in direct conflict with the wishes of Baldini and Casazza, who had undertaken the restoration with the intention of dismantling the altar, and whose conviction was reinforced by the discovery of the fresco fragments and decorative bands beneath the marble structure, there were many who felt that the council's decision was based as much on hierarchy as it was on history.

"This is the sort of thing which happens to a historian when he retires," Procacci comments sadly. "He loses all his influence. It happened to me. And now it has happened to Baldini."

Whether based on personal rivalry, or on the ethics of restoration, the Superior Council was aware that its decision would be extremely unpopular. The council spent months trying to engineer an unlikely compromise that could placate both camps. One historian suggested that the lateral columns of the altar be replaced with a transparent crystal which would afford a vision of the underlying *fresco* fragments. A second member of the council wanted to remount the *pala d'altare* (the upper section of the altar) leaving a sixty centimeter (24 inch) space between the marble and the wall so that visitors willing to crane their necks could glimpse Masaccio and Masolino's window decorations. In the end, and wisely, the council opted to remount the altar as Baldini's team had found it.

"There's nothing to be done now," comments Ornella Casazza, trying to mask her bitterness with a resigned gaiety. The remounted altar, aside from concealing the fragments of the chapel's central panel and the window decorations that had been hidden from view since 1748, will also cover up the newly-unearthed sections of *St. Peter Healing with his Shadow* and *The Alms Giving*. Moreover, the altar's imposing presence will decidedly alter the geometry and character of the chapel.

"The Brancacci chapel will reopen with the altar back in place," Casazza says dryly. "This was decided by a *select* committee, composed of *select* individuals."

Objectively, the argument for the insertion of the altar is just as cogent (or just as subjective) as the argument for its permanent removal. The Superior Council of Fine Arts, composed of both art and architectural historians, ruled that the altar was one of the many historical vicissitudes that had transformed the chapel during its six hundred years of existence. And, unlike the branches covering the genitals of Adam and Eve, the altar was a piece of history that could not be erased.

"The shadow of history has passed over the chapel which was the glory of the Brancacci and transformed it into a largely baroque setting dedicated to an ancient icon," says restoration historian Antonio Paolucci. Baldini's successor at the Opificio Delle Pietre Dure, Paolucci is currently Fine Arts Superintendent for Florence. He compiled the technical report for the Superior Council's debate on the Brancacci altar.

"There are those who say the altar is mediocre," Paolucci continues. "Of course it is, as are the marble basements, the floor, the baroque window, and the Meucci vault frescoes, at least compared to the work of Masaccio and Masolino. But this is how history has progressed, and I don't see how we can change that. With the insertion of the altar, the *fresco* cycle of Masaccio and Masolino will undoubtedly be sacrificed in part. But the chapel will be compensated by the connotations of the 1700s, which by now are indelible elements. This is an opinion, as are the opinions of those who would prefer that the rear wall be left as it is. What is certain is that we are planning to reopen the Brancacci Chapel in the spring, with the altar in place."

The anathema against an arbitrary revision of history has always constituted one of the primary postulates of Baldini's theory of restoration. And the inherent subjectivity of the restoration field could ask for no better illustration than that of Baldini and Casazza's readiness to bend their own rules out of a preference for Masaccio and Masolino.

Yet the directors of the Brancacci Chapel restoration contend that the inherent beauty and the intrinsic historical value of the exquisite *fresco* cycle eclipses all other considerations. In an almost Orwellian logic, they seem to be saying that although all moments of history are worthy of conservation, some of them are more worthy than others. Baldini and Casazza feel that the wall paint-

ings merit absolute priority in the chapel. And they are far from
alone.

"It's a scandal," inveighed Federico Zeri, the reigning authority on Italian painting. "To disrupt a text of this importance for the work of some fourth-rate scalpel-wielders. And enough with this business of history. What did they clean the paintings for then? Wasn't the layer of grime which coated the frescoes also history? And what about the repaintings? These days they want to consider everything as history, a meaningless rock, anything. If it were up to me, I'd detach the frescoes on the vault as well."

Like the rest of his Brancacci teammates, Professor Paolo Parrini is hardly enthusiastic about the restoration's unexpected epilogue. "Naturally, I share Baldini's opinion," says Perrini from his Syremont office in Milan.

"The frescoes are far too important to be compromised by an altar which is hardly exceptional. I can see, however, how someone else might feel differently. What is truly scandalous is that they've let all this time pass without making a decision. The public has waited long enough already to see the Brancacci."

Technically, the reinsertion of the Brancacci altar will require Parrini to modify the chapel's ventilation system. "We'd originally placed our two main vents on the rear wall where the altar had stood," he explains. "Now that they've decided to put it back, our circulation will have to be rerouted. This will mean another delay."

Naturally, the Brancacci restorers were crestfallen. "It's not so much for the fragments or the window decorations," says Gioia Germani. "But for a faithful reading of the paintings, and of the visual geometry. The altar interrupts the entire structure of the fresco cycle."

Sabino Giovannoni acts almost as if he'd suffered a personal affront. "It's not for me to say," he observes, spreading a cloud of self-deprecation to screen his true sentiments. "I've been working as a restorer for thirty years and I still haven't learned to do it well. These people are on the Council because they know what they're doing. I'm certainly not qualified to approve or disapprove. I'm only happy that someone didn't decide to detach the fragments and the window jamb decorations so they could be moved into a museum. Because I would have refused."

224   Giovannoni pauses to reconsider, and to recompose. "No. That's not true. I would have done it. I would have done it because that's my job. I'm just glad I didn't have to do it. Because when you remove a fresco from its natural setting, you rob it of its significance. It becomes a postage stamp, void of context or meaning. The Brancacci fragments have been cleaned and consolidated. They're out of danger. And in twenty or thirty years, when the people who make these decisions come to their senses and realize that they've saddled the wrong horse here, those fragments will still be there when the altar is removed for good."

Epilogue

On June 7, 1990, in the presence of Italian President Francesco Cossiga, the Brancacci Chapel was at last reopened. Before a bulging crowd of journalists, dignitaries, and socialites, Baldini and Casazza escorted Italy's head of state through the chapel, pointing out the subtleties of the fresco cycle, and tracing the highlights of their own project, a project which had begun nine years earlier. As the Fine Arts' marble restorers were unable to remount the entire altar in time for the opening, only the bottom half of the altar was in place. The *pala d'altare* was to be reinserted in September.

After his visit to the chapel, Cossiga moved on to Florence's Palazzo Vecchio to inaugurate a complimentary exhibit called "The Age Of Masaccio." In the afternoon, Cossiga's motorcade climbed the hills on the south side of the Arno to inaugurate an exhibit of vintage Ferrari race cars at the Forte Belvedere.

All of the exhibits, including the Brancacci Chapel, were planned to coincide with the World Cup Soccer Championships that Italy hosted from June 8 through July 8. And it is telling that it took an event like the World Cup to finally return the Brancacci Chapel to the public.

Given the enormous numbers that were expected to flock to the chapel, it was unthinkable that they enter through the main body of the Carmine church. At present, a temporary barrier separates the Brancacci Chapel from the rest of the Carmine. To reach the chapel, visitors must pass through the adjacent cloister and through a waiting room where the two *synopie* that Baldini found beneath Meucci's upper-register frescoes are displayed. Meucci's eighteenth-century *synopie* are on display as well.

226   Tickets to the Brancacci Chapel are priced at five-thousand lira (four dollars) apiece. In order not to upset the chapel's delicate climatic equilibrium, no more than thirty people are allowed into the Brancacci at any one time. Visits are currently limited to fifteen minutes, after which the chapel is cleared for the next group.

With the *beverone* removed, and with the sparse, effective artificial lighting that illuminates the frescoes without spotlighting them, the Brancacci Chapel is simply glorious. The colors are not those of Masaccio or Masolino or Filippino Lippi. As Ornella Casazza says, those colors are gone. What remains, and what Baldini and Casazza's team has recovered, is the visual harmony of the chapel; a harmony that lay muffled beneath layers of egg and dust and smoke, and that once more rings limpid and pure, like the spirit of the Renaissance that inspired them.

Glossary of Terms

a fresco: Literally meaning "when fresh," *a fresco* is a method of mural painting where earth pigments are applied to a still-damp lime-based plaster without a binder.

arriccio: The first layer of *malta* applied onto the stones or bricks of a wall.

asecco: Meaning "when dry," another mural painting technique where the artist applies his pigments to dry wall plaster with the aid of a binder, usually an egg or glue mixture.

battistero: A baptistry.

beverone: A generic term used to refer to the various proteic mixtures applied to wall paintings by restorers. Usually egg- or glue-based, these substances degrade over time.

borgo: A country town.

bottega: An artist's workshop, the center of production and education for artisans and artists from the middle ages onward. Many restorers learned and continue their trade in a restoration *bottega.*

cartone: A full-sized drawing or "cartoon," which was traced into the damp *intonaco* to serve as the artist's outline, allowing the artist to work more complex spatial effects than the *synopia.* The *cartone* was widely used from the middle of the fifteenth century onward.

228   *chiaroscuro:* Literally meaning "light and dark." This is a painter's technique, which uses shading to create the illusion of space and depth.

collegiata: An ecclesiastical college.

Dottoressa: Doctor.

garzone: The most humble member of a *bottega*. A "gopher."

gesso: Calcium-sulfate, an extremely common mineral compound and a major threat to the calcium-carbonate *intonaco* used in *fresco*.

giornata: Literally meaning "a day's work," the area of *intonaco* painted by an artist in one sitting, before the *intonaco* is too dry to absorb any more color. The *giornata* of a *fresco* allow historians to trace an artist's progress in the painting of a mural.

intonaco: The second, thinner layer of *malta* spread over the *arriccio* onto which the artist will apply his pigments.

malta: The artist's mix of limestone and sand that is applied onto the wall to form the support of his mural.

maestro: Literally "master," the *maestro* of the *bottega* directed assistants, apprentices, and journeymen collaborators through the various phases of artistic production.

mural: Any wall painting.

patina: The term used to indicate the natural aging of a painting's surface. A real phenomenon in panel and canvas painting, the existence of the *patina* in *fresco* is widely contested.

pietra serena: A type of stone, generally referred to by its Italian name.

predella: A small, complementary panel painted beneath the major scene of an altarpiece.

stacco: A restorer's technique for the removal of wall paintings from their supports. In the *stacco*, the *intonaco* is separated from the underlying *arriccio*.

strappo: Another restorer's technique for the removal of wall paintings. In the *strappo*, the artist's color layer is stripped off of the *intonaco*.

synopia: The artist's preparatory sketch, done in red on the *arriccio*. Named for the Turkish town of Sinope, renowned for its iron-based red pigment.

tempera: From the Greek for "medium," *tempera* is an egg or glue-based binder that causes the artist's pigments to adhere to a dry surface.

verde terra: A green earth pigment used in *fresco*.

Bibliography

F. Albertino. *Memoriale di Molte Statue e Pitture di Florentina* (Memorial of Many Statues and Paintings of Florence) Firenze: 1510.

Frederick Antal. *Florentine Painting and its Social Background*. London: 1948.

Giuseppe Bacchi. "La Cappella Brancacci" (The Brancacci Chapel) in Rivista Storica Carmelitana. 1929, n.1: pp 54-68.

————. "Gli Affreschi Delle Sagra di Masaccio" (The Frescoes of Masaccio's Sagra) in Rivista Storica Carmelitana. 1929, n. 1: pp 107-126.

Mauro Bacci, v. Cappellini. "Diffuse Reflectance Spectroscopy: An Application To The Analysis of Art Works" IROE-CNR (in-house publication). Firenze: 1986.

Umberto Baldini. *Teoria del Restauro e Unita di Metodologia* (Theory of Restoration and Unity of Methodology) vols I + II. Firenze: 1978.

————. La Primavera del Boticelli: Storia de un Quadro e di un Restauro (Botticelli's Primavera: Story of a Painting and of a Restoration). Milano: 1984.

————. "Restauri di dipinti Fiorentini, in occasione della mostra di quattro maestri del Rinascimento" (Restorations of Florentine Paintings, on the Occasion of the Exhibit of Four Renaissance Masters) in Bolletino D'Arte. 1954, n. 39: pp 221-240.

————. "Il Crocifisso di Cimabue" (Cimabue's Cricifix) in Amici Dei Musei. 1977, n. 8: pp 1-3.

————. "Nuovi Affreschi Nella Capella Brancacci" (New Frescoes in the Brancacci Chapel) in Critica D'Arte. 1984, n. 49: pp 65-72.

————. "Michelangelo Ritorna" (Michelangelo Returns) in Critica D'Arte. 1985, n. 6: pp 69-70.

————. "Restauro Delle Cappella Brancacci Primi Risultati" (Restoration of the Brancacci Chapel, First Results) in Critica D'Arte. 1986, n. 9: pp 65-68.

————. "Le Figure di Adamo e Eva Formate Affatto Ignude in una Cappella di una Principale Chiesa di Fiorenza" (The Figures of Adam and Eve in Fact Nude in a Chapel in a Principal Church of Florence) in Critica D'Arte. 1988, n. 16: pp 72-77.

————. "Masaccio" in Enciclopedia Universale Dell'Arte Vol VIII Roma. 1962, coll 865-877.

————. "Masolino" in Enciclopedia Universale Dell'Arte Vol VII Roma. 1962, coll 920-924.

Umberto Baldini. ed. *Metodo e Scienza* (Method and Science) Firenze, Sansoni. 1982.

Eugenio Battisti. *Brunelleschi.* Milano. 1978.

J.H. Beck. *Masaccio, The Documents.* Locust Valley. 1978.

————. "Una Prospettiva. . . .di mano di Masaccio" (A Prospective..by the Hand of Masaccio) in Studies In Late Medeival And Renaissance Painting In Honor Of Millard Meiss. NYU. 1978, pp 48-53.

Bernhard Berenson. *The Florentine Painters of the Renaissance.* New York. 1909.

Luciano Berti. *Masaccio.* Milano. 1964.

————. *L'Opera Completa di Masaccio* (The Complete Works of Masaccio) Milano. 1968.

————. *Masaccio.* Firenze. 1989.

————. "Masaccio 1422" in Commentari. 1961, n. 12: pp 84-107.

————. "Massacio A San Giovenale Di Cascia" (Masaccio at San Giovenale di Cascia) in Acropoli. 1962, n. 2: pp 149-165.

L. Berti, U. Baldini. *Filippino Lippi.* Firenze. 1957.

Eve Borsook. "A Note On Masaccio In Pisa" in Burlington Magazine. 1961, n. 103: pp 149-165.

Guido Botticelli. "Metodologie Di Pulitura Dei Dipinti Murale Anche In Funzione Al Consolidamento Con Un Materiale Minerale" (Methodology of Cleaning Wall Paintings Also Using a Mineral Material as a Consolidant)

Cesare Brandi. "Restauri A Piero Della Francesca" (Restorations of Piero Della Francesca) In Bolletino D'Arte. 1954, n. 39: pp 241-258.

————. "Filippino Lippi: L'ultimo Pittore Del 1400" (Filippino Lippi, the Last of the 1400's Pinaters) in *Saggi su Filippino Lippi.* Firenze. 1957, pp 34-50.

Carlo Carnesecchi. "Messer Felice Brancacci" in Miscellanea D'Arte. 1903, n. 11: pp 190-192.

Ornella Casazza. *Il Restauro Pittorico* (Pictorial Restoration). Firenze. 1981.

————. "Trattamento Digitale Delle Immagine e Conservazione e Restauro di Opere D'arte" (Digital Treatment of the Images and Conservation and Restoration of Artworks) in Critica D'Arte. 1985, n. 4: pp 71-78.

————. "Ill Ciclo Delle Storie di San Pietro e La Historicus Salutis; Nuove Lettere Della Cappella Brancacci" (The Cycle of the Stories of St Peter and their History: New Letters from the Brancacci Chapel) in Critica D'arte. 1986, n. 9: pp 69-82.

————. "Il Settecento Nella Cappella Brancacci" (The 1700's in the Brancacci Chapel) in Critica D'Arte. 1986, n. 11: pp 68-72.

————. "La Grande Gabbia Architettonica Di Masaccio" (Masaccio's Grand Architectonic Cage) in Critica D'Arte. 1988, n. 16: pp 78-97.

Dante Castellacci. ed. *Il Diario di Felice Brancacci* (The Diary of Felice Brancacci) Archivio Storico Italiano (Florentine Historical Archive). 1881. vol 8, pp 157-188.

Cennino Cennini. *Il Libro Dell'arte o Trattato Della Pitture* (The Book of Art or Treatise on Painting) Neri Pozza, ed. Vicenza. 1971.

H. Cinelli. *Fortuna Visiva di Masaccio* (The Visual Fortune of Masaccio). San Giovanno Valdarno. 1979.

Kenneth Clark. "An Early Quattrocento Triptich for Santa Maria Maggiore, Rome" in Burlington Magazine. 1951, n. 51: pp 339-347.

Bruce Cole. *Masaccio and the Art of Early Renaissance Florence.* London/ Bloomington. 1980.

————. "A Reconstruction of Masolino's True Cross Cycle in Santo Stefano, Empoli" in Mitteilungen des Kunsthistorisches Institutes, Florenz. 1967-68, n. 13: pp 289-300.

Enrico Colle. *Masaccio.* Siena. 1987.

Alessandro Conti. Storia del Restauro (A History of Restoration). Milano. 1978.

E. Ferroni. "Utilisation De Techniques Diffractometriques Dans L'etude De La Conservation Des Fresques" (Utilisation of Diffraction Techniques in the Study of Fresco Conservation) in Beme Colloque Sur L'analyse De La Matiere, Florence Septembre. 1969.

————. Contributi E Prospettive Della Ricerca Chimico Fisica Nel Restauro Degli Affreschi" (Contributions and Prospectives in Physical Chemistry Research in Fresco Restoration) in Atti e Memorie dell'Accademia Petrarca di Lettere, Arti e Scienze di Arezzo vol XL. Nuova Serie, 1970-1972, pp 169-179.

E. Ferroni, D. Dini. "Restauro chimico-strutturale di affreschi solfatati" (Chemical-Structural Restoration of Sulfatated Frescoes) in *Metodo e Scienza* op. cit.

————. "Prospettive Per La Conservazione Degli Affreschi" (Prospectives for Fresco Conservation) in Scritti Di Storia Dell'Arte In Onoroe Di Ugo Procacco. Firenze. 1980, pp 19-23.

234   *Giuseppe Fiocco.* "Masaccio Incompreso" (Masaccio Misunderstood) in
Rivista Storica Carmelitana 1929, n. 1: pp 88-108.

————. "Incontro Tra Filippino E Masaccio" (The Meeting of Filippino and Masaccio" in *Saggi su Filippino Lippi* op. cit.

Richard Freemantle. "Some Documents Concerning Masaccio and His
Mother's Second Family" in Burlington Magazine. 1973, n. 115:
pp 516-518.

————. "Some New Masolino Documents" in Burlington Magazine.
1975, n. 97: pp 658-659.

Frey. ed.   Codice Magliabecchiano (Magliabecchiano Code). Berlin. 1892.

Frey. ed.   Libro Dal'Anonimo Billi (The Book of the Anonymous Billi).
Berlin. 1982.

Richard Friedenthal.   Lettere di Grandi Artisti: Da Ghiberti a Gainsborough.
(Letters of Great Artists: From Ghiberti to Gainsborough). Milano.
1960.

Fiammetta Gamba.   Filippino Lippi Nella Storia Della Critica (A Critical
History of Filippino Lippi). Firenze. 1958.

Henrick Lindberg.   To the Problem of Masolino and Masaccio. Stockholm.
1931.

Roberto Longhi.   Fatti di Masolino e di Masaccio (Facts of Masolino and
Masaccio). Firenze. 1941.

————. "Recupero Di Un Masaccio" (Recovery of a Masaccio) in Paragone. 1950, n. 5: pp 3-5.

————. "La Presenza di Masaccio nel Trittico della Neve" (Masaccio's
Presence in the Tryptich of the Snow" in Paragone. 1952, n. 25:
pp 8-16.

Joseph Manca. "La Natura Morta di Masolino a Palazzo Branda di Castiglione Olona" (Masolino's Still Life in the Palace of Branda Castiglione Olona" in Prospettiva. 1981, n. 25: pp 45-46.

Antonio Manetti.   Operette Istoriche (Historical Essays, or Fourteen Outstanding Men Of Florence) ed Gaetano Milanesi. Firenze. 1887.

Valerio Mariani. "L'arte di Filippino Lippi" (The Art of Filippino Lippi)
in *Saggi su Filippino Lippi.* op. cit.

B. Marrai. "Masolino e Masaccio" (Masolino and Masaccio) in Miscellanea D'Arte. 1903, n. 12: pp 164-174.

Frank Jewett Mather, Jr. "The Problem of the Brancacci Chapel Historically Considered" in The Art Bulletin. 1944, n. 26: pp 175-187.

Mauro Matteini, Arcangelo Moles.   Scienza e Restauro: Metodi D'Indagine
(Science and Restoration: Methods of Investigation). Firenze. 1986.

Peter Meller. "Problemi Ritrattistici e Iconografici nella Cappella Brancacci" (Problems of Portraiture and Iconography in the Brancacci
Chapel) in Acropoli. 1960-61, n. 3: pp 186-228.

J. Mesnil.   *Masaccio e Les Debuts de la Renaissance* (Masaccio and the Beginnings of the Renaissance). La Haye. 1927.

————.   "La Data di Morte di Masaccio" (The Date of Masaccio's Death) in Rivista D'Arte. 1912, n. 2:
pp 31-34.

————.   "Per la storia della Cappella Brancacci" (For the History of the Brancacci Chapel) in Rivista D'Arte. 1912, n. 2: pp 34-40.

Emma Micheletti.   *Masolino da Panicale* (Masolina From Panicale). Milano. 1959.

A. Molho.   "The Brancacci Chapel: Studies in its Iconography And History" in Journal Of The Warburg And Courtald Institute. 1977, n. 40: pp 50-98. (taken from an address given at I Tatti)

P. Mora, L. Mora, P. Philippot.   *The Conservation of Wall Paintings.* Glasgow. 1983.

Antonio Paolucci.   "Il Crocifisso Di Brunelleschi Dopo Il Restauro" (Cimabue's Crucifix After Restoration) in Paragone. 1977, n. 28: pp 3-6.

————.   "Il Restauro Del Cenacolo Di Leonardo" (The Restoration of Leonardo's Last Supper" in Amici Dei. 1982, n. 23: pp 5-8.

————.   "Una Inedita Relazione Di Roberto Longhi Sul Restauro Di Mauro Pellicioli Alla Camera Degli Sposi Del Mantenga" (An Unpublished Paper by Roberto Longhi about Mauro Pellicioli's Restoration of Mantegna's Camera Degli Sposi) in Paragone. 1985, n. 1: pp I 331-335.

————.   "I Grandi Cantieri Di Restauro" (The Great Restoration Projects) in Amici Dei Musei. April 1986, n. 34: pp 22-23.

————.   "Quale Politica Per Il Restauro" (What Policy For Restoration) in Amici Dei Musei. 1987, n. 39: pp 1-3.

Paolo Parrini. ed.   *Scienza, Conservazione, e Restauro* (Science, Conservation, and Restoration) Montedison Cultural Project Arcadia Edizioni. 1986.

————.   "Non Destructive Methods for Determination of Surface Alteration of Stone" in Vth International Congress of Determination and Conservation of Stone. (Lausanne, 25-27. September.)

P. Parrini, Giuseppe Pizzigoni.   "Lorenzo Ghiberti: Sulla Tecnica Di Esecuzione" (Lorenzo Ghiberti: His Working Technique) in *Metodo e Scienza.* op. cit.

————.   "Primi Risultati Delle Ricerche Relative All'Ambiente E Allo Stato Di Conservazione Degli Affreschi Della Cappella Brancacci Nella Chiesa Del Carmine A Firenze" (Preliminary Results of the Research Regarding the Environment and the State of Conservation of the Frescoes of the Brancacci Chapel in the Carmine Church of Florence) in *Scienza, Conservation, e Restauro.* op. cit.

Bibliography

236   Mary Pittaluga. *Masaccio*. Firenze. 1935.

Rosanna Proto Pisani. ed. *Masolino a Empoli* (Masolino at Empoli). Empoli. 1987.

G. Poggi. "La tavola di Masaccio per il Carmine di Pisa" (Masaccio's Panel for the Carmine of Pisa" in Miscellanea D'arte. 1903, n. 10: pp 182-187.

————. "Masolino e la Compagnia della Croce in Empoli" (Masolino and the Company of the Cross of Empoli) in Rivista D'Arte. 1905, n. 3: pp 46-52.

Ugo Procacci. *Masaccio*. Firenze. 1980.

————. *Tutta la Pittura di Masaccio*. (The Complete Paintings of Masaccio). Milano. 1961.

————. *Mostra di Opere D'Arte Restaurate*. (Exhibit of Restored Artworks). Firenze. 1946.

————. *Mostra Degli Affreschi Staccati*. (Exhibit of Detached Frescoes). Firenze. 1958.

————. *Sinopie e Affreschi*. (Synopies and Frescoes). Milano. 1960.

————. "L'incendio della Chiesa del Carmine del 1771" (The Fire of the Carmine Church in 1771) in Rivista D'Arte. 1932, n. 14: pp 141-212.

————. "Recent Restoration In Florence: Masaccio's Madonna With St. Anne" in Burlington Magazine. 1947, n. 89: pp 309-310.

————. "Sulla Cronologia Delle Opere di Masaccio e Masolino tra il 1425 e il 1428" (On the Chronology of the Works of Masaccio and Masolino from 1425 through 1428) in Rivista D'Arte. 1953, n. 28: pp 3-55.

————. "Nuove Testimonianze Su Masaccio" (New Testimonies on Masaccio) in Commentari. 1976, n. 27: pp 223-247.

————. "Le portata al catasto di Ser Giovanno detto lo Scheggia" (The results of the census of Ser Giovanni, known as the Scheggia) in Rivista D'Arte. 1984, n. 37: pp 235-257.

Rizzoli. ed. *L'Opera Completa di Masaccio* (The Complete Works of Masaccio). Milano. 1968.

Mario Salmi. *Masaccio*. Milano. 1947.

————. *Mostra di Quattro Maestri del Primo Rinasciamento* (Exhibits of Four Early Renaissance Masters). Firenze. 1954.

Roberto Salvini. "Botticelli E Filippino Lippi" (Botticelli and Filippino Lippi) in *Saggi su Filippino Lippi*. op. cit.

A. Schmarsow. Masolino und Masaccio (Masolino and Masaccio). Liepzig. 1928.

K. Steinbert. *Masaccio*. Wien. 1948.

Secco Suardo. *Manuale Per la Parte Meccanica Dell'Arte del Restauratore dei*

Dipinti (Manual for the Mechanical Part of the Art of the Restorer of Paintings). Milano. 1866.

Elena Berti Toesca. "Per La Sagra di Masaccio" (For Masaccio's Sagra) in Arte Figurative. 1945, n. 1: pp 148-150.

Pietro Toesca. *Masolina da Panicale* (Masolino from Panicale). Bergamo. 1908.

Charles de Tolnay. "Note sur l'iconographie des fresques de la Chapelle Brancacci" (A Note on the Iconography of the Frescoes of the Brancacci Chapel) in Arte Lombarda. 1965, n. 10: pp 69-74.

Giorgio Vasari. *Le Vite de'Piu Eccellenti Architetti, Pittori, et Scultori Italiani, da Cimabue Insino A'Tempi Nostri* (The Lives of The Artists) Giulio Einaudi, ed. Torino. 1986.

M.L. Eiko Wakayama. "Novita di Masolino a Castiglione D'Olona" (News about Masolino at Castiglione D'Olona) in Arte Lombarda. 1971, n. 16: pp 1-16.

―――. "Masolino o non Masolino: Problemi di Attribuzione" (Masolino or not Masolino: Problems of Attribution) in Arte Cristiana. 1987, n. 75: pp 125-136.

Index

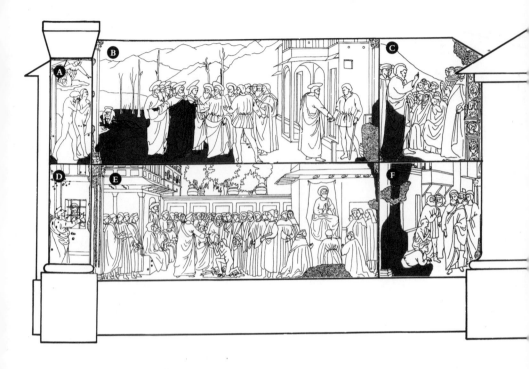

A Masaccio: *Adam and Eve Driven from Paradise.*

D Filippino Lippi: *St. Paul Visiting St. Peter In Prison*

B Masaccio: *The Tribute Money*

E Masaccio and Filippino Lippi: *The Resurrection of Teofilo's Son and St. Peter Enthroned*

Masolino: *St. Peter ...hing to the Crowd*

F Masaccio: *St. Peter Healing with his Shadow*